From The WA State Strong Foundations Reentry Team

We're glad you picked up the *Washington State Strong Foundations Reentry Guide.* Whether you spent many years in prison or just a few, it can help you start your life on the outside. This guide gives you information about employment, housing, education, healthcare, and more.

If you are a family member, friend, or service provider for someone who is coming home, this book can help you too. We hope you will find resources in this book that will assist you in helping your loved one.

There are five main sections in Strong Foundations:

- **Before You Leave** advises about getting ready for release.
- **Personal Reentry Plan** is for use to write out your plan before release.
- **Once You're Out** helps you set up your life once you're out.
- **Healing and Moving Forward** is about getting used to life after prison.
- **Our Reentry Directory** contains contact information for useful resources by county.

Getting used to life on the outside can be hard. You may face challenges because of your criminal record. You may have trouble finding a job. People might treat you differently. Your parole/community custody may feel unfair.

Strong Foundations will help you meet these challenges. Maybe it will even make you want to work for change. We believe in YOU and your ability to make a difference in the world. Don't stop believing in yourself.

In this book, you'll find helpful words from people like you who went through reentry. Many of them are alumni of the House of Mercy, a nonprofit community organization focused on reentry in Washington State. They, and so many others, have successfully reentered the outside world. You can too!

Please keep in touch. We'd love to know how you're doing and how we can make *Strong Foundations* better. Your comments can help those who follow in your footsteps.

Again, welcome home. We're glad you're back.

In solidarity,

Washington State Strong Foundations Reentry Team

About Strong Foundations

Strong Foundations was made by members of House of Mercy (HOM). HOM is a nonprofit community organization focused on reentry Washington State. Since 2005, HOM has provided transitional housing, case management, peer-to-peer mentorship, employment, life skills training, and an increasing number of wrap-around services to thousands of people going through reentry. 90% of HOM employees are previously incarcerated individuals.

We created Strong Foundations because we care about people like you who are being released from prison. This guide was made under the philosophy of "by us, for us."

The world is changing all the time. That means we can't be sure everything in this guide is right. We've tried to use the best, most up-to-date information from trusted sources.

≫ DISCLAIMER

We have listed a lot of programs, services, and businesses in this guide as resources for formerly incarcerated people and their families. We don't endorse any of these organizations. We also don't guarantee that these resources will be helpful (although we hope they are).

Request Our Guides!

Strong Foundations is free for incarcerated or detained people and can be ordered the following ways:

- Get them online through ReentryWA.com. You can download a pdf for free.
- Request one at the reentry resource room in your facility.
- Request by phone at (206) 651-7840, or by email at reentryguide@hom.church
- Send a request by mail: House of Mercy, P.O. Box 4240, Federal Way, WA 98603

Paying for Guides

Please help us give Strong Foundations to every person who wants it. If you can, please send a check to the address above, or donate online at ReentryWA.com/donate. We don't get money from the Washington Department of Corrections. Each copy of Strong Foundations costs $12 to print and send. Thank you!

Mission Statement

House of Mercy is committed to healing our culture by investing in the lives of people in transition by providing safe & supportive housing, transitional care management, supportive services, connections with employers, life-skills training, leadership training, digital-skills training, community, and reentry resources such as this guide.

Part 1: Before Your Release

This main section addresses what an incarcerated person can do before their release to feel more in control of their situation. It includes the following chapters:

1. Prepare Mentally for Release
2. Gather Your Documents
3. Prepare for Your Job Search
4. Health Before Release
5. Preparing for Reunification
6. Parole/Community Custody

1. Prepare Mentally for Release

It's never too early to get ready to leave prison. Even if you have a very long sentence, keep your eye on life after release. Find ways to learn and grow while you are there.

- Take Adult Basic Education classes or get your GED.
- Take college classes or vocational classes.
- Get involved in cultural and positive programs.
- Play an instrument, exercise, draw, join a choir, or read a book.
- Start going to religious services.
- Attend substance use programs or anger management classes.
- Get involved in volunteer activities.

These activities can help you meet other people who can support you. They will help you think about what you have to offer.

You can still make a difference in prison. There are many programs within Washington State prisons that you can participate in and help to promote a positive culture within your facility. Complete list of DOC approved programs: Current Programming | Washington State Department of Corrections (*See list in resource directory*).

Many incarcerated people donate to local charities and Churches like food pantries, Habitat for Humanity, St. Jude Children's Hospital, and more. What can you do?

If you're getting released soon, there is a lot more you can do to prepare. In this chapter, we address how to build your support network and prepare mentally for the challenges of reentry.

Build your Support Network

People often isolate themselves during tough times. But it can help to stay connected to positive friends and family members. Think about the people you know. Contact family members and friends. Be honest about what you need from them, whether it's housing, help with money, or just support and love. Find out what they expect from you.

Reflect

1.   What does "support" mean to you?

2.   Who are the people you're counting on to be there for you? Do they know what you expect?

3.   Who do you know and trust to help you build your support network?
4.   Are there people in your life you'd like to reconnect with as you prepare for reentry?

5.   Are there people in your life who might make reentry more difficult? If so, how can you set yourself up for success?

6.   How can you strengthen relationships to prepare for reentry?

Prepare for Challenges

Before leaving prison, work on practicing patience, both with others and with yourself.

You will need to accept that things may not be perfect or easy. Forgive yourself if you make mistakes. You will probably have some awkward talks with people on the outside. Let yourself laugh them off. People in the outside world have awkward experiences all the time! You may think everyone will know you've just gotten out of prison, but they probably will not.

Patience is important on the outside. Everything may not go the way you want it to. Sometimes you will feel confused by how much things have changed since you went away. Go slow. Breathe. It is normal to feel stressed sometimes, but you don't want it to get out of hand.

How will you relax once you're out in the world? Life on the outside can feel very rushed. HOM alumni said visiting the waterfront, taking long walks, biking, and gardening have helped. How can you include activities like this in your life?

"Best thing that can reduce anxiety is to have a plan. You don't have to be rigid with that plan, because you're going to get out and realize that the world isn't what you expected it to be." —Joe-Joe

 Reflect

1.   What skills do you use to manage stress?

2.   When things go wrong, what can you do to keep yourself on track?

3.   What have you done in the past to adjust to major life changes?

2. Gather Your Documents

You will need your birth certificate, Social Security card, and ID on the outside. As your release date gets closer, you should start the process of getting them. It is harder to get them on the outside. Try to begin this process at least **one year** before you are released.

There may be counselors or departments at your facility that can help you get your documents. You will need to reach out to them and ask.

——— 🙶 ———

"Do not depend on your counselor, this is your release, not theirs. If you sit around waiting, only the minimal will be done for you." -Anonymous

"Take responsibility and look for as much information as you can. Go talk to the law clerks, everybody that you can to get information." -Anonymous

——— 🙶 ———

 Step 1. Verification of Incarceration.

To get started, ask your counselor for a document that verifies that you are incarcerated. You may need this to get your other documents. It's also a good idea to gather any transcripts or certificates from classes you've taken in prison. You can use those documents to get your birth certificate, Social Security card and ID.

 Step 2. Birth Certificate.

Next, you will need a certified copy of your birth certificate. This means a birth certificate that has a state seal and is signed and dated by the county registrar.

How Do I Order a Birth Certificate If I Was Born in Washington?

In Washington, the Department of Health issues certified copies of vital records (or "certificates") for births that took place in the state of Washington. Below is a chart showing a few

ways to order a certified copy of your birth certificate. If you are still incarcerated, talk to your counselor to determine the best way to start the process from your facility (*you may be eligible for a free birth certificate, see below*). If you apply by mail, you will need a copy of the order form, which is called Washington State Department of Health Birth / Death Certificate Mail Order Form. This form can be found online at 422-182-BirthCertificateOrderForm.pdf (wa.gov), or your counselor may be able to help you get a copy.

Ways to Order	Cost per Certificate	Order Fulfillment	Links and Info
Mail	$25.00	Shipped within 1-3 weeks of the department receiving the order and processing payment. A record problem may cause delays.	Fill out the order form (available at 422-182-BirthCertificateOrderForm. pdf (wa.gov)) Requirements: • Required information • Signature • Photocopy of valid ID • Proof documentation
Online	Starting at $40.50 depending on shipping method.	Shipped within 3-7 business days of the Department receiving the order from VitalChek, depending on the shipping option you select. A record problem may cause delays.	Go to www.vitalchek.com Requirements: • Required information • Valid ID (En Español) • Proof documentation (En Español)
Phone	Starting at $40.50 depending on shipping method.	Shipped within 3-7 business days of the Department receiving the order from VitalChek, depending on the shipping option you select. A record problem may cause delays.	Call 1-866-687-1464 at any time. Payment by credit/debit card.
Walk-In	Varying Fees	DOH partners with local Washington health departments for in-person services of most birth and death certificate purchases. There might be an additional fee for this service. Customers will receive most orders within the same day.	local Washington health departments

Additionally, it is helpful to know that Washington is a public records state by law. This means that a loved one or family member can use any of the options detailed in the chart above to order a birth certificate for you if they are able to fill out the order form with your complete and accurate information. Your loved one or family member will need the following information about you to order your birth certificate:

• Your full name as it appears on your birth certificate.

To prove you're a qualified applicant, you must submit documentation proving your relationship.

• Your date of birth (Month/Date/Year).
• Your city or county of birth; and
• Your parents' full names at the time of your birth.

Qualified applicants are self, spouse or domestic partner, parent, stepparent, legal guardian, child, stepchild, sibling, grandparent, great grandparent, legal representative, authorized representative, or government agency or the courts if the birth certificate is used for official duties. If you are not one of the people listed above, you will not receive a birth certificate.

The acceptable documentation to prove qualifying relationship includes:

- Copies of vital records such as birth or marriage certificates from this or another state that links you to the requested birth record
- Copies of certified court orders linking you to the requested birth record (e.g., legal guardianship court order)
- Authorized Representative form
- Document of letter from a government agency or court stating that the birth certificate will be used for official purposes (for government agency or court only)

How Do I Get a <u>Free</u> Birth Certificate If I Was Born in Washington?

To qualify:
- Born in Washington
- Within 6 months of release
- Will need to be going to some sort of partial confinement (*GRE, Work Release, CPA*)
- Have an ORP submitted as homeless (***see definition below***)
- Have an ORP submitted for an approved housing voucher program.

If you qualify:
- Ask your counselor for the application and the letter that are needed to proceed (*By the incarcerated individual filling out the Birth Certificate form and giving the form to the counselor they agree to DOC staff making a copy of their WA ID card or DOC ID card*).

- Once returned, your counselor will prepare a letter to DOH.
- The counselor will make a copy of both the individual's DOC ID and the counselor's staff ID with the word copy across it.
- The counselor will mail the application, letter and both IDs to the address listed on the application in the upper left corner.
- The counselor will Chrono that they have mailed Birth Certificate application, Birth Certificate letter, copy of Individuals DOC ID and Staff ID to the Department of Health for processing.

Definitions: (12) **"Homeless person"** RCW 43.185C.010
- Individual living outside or in a building not meant for human habitation,
- or they have no legal right to occupy,
- an emergency shelter,
- or in a temporary housing program which may include transitional and supportive housing (Reentry Center, transitional housing, treatment center, housing voucher program) if habitation time limits exist.
- substance abusers,
- people with mental illness,
- and sex offenders who are homeless.

How Do I Order a Birth Certificate If I Was Born in a Different State?

The process for ordering birth certificates varies from state to state. If you were born outside of Washington, you will need to research how to order a birth certificate directly from the state or country in which you were born. Unless you have internet access, or can ask for help from someone who does, you may need to wait until you are released to find this information. However, it is a good idea to also talk to your counselor and see if he or she can provide you with any assistance. If you are able to have someone assist you with finding this information while you are incarcerated, the State Vital Records website https://statevitalrecords.org contains information on locating vital records and includes links to information and guidelines for ordering birth certificates from various states and US territories.

Another way is to order a birth certificate using www.vitalchek.com. (See chart below)

Ways to Order	Cost per Certificate	Order Fulfillment	Links and Info
Online	Starting at $40.50 depending on shipping method.	Shipped within 3-7 business days of the Department receiving the order from VitalChek, depending on the shipping option you select. A record problem may cause delays.	Go to www.vitalchek.com Requirements: • Required information • Valid ID (En Español) • Proof documentation (En Español)
Phone	Starting at $40.50 depending on shipping method.	Shipped within 3-7 business days of the Department receiving the order from VitalChek, depending on the shipping option you select. A record problem may cause delays.	Call 1-866-687-1464 at any time. Payment by credit/debit card.

If you cannot get your birth certificate before you get out, another option is to request it at a county clerk's office after you are released. Call them before you visit to get instructions.

 ## Step 3: Social Security Card.

All US citizens and permanent residents have a Social Security number (SSN). This number is used by the government to keep track of your taxes and Social Security benefits. You will need your Social Security card when you get a job or open a bank account. If you have lost your card, you can apply for a new one. There is no fee for requesting your Social Security card.

Per DOC 380.550:

II.   Social Security Card Application
A.   Individuals who have never had a social security card may apply for an original card with the Social Security Administration upon release.
B.   Individuals who are United States citizens may request a replacement social security card within 180 days to the earliest transfer date to partial confinement, the release date, or any known court date for individuals impacted by sentence reform.
license. You may be able to apply for a replacement card online using my *Social Security* web portal www.ssa.gov/myaccount/. For more information on setting up an account on *my* Social Security, visit www.ssa.gov/myaccount/. You can

1.   Requests will be submitted using SS-5 Application for a Social Security Card and SSA-3288 Consent for Release of Information (*You can also request a form from your prison library or your counselor. You can also request one by calling the Social Security Administration (SSA) at 1-800-772-1213. They can mail you a form*).
2.   The individual's signature is required and should reflect the legal name, not the court/committed name. All aliases and social security numbers used should be listed under "Other Names Used".
3.   The DOC number should be included in the address
Your Social Security card must be placed in your central file, until you are released. If you get it in the mail, give it to your counselor. Be aware that sharing it with another person could put you at risk for fraud.

To get your Social Security card replacement after releasing you will need to have a valid U.S. mailing address and Washington state ID or driver's

also use go to http://www.ssa.gov/locator to find the nearest office to your location and go in person.
To obtain a replacement Social Security card, you also must provide one document to prove your

identity. Documents that may be accepted as evidence of identity include:

- Washington State ID Card;
- Driver's license; or
- U.S. passport.

"I needed a second form of identification to get my social security card. If you are in this sort of dilemma, you can retrieve a copy of your medical record as a second ID. If you do not have your medical record you can go to a free clinic, take an H.I.V. test and request a copy of the record; you can use this document along with your birth certificate to get your Social Security card." –Antonio

 Step 4: WA State ID Card.

Per DOC 380.550:

I. Identification Card Application
A. Individuals must provide a Washington State mailing/residential address to receive an identification card.
B. In Prisons, the case manager will initiate applications for individuals who need Washington State identification up to one year before the earliest transfer date to partial confinement, the release date, or any known court date for individuals impacted by sentence reform.
1. Applications will be initiated through the Department of Licensing application portal via https://www.dol.wa.gov.
2. For individuals with less than 30 days before transferring to partial confinement or to the Earned Release Date (ERO), the case manager will initiate DOC 21-777 DLE-520-090A Post-Release Application.
C. In Prisons, facility records employees will:
1. Photograph the individual using the background provided by the Department of Licensing and obtain the individual's signature.
2. Update the application with the current photograph and signature and submit it via dol.wa.gov.
3. Document the application status in the individual's electronic file as a chronological event.
D. If an application has not been previously submitted, the case manager/designee will

initiate DOC 21-777 DLE-520-090A Post-Release Application during intake for individuals housed in partial confinement or on community supervision.

How Do I Get or Renew My Washington State ID Card After I Am Released?

You can get your Washington State ID card after you are released by visiting a DOL office. You can find DOL office locations by visiting : https://fortress.wa.gov/dol/dolprod/dsdoffices/. When you visit the office, you will need to bring the following items with you:

- **Proof of identity.** There are several different documents that DOL will accept as proof of your identity.
  See http://www.dol.wa.gov/driverslicense/id proof.html for a detailed list of identity documents that DOL accepts, and what combinations will be enough to proof who you are.
- **Form of payment for the fee** A standard ID card costs $9 per year, an enhanced ID (EID) card $13 per year. You can choose to renew every 6 or 8 years.
  - A standard ID card is $54 for 6-year renewal and $72 for 8-year renewal.
  - An EID card is $78 for 6-year renewal and $104 for 8-year renewal.
  - Replacing a lost or stolen ID card costs $20.

- **Your Social Security number or proof of address.** If you are 18 or older, you must provide your Social Security number. You do NOT need to show your Social Security card. If you do not have a Social Security number, you must prove that you have a valid address in Washington.
  See www.dol.wa.gov/driverslicense/idproof.html (at item #3) for more information about how to prove your address.

You will also need to have your picture taken at the DOL office. Once all your information is verified, you will be given a temporary ID card before you leave the office. Your permanent ID will be mailed to you and will arrive within 7-10 days.

If your ID card is expired, renewing it is easy. You can renew by visiting a DOL office or by using the online tool at:
https://fortress.wa.gov/dol/olr/. To renew online, you will need your ID card number, the last four digits of your Social Security number, an email address, and a credit card. The fee to renew your ID card is $54 for 6 years or $72 for 8 years†.

†You may qualify for a reduced fee ID card when you are in person at a Licensing Services Office. If you are eligible for a

reduced fee ID card, your cost for a standard ID card is $5, (RCW 46.20.117). For DOL to issue at the reduced cost, you must:

- *Have a 'Request for "Identicard" form issued to you by Department of Social and Health Services (DSHS). Present this form in person at a Licensing Services Office, or*
- *Be under age 25 and do not have a permanent home address, or*
- *Have been recently released from a Department of Children, Youth, and Families (DCYF) Juvenile Rehabilitation Administration (JRA) facility.*

If you choose to enhance your reduced fee ID card, the enhanced fees still apply. There is an extra $4 per year until it expires.

 If you are under an alias: *If you are locked up under an alias, it is important that you start gathering your documents early. First, write to the county where you are convicted or the state's attorney office. Ask them to change the charging document to reflect your real name. The court probably will not change all the court documents to fix this problem. You may need to talk to a lawyer to see if there are any legal steps you can take.*

99

"I recommend going to DSHS before going to get your ID. In most cases, DSHS will give you a voucher so that you only have to pay $5 for your ID" -Anonymous

---
♪♪
---

3. Prepare for Your Job Search

If you are getting ready to leave prison, you're probably thinking about getting a job. This is an area where you may hit many roadblocks and challenges. The good news is that there are employers who are willing to give you a chance. There are ways you can prepare while still in prison to find a good job. Be hopeful. Many people have found good jobs after incarceration. If you're prepared, persistent and have the right attitude you can find one too.

 Step 1: Build Experience

In the facility where you're locked up, can you earn certificates, learn new skills, or work? Any experience like this can help you find a job on the outside. They can also make you more confident and help you build skills you didn't know you had.

School is another good way to get ready for work on the outside. Enroll in school programs, from Adult Basic Education to college programs. School records can also show employers you are intelligent and dedicated. Try other things too. Arts, parenting classes, and other programs will give you new skills and confidence.

 Step 2: Write Your Resume

Another important thing you can do while you're in prison is to write your resume. A resume is a summary of your skills, strengths, and work experience. You will need a resume to search for and apply for jobs. Even if you don't have a computer or typewriter, write your resume out while you are still incarcerated, use the resume writing worksheet in the back of the book to guide you. You can type it out after your release. Your resume should have several parts:

1. Your name, address, and contact information. If you are not sure of your address yet, ask a friend or family member if you can use theirs.
2. Education. Your resume should have a list of schools you've attended. You can add any education you had in prison, especially If you earned any degrees or certificates.
3. Work experience. List your jobs, including volunteer work. Include where, when and for how long you held each job.
4. Other professional skills. This includes certifications, technical skills, and languages you speak other than English.
5. Awards (optional). If you've ever received an award for your work, like employee of the month, or a scholarship, list them at the end of your resume.

Are you worried about what people will think when they see school or work you did in prison? You do not have to put those on your resume if it worries you. The sample resumes in the back of the book can show you how other formerly incarcerated people have created their resumes.

"Be ready to pivot. Be patient with yourself. You're eager to get out, eager to do all of those things. Be realistic with yourself, what you can really do, what is within your control. You're going to be facing a lot of things." —Roberto

"If you sat at a table playing cards for ten years and now you want to come out and you want to go out and get yourself a job that's paying $18-20 an hour – well, be realistic. You're not gonna do it. You're not going to have that job because you didn't do anything to prepare. What are you going to put on your resume, that you played cards for ten years?" —Anonymous

For information about how to prepare for employment once you are released, see the employment section of the personal reentry plan on page 39.

4. Find Housing

One of the most important decisions you will make is where to live after release.

Some people choose to live with family or friends after release. You may need to submit the address where you plan to live as part of your release plans. The people you live with will need to fill out forms. Talk to them to make sure they understand the rules that you need to follow. Some of these rules will affect them, too. A Community Corrections Officer may visit the home and decide if it's OK for you to stay there. See our *Release* chapter for more information.

If you are not able to live with family members or friends upon release, you may need to find a halfway house (also called transitional house). You may also be eligible for housing vouchers for up to 6 months to cover the cost of living at a WADOC approved transitional house. Speak to your counselor about this.

Advantages

Living in a halfway house after release has some advantages.

- Many halfway houses provide support services, such as employment help, case management, life skills training and medical referrals. Having this support can be helpful while you navigate reentry.
- Halfway houses can provide structure and community. They can help set you up for success. They can remove some unknowns and allow you to focus on your priorities.
- With a housing voucher, up to 6 months of your housing fees will be covered by the state.
- If you do not have an approved release address, you may be held in confinement until your Max release date. This makes a transitional house a very viable option to ensure that you are released prior to your Max release date.

Challenges

Be aware of possible challenges with halfway houses, too.

- The quality of halfway housing varies a lot, and different halfway houses may specialize in different things. Do your research. Find out about other people's experiences with a halfway house. Ask for information before committing.
- Living in a halfway house can be costly. Some programs may be free or low cost. Other programs might charge very high fees. Be sure to ask about payment and the payment schedule.
- Program rules and expectations vary widely. Many have strict rules. Depending on your needs, these rules may provide helpful structure, or they may feel punitive and strict. Make sure you understand the rules before you commit

How to Find Halfway Housing

Per DOC 350.200 Section 4:

D.   Individuals who require an approved release address will be returned to their county of origin/alternate county of origin as determined and approved per Attachment 1.
1.   Individuals under Board jurisdiction are not subject to the county of origin requirements.
E.   Within 30 months of the ERD, eligible individuals may be referred for partial confinement.
F.   At least 12 months before the ERD, the case manager will directly assist the individual to identify a release address(es).
1.   Facility records employees will provide individuals with information to resolve warrants, if applicable.
G.   At 6 months before the ERD, the case manager will:
1.   Develop the release plan in the electronic file and verify the proposed address(es). "At least 12 months before the ERD, the case manager will directly assist the individual to identify a release address(s)." and
a.   Before submitting an investigation release plan, the case manager will complete DOC 11-012 Release/Transfer Sponsor Orientation Checklist with each prospective sponsor, determine the appropriateness of the proposed plan(s), and complete and send DOC 11-013 Sponsor Letter to each prospective sponsor.
1)   The sponsor checklist and letter are not required for individuals releasing to housing vendors listed in the Statewide Transitional Housing Directory located on the Department's internal website.

b.   If the individual cannot provide an address, the case manager will directly assist the individual in locating appropriate housing.

1)   If an address cannot be secured, eligible individuals should be referred for financial housing assistance using the Reentry Housing Assistance Program Job Aid located on the Department's internal website.
a)   Release plans for individuals using reentry housing assistance will only be submitted after benefits are approved.

In WADOC, case managers have access to an approved housing vendor list for those qualified for the housing voucher program. There are many types of transitional housing programs, and they are in most counties in the state. If your case manager determines you are approved for the housing voucher program, you will have to use housing vendors from this list. If you are not approved for the housing voucher program, you may still be able to arrange to be released to one of the approved housing vendor's houses. In this case, you will be responsible for all fees associated with going to said halfway house.

Ask your counselor to help you contact housing vendors in your county of origin. A lot of people need the spots. It's hard for them to know ahead of time what will be available. This can create a lot of stress. It may be useful to bring a list of halfway houses to your counselor. It's also a good idea to apply to a few halfway houses just in case.

For help finding housing, our directory provides a list of different reentry organizations organized by county that may be able to connect you to housing. In addition, here are a few websites that can help:

- Transitionalhousing.org

- Soberhousedirectory.com

Applying to Halfway Houses

While the application process for each halfway house may be different, here are some general steps you may follow:

1. Fill out an application. Your re-entry counselor can help you, or you can write to a halfway house to request one. You may need to share documents like disciplinary history, convictions, programs, and letters of recommendation.
2. Interview. If you meet the requirements, the halfway house may schedule an interview to see if you are a good fit.
3. Waiting list. If you are accepted, you can ask for a letter to show whatever board you may be under. You may have to wait to see if there is a bed available. This is one reason why some people apply to multiple halfway houses.
4. Payment. Another factor impacting your acceptance will be your ability to pay. Talk to your counselor about the voucher program. The voucher program will help you cover the housing fees for up to 6 months and will need to ensure payments can be made at the time of your release.
5. Transportation. When your release date is confirmed, usually a prison official will talk to the halfway house to make sure they have a space for you. They will help plan for your release day transportation.

Finding the Right Fit

There are a lot of good and bad halfway houses out there. Here are a few questions you can ask your counselor or the people at the halfway house to see if it is a good fit for you:

- Who do you serve?
- How long can I stay?
- What is the cost? What is the payment schedule?
- What programs and services are offered? What will I be doing when I live there?
- Do you provide mental health or substance use treatment?
- What rules will I have to follow while I am there? What freedoms will I have?
- Is this a faith-based program? Will I be required to attend services?

Unfortunately, almost all transitional houses do not let in people who have been convicted of sex-based offenses, and some do not let in people who have been convicted of violent offenses. Our Housing After Release chapter has some advice about how to find housing if you have a sex-based offense.

5. Health Before Release

Planning for healthcare before you leave prison saves money and helps you avoid problems. There are a few steps you should take before you are released.

 Enroll in Medicaid

Per WADOC Publication 600-HA003, Health Services Orientation Handbook:

"Medicaid Pre-enrollment Program: If you meet certain criteria, this process enables DOC to help you enroll in Washington Apple Health so that you have medical coverage before you release from incarceration. If you do not meet the criteria for Apple Health, you may also qualify for a temporary or conditional benefit until your Medicare benefits get fully activated. To qualify for the pre-enrollment, you must be within 60 days of your release, a US citizen or legal resident alien, and upon your release you must not be residing with a spouse or dependents (children for which you are financially responsible for at least 6 months out of the year). DOC will not pre-enroll you in a program that will cost you money. If you qualify and are successfully enrolled, DOC will notify you via letter. You will also receive two identification cards (ProviderOne, Managed Care Plan) and a Washington Apple Health Benefits Book. If you do not qualify for pre-enrollment or are denied coverage by Washington Apple Health, DOC will send you a letter explaining the reasons for the denial. Just because you are denied/not eligible for the Pre-enrollment Program, it does not mean you are not eligible for Washington Apple Health." (Washington State DOC, 2017)

Ask your counselor to help you get started. As part of your release plan, facility health services will be contacted to facilitate this process.

If you have a loved one with internet access, they may be able to help you apply at wahealthplanfinder.org. Once you submit your application, it takes 30 days to get insurance, so get started early! This is especially important if you have a health problem that requires treatment.

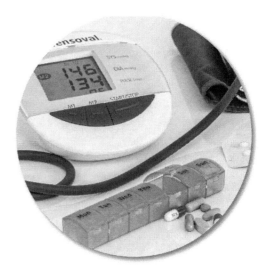

Get Your Health Records

Per DOC 640.020
V. Health Information Disclosure
A.　　Information contained in the health record, including information shared with health care professionals, is confidential and will only be disclosed/photocopied as authorized by statute. Requests will be processed per the HRP.
B.　　Patients may request, in writing, to examine or obtain a copy of all or part of their health information. A response will be made within 15 business days upon receipt of the written request.
1.　　Requests for copies will be submitted to the Department of Corrections Public Records Unit at P.O. Box 41118, Olympia, WA 98504.
2.　　The individual will be notified of the fees for copies.
a.　　For individuals who are indigent, copies from the previous 6 months will be provided at no charge. Individuals will be charged for duplicate copies.

Ask your counselor about how to get your health records. You may need to fill out a form. We recommend that you start this process a few months before your release

 ## Get Your Exams

Request a dental exam, an eye exam, and a physical exam before you leave prison. Start early (a year before release) in case they find something you will need to address.

 ## Make A Birth Control and Sexual Health Plan

If you plan to be sexually active after release, discuss birth control and safe sex during your physical exam. This may help you avoid unwanted pregnancy and STDs. Women should request a gynecological exam with a PAP smear and ask for a mammogram if over age 40.

Consider your options carefully. Some forms of birth control, like condoms, are easy to get and are cheap. They need to be used every time you have sex and may not be as effective as other options. Other kinds of birth control require a prescription from a doctor or a medical procedure. When you have your physical exam, you may be able to request longer-term birth control options, like pills, patches, or intrauterine devices (IUDs). Implants or IUDs can protect you for several years from unwanted pregnancy.

No doctor should pressure you into a permanent or long-term birth control or sterilization procedure. Unfortunately, some doctors at prisons have pressured women to have hysterectomies (sterilization) and men to have vasectomies. While vasectomies are reversible, hysterectomies will prevent you from ever conceiving. Take time to ask questions and decide what is best for you. If you are feeling pressured, remember it's your right to say no.

 ## Make A Medication Plan

WADOC offers people a 30 to 90-day supply of medication upon release. Generally, you will pick up your medications the day you are released, but you may want to request these medications ahead of time, just to be safe. The doctor will usually give you a prescription so you can get more. Plan to get more medication after you leave. Set up an appointment with a doctor on the outside so that you don't run out. This can help you avoid going to the ER to get medications filled, which can be costly.

 ## Plan For Doctor Visits After Release

Before you are released, ask for a list of healthcare providers that accept Medicaid or low-cost community clinics. If you have a serious mental or physical health issue, be proactive and set up appointments ahead of time. A counselor or family member may be able to set up the appointment for you.

You may have been in a drug or alcohol treatment program while in prison. Continue treatment after release to make sure you don't relapse. Ask your doctor, clinical services, or a family member to help you find a treatment center. Try to schedule the appointment for a few days after your release. Our directory includes a list of many low-cost health clinics and substance use treatment centers.

Health checklist

	Taken care of	Need to tackle	Where to get help
Enroll in Medicaid			
Enroll in SNAP			
Get health records			
Physical exam			
Eye exam			
Dental exam			
Contraception plan			
Medication plan			
Set up doctor visits after release			
Set up mental health treatment after release			
Set up substance use treatment after release			

For more information, see our Health chapter, our Trauma and Mental Health chapter, and our Substance Use chapter.

A Warning: The first few hours, days, and weeks after release are often the hardest. People are at greater risk for suicide. Many return to old habits, like drug or alcohol use. People are at greater risk for overdose because their bodies aren't used to drugs anymore. If you can, be proactive and schedule appointments with health care providers ahead of time. You may not need them, but you'll have a plan just in case.

6. Prepare for Reunification

This chapter covers the following topics:

- Staying Close to Loved Ones While in Prison
- Preparing for Reunification
- Preparing to Reunite with Children

Staying Close to Loved Ones

For many, the hardest part of being locked up is the strain it places on relationships. Separation is hard for both you and your loved ones. While you may feel love, concern, and care, there may also be feelings of guilt, loss, frustration, anger, and grief.

If you have any emotions at all, you're going to have guilt about making your family suffer the pains that you're going through. Because you're not suffering alone. They suffer with you while you're in there. – Tony C.

Healthy relationships are open, honest, and deep. Try to maintain regular, open lines of communication through letters and phone calls, when possible. Staying in touch with your loved ones will make reunion smoother.

The complexities of being in prison can startle any relationship. That's why understanding and communication is key. In reality no one wants to be a burden; however, everybody needs someone. The pressure of maintaining a healthy relationship is hard for two people in the free world. When I was doing time, I had to understand the sacrifices I needed to make to maintain a healthy relationship with the people that mattered the most to me. I had to remember what it was like to be free, and I had to educate my family and friends of what it was like to be incarcerated. --Antonio

A lot of times people get discouraged when family don't take their phone calls. They don't get a response, and they get discouraged. They think, 'To hell with it, they don't want to hear from me.' Even if they don't respond, you still have to try to cultivate those relationships. A lot of times people are super busy out here. It's not that they don't want to talk to you. Keep cultivating those relationships because they are what's going to help you when you get out. --Anonymous

It's hard, but you must make your kids understand that you don't want to be away from them... You love them and you're going to do everything you can to make sure you're in their life. – Tony C.

During incarceration, some relationships may end, and all relationships will be challenged. Some find it so difficult that they distance themselves as a form of self-preservation. Be aware that this distance can be very hard to overcome upon release.

You spend so many years in there and so much time keeping people at an arm's distance. You never let anybody get close... But when you come home, you've gotten so used to keeping people at a distance that you just continue to do it. It's hard to make new friends. – Tony C.

You don't want to worry your family with those issues. You get on the phone, and you grind your teeth. Regardless of what you're feeling, you're going to tell them that everything is going to be OK. You get in this habit of keeping things bottled up, and you're dealing with some degree of loneliness and emptiness, because you're not sharing it with your family. --Roberto

Explore other ways to maintain relationships. While it's painful to not be physically present in your loved ones' lives, there are other ways to be present. Talk, listen, and provide emotional and mental support when and how you can.

Try to find ways to make it easier for them to accept you being gone. Because if you just sit and tell them how horrible it is and you bark at them every time they come to visit you or you yell at them in letters or on the phone, then they're gonna get frustrated with dad and say, "Well hey, you're not even here, so what can you do?"
– Tony C.

Relationships aren't a one-way street. Family members can also do a lot to maintain relationships. They can help those who are incarcerated feel included. Share everyday things to help them feel connected.

I send him a little bit of money, enough to keep phone calls going, you know, and pictures and stuff and try to set up options for him so he knows he doesn't have to go back to the same stuff. Just let him know that there's help, there's better things in life. I try to talk to him about the good stuff, about working and going to church, when we're playing games with his little sister and stuff like that. – Heather B.

Preparing for Reunification

You might be scared, worried, or excited about reuniting with family and friends. You can prepare by reflecting on your relationships. Be honest about who is likely to be a positive, supportive influence in your life. You and your loved ones can also set realistic expectations. You are all in transition. A period of adjustment will be necessary.

It is hard to be left at home and hard to come home, even if you were only away for a few months. For loved ones, having the person come home can take some getting used to as well.

You might begin by letting your loved ones know what you are hoping for and what you will need from them during your reentry. This could include both emotional and financial support. Never be afraid to ask for patience.

Listen to the needs and concerns of your loved ones, too. Reuniting will be easier if you can talk ahead of time and learn to compromise.

The key thing is honesty. [If] you come out being honest with yourself and with [your loved ones], you can't go wrong, because you're not feeding them a fairy tale. You're giving them you. – Keke

Keep in mind that you are entering somebody else's space. You must be mindful of the relationships around you. --Pablo

If you were locked up for a long time, you'll need to relearn who you are and who your loved ones are. Children who were young when you left may be teenagers or even grown up with children of their own. You may have different ideas of what the new relationship should look like.

Don't come in like they're supposed to know you or even respect you a little bit, because you've been gone. You gotta gain that respect and that trust back when you've been gone so long. – Keke

Recognize that we haven't been part of that house for years, so I can't come in and put down my dominance, something we're used to doing when we're in the cell. We're used to carving up space and making it our own. --Joe Joe

Acknowledge the ways you have changed. You and your loved ones have both grown. Allow for this growth. Be open to the person before you and who they are now.

First you gotta get yourself together, mentally. Because you might think you know them because they're part of you, but you really don't know them and what they've been through. You know what they tell you. Same thing with you. – Keke

Never expect anyone to evolve at your pace. When you are dealing with people you haven't lived with in a while you have to be analytical, you have to examine the structure of your own character. And the character of those you live with. Once you are fully in tune with the compound presence of your household you should become as flexible as a bamboo stick, but it won't be easy. So, get an evaluation and accept some help from those who can help you with your transition. --Antonio

Oftentimes when people are anticipating going home, they have ideals and expectations on how their reunification with family will be. There's the dream and there's the reality. It's good to have these great expectations, but don't set yourself up for disappointment if people don't live up to the expectations you have of them. People have lived experience that might color the way they interact. –JoeJoe

---
♪♪

Preparing to Reunite with Children

You may have young children you are looking forward to being with. You may be excited to see your kids again or you might be nervous and stressed. It's ok to have mixed feelings. There's no right way to feel.

There are things you can do to parent from prison and prepare yourself for regaining custody of your kids, if that's your goal. Show your commitment to your children. This will make it easier to get them back when you are out. Here are some ideas:

Before Your Release

- Stay in touch with your kids through regular phone calls and letters. Record the dates and times so that you have evidence of your involvement.
- Attend all hearings about your child. It's your right!
- Take parenting classes if offered.
- Take job training as well as academic and technical classes.

After Your Release

- Prioritize getting safe and stable housing.
- Follow all parole rules and requirements.
- Visit your kids as often as you can. Record details about the visits.
- Continue to attend parenting, job training or other classes. This shows your commitment to providing a stable home for your child.

If you've been separated from your children, you may be eager to reunite with them as soon as you can. But don't rush things. First you need to have a stable job, safe housing, and sobriety. Getting your kids back too soon can cause more harm than good if you are unable to provide a healthy and safe environment for them.

If your parental rights have been terminated, you will need the court's permission to get your children back. To find legal aid in your area, search for the name of your city and terms like "child custody" "legal aid" or "pro bono." Please reference the resource directory for additional resources.

Even if you don't get your kids back as soon as you would like, you can still make changes and be involved in decisions about them. If getting your kids back is what's right for your family, don't give up, even if there are roadblocks!

7. Community Custody or Parole

When you are released from prison, you will probably be in some form of parole or community custody. This means you will be supervised by the Department of Corrections for your state until the set period is over.

While in community custody, you'll have to follow some rules. We realize that it is frustrating to know that even though you are getting out of prison, you will not be completely free. Hang in there. Community custody is difficult, but many people have gotten through it. You can, too.

This chapter covers:

- Preparing for community custody/parole
- Community custody/parole after release
- Community custody/parole rules and violations
- Registries (sex offense registry)

Preparing for Community Custody/Parole

The release process usually begins around twelve months before your release date.

 Step 1. Educate yourself about the conditions of your release.

As you get closer to release, your counselor will call you in to complete a reassessment. The outcomes of this assessment will determine the type of restrictions that will be placed on you and the type of programming that you will be required to complete upon release. Make sure you understand the results of your assessment, ask your counselor questions if you do not understand. The assessment is used to structure your release plan, which will be transferred over to the Community Corrections Officer (CCO) you are assigned to. The CCO will be the one responsible for monitoring you to make sure you are in compliance with your release conditions, this is why one of the first places you must go upon release is to see your CCO. If you are under the ISRB (*Indeterminate Sentence Review Board AKA Parole Board*), your assessment outcomes and release plan will be forwarded to them. The Board has the discretion to alter or add to your conditions. For example, they may require you to be placed on electronic monitoring for a while.

 Step 2. Find a place to live.

One of the requirements for your release from prison is to provide a valid address where you intend to live. This address must be approved by a Community Corrections Officer (CCO) who may visit the place and check if it is suitable for you, especially if you must wear an electronic monitoring device. If you do

31

not have a place to stay, your counselor will help you find one, and you may be eligible for a voucher program that can pay for your transitional housing for up to six months. Unless you are under the Board, you will most likely have to be released to your "County of Origin." The county of origin is the county where you lived at the time of your first felony conviction, including a juvenile conviction, in Washington State.

 ## Step 3. Talk to the people you will be living with.

Many of the community custody rules you'll follow will affect the people you live with. Talk to them early and clearly. Let them know what your release conditions will mean for them. They can contact your counselor and/or assigned CCO with their questions.

 ## Step 4. Complete paperwork.

The people you plan on living with will have to complete a document called the "Release/Transfer Sponsor Orientation Checklist" that allows them to host you in their home. It may come in the mail, or the CCO may bring it when they visit the home.

 Transferring to another state: *If you plan to live in another state, talk to your counselor about filing for an interstate compact. Your counselor will guide you through the process. You can also review policy in DOC 380.605 by visiting your facility's law library.*

Community Custody/Parole After Release

When you are released, you will usually be required to visit your local community field office to check in with your CCO, often within 48 hours, but it is highly recommended to make that one of the first activities upon release, doing it that same day if possible. Before you leave, make sure you have your CCO's name and phone number. It is your job to get in touch with your CCO. If you cannot reach your CCO or do not know who they are, contact your local community field office for help.

Electronic Monitoring

Many people are given Electronic Monitoring (EM) with their parole or as a part of an early release program. If you have EM, you will have to follow some extra rules.

You will likely be given instructions before you are released. You may need to go straight home and check in with your CCO and in many cases your CCO will be the one to pick you up upon release so that they can monitor and guide you through all the necessary steps. A technician will generally come to your home to set up the electronic monitor. The monitor may have an anklet and a box that plugs in the wall. Make sure the monitor stays plugged in. Once the monitor is set up you and your CCO will decide what times you will be allowed to leave your home.

You will be required to check in regularly with your CCO. Remember, it's very important you answer the phone when your CCO calls. Not answering could get you in trouble.

Electronic monitoring can be hard for everyone in your house. Until you find a job, you will be home most of the time, which can cause stress. If you need rides during your movement times, you will need to work that out. Talk clearly with the people you will live with. Let them know what you need from them, what they need from you, and how you will address problems.

Community Custody/Parole Rules & Violations

CCO's have the responsibility and authority to hold you accountable for your release conditions. These conditions are written on a legal document. Make sure you understand all the rules and instructions before you sign. Ask questions! Some of the most common rules include:

- Do not commit any criminal acts.
- Report to your CCO on a regular basis.
- Do not possess firearms.
- Allow the CCO to inspect and search you and your residence.
- Refrain from using drugs.
- Do not leave the state.

If you break the conditions of release, you may be violated and sent back to prison. Sadly, this happens a lot. Follow the rules very carefully so you can stay on the outside. If something happens that makes it look like you violated your conditions, call your CCO right away to explain what happened. If you haven't broken any rules, your CCO can ask that you not be charged.

If you are charged with violating conditions, you may be able to appeal. You may be assigned a lawyer. The lawyer can show evidence and bring witnesses to help you make your case. Please reference **RCW 9.94A.737** which can be made available to you at your facility's law library.

Registries

If you have a sex offense you will be required to register after release, depending on your conviction and offense level. Washington state has sex offense registries. These registries are online databases that anyone can see. They have photos and information such as your name,

address, birthday, place of work, crime conviction history, age, and victim gender.

If you have to register, you will likely face many challenges. People will make hurtful comments. It will be very hard to find housing and a job. Focus on your self-worth. You are more than your conviction. We believe in you.

Ask your counselor before you are released if you need to register. You can also ask someone you trust to contact the authority that maintains the registries. Make sure you know and understand the rules. It's easy to make a mistake and go back to jail. You may be charged with "failure to register" because you missed a deadline or didn't know you needed to register again.

Where will I register? Typically, you will register at your local police or sheriff's department. This is something you will likely need to do right away when you get to your host site.

How often will I need to register? It depends. You may have to register every 90 days or once a year. Keep a calendar of all your deadlines and dates to re-register. Call ahead and make appointments if you can.

What should I bring when I register? It varies by state. You will likely need proof of address (rent or utility bill, official document with address) and your state ID. They will take a photo of you and post it on the sex offense registry website. They may also take fingerprints or a DNA swab. You will have to sign registration documents. Be sure you understand what you are signing. Keep your documents in a safe place so you can get to them easily. Hold onto documents that explain the conditions of probation or parole, your registration documents, and certified receipts.

How long will I have to register? It depends on your conviction and the state you live in. You may be required to register every year for a few years after release. For more serious convictions, you may have to register for the rest of your life.

Do I have to register every time I move?
Yes—though if you move out of state, check to find out their requirements. Some states do not have a registry. Generally, you have a few days to let law enforcement know that you have moved. You may also have to re-register if you have a change of job or if you change your email address or your online identifiers.

Will I have to pay to register? Check with your state. Illinois requires a fee of $100 or 100 hours of community service per year, and failure to pay is a felony.

What other restrictions may I face? Common restrictions, especially for those convicted of child sex offenses, include not being allowed to go in school buildings or on grounds, or live near a school, playground, or childcare facility. You may not be allowed in parks or public park buildings. You may not be able to use social media, like Facebook or Instagram.

Where can I get help? You don't have to figure it out alone. There may be organizations in your state that can support you. The Sex Law and Policy Center publishes a reentry guide called *Registering with Dignity*. Check it out here:

- https://narsol.org/wp-content/uploads/2017/12/RegisteringWithDignity-Handbook.pdf
- Restrictions for Washington - PROBATION INFORMATION NETWORK

Note: It is against the law to harass or threaten people on the sex offense registry or their families. If this is happening to you, call the police or your probation or parole officer.

Part 2: Personal Reentry Plan

Planning for your release is a crucial step to ensure your success and well-being after incarceration. This section helps you create a personal release plan that covers different aspects of your life, such as housing, employment, education, health, and family. By completing this exercise, you will have a clear vision of your goals and the resources you need to achieve them. You will also be prepared to overcome any obstacles or challenges that may arise along the way. This section is divided into the following chapters:

1. Getting Organized/Barriers
2. Identification
3. Housing
4. Employment
5. Clothing
6. Transportation
7. Food & Other Benefits
8. Money Management
9. Medical/Health
10. Education
11. Selective Services
12. Mental Health Services
13. Recovery
14. Family Reunification
15. Technology
16. Living Under Supervision
17. Appendix: S.M.A.R.T. Goals

1. Getting Organized/Barriers

Use this checklist to assist in planning your **PERSONAL** reentry plan by recognizing some of your barriers. What do you need for a successful reentry?

Item	Y	N
Social Security Card		
Birth Certificate		
Driver's License/ State Identification Card		
EBT Card		
Credit Report		
Registration/Status of Information exemption for Selective Service		
Résumé		
Housing (i.e., House of Mercy)		
Medical Care (Apple Health)		
Support Groups (Church, Recovery, etc.)		
Child Support Issues/Problem Solving Court		
Transportation		
Education/ Certifications		
Veterans Assistance/DD214		
Employment		
Legal Assistance		
Telephone		
Other		

What are some barriers you will need to overcome as part of your reentry success? What are some solutions to those barriers? Remember that solutions must be REALISTIC and ATTAINABLE to be successful. For example: lack of money may be a real barrier but winning the lottery would not be a very realistic solution! (*See the Appendix for how to write S.M.A.R.T. Goals*).

_____
_____
_____
_____
_____
_____
_____
_____
_____

2. Identification

Having approved identification is a critical tool for successful reentry! Which documents do you have and/or how will you get them? (Review *Part 1, Before You Release*)

Identification	Have Y/N	Plan to Get
Birth Certificate (certified)		
Social Security Card		
DL/State ID		

Use additional paper if needed

3. Housing

The place where you live after you get out of prison can make a big difference in how you get the help you need. You might start by staying in a transitional house or somewhere else for a while, but you probably want to have your own place someday. You should think about where you want to live and what services are available there. This workbook can help you find out.

If you are going to live in a House of Mercy house at first, that's awesome! You can stay there as long as you need to get ready for your new life. But we guess you don't want to stay there forever. Do you know where you want to live next? Have a plan B, and then have a plan C! You never know what might happen. When looking for housing, keep in mind where it is located relative to your work, what transportation is available, what your release stipulations are, and what stores are in the area.

Primary Residence Plan:

Living with (Name/Relationship):

_____.

Address (physical/mailing):

_____

_____.

Contact Number(s): _____.

Notes:

_____
_____
_____
_____
_____.

Secondary Residence Plan:

Living with (Name/Relationship):

_____.

Address (physical/mailing):

_____

_____.

Contact Number(s): _____.

Notes:

_____
_____
_____
_____
_____
_____
_____
_____

Third Residence Plan:

Living with (Name/Relationship):

_____.

Address (physical/mailing):

_____

_____.

Contact Number(s): _____.

Notes:

_____
_____
_____
_____
_____
_____
_____
_____
_____
_____
_____
_____

Use additional paper if needed

4. Employment

Information in this section will help you when filling out employment applications, putting together a résumé, interviewing, and keeping a job.

Job Objective Worksheet

The questions below can help you determine what your **resume objective statement** should look like, what type of employment you are seeking, what you can offer the employer, where you want to go with your career, etc.

List courses you have taken during incarceration.

1. _____   3. _____

2. _____   4. _____

Which subjects do you enjoy and do well in?

1. _____   3. _____

2. _____   4. _____

What qualifications and/or skills do you possess?

1. _____   3. _____

2. _____   4. _____

List work and/or details you have had while incarcerated.

1. _____   3. _____

2. _____   4. _____

Based on the information provided above, what are some job choices in your area of interest?

Option 1: _____

Option 2: _____

Use additional paper if needed

Next, list possible job types available in your area.

Option 1: _____

Option 2: _____

Option 3: _____

Option 4: _____

Option 5: _____

Job Search Plan

To succeed in your job search, you must be organized. You will be competing with others and your goal is to present yourself as the best candidate for the job.

Where will you go to find employment assistance?

Friends & Family	
Online Employment Resource (Honest Jobs, Indeed, Monster, Etc.):	
WA Department of Labor:	
Community Reentry Service (House of Mercy, The Journey Project, WELD, Etc.):	
WorkSource/Goodwill Resource Ctr.	
Other Community Resources (Public Libraries)	

Employment/Job Placement Record – Tracking Log

1. Make a list of who you plan to call (use table below & additional paper as needed).
2. Find all the phone numbers and write them in the table.
3. Call and get the name of the person in charge of hiring. Keep calling until you get it.
4. Call the person in charge of hiring. Are they hiring now? Keep calling until you find out.
5. If they are hiring, schedule an appointment with them. Keep calling until you get one.

6. Show up on time, do the interview and application, and agree on the next steps before you leave.
7. Call back and thank them for the interview and opportunity. Keep calling until you reach them.

Company & Phone	Name of person hiring, are they hiring now?	Date & time of appointment	Interview and application done?	Thank You Note completed & sent?	Got an answer on the job?

Resume Writing Worksheet

The following worksheet was compiled from multiple online sources and will help you complete your resume. Think about the following areas and make notes for each section. This will help you develop a professional resume with relevant and necessary content. If a category does not have enough space, please use additional paper.

Heading – Personal & Contact Info

You may use an alternative address to indicate where an employer may contact you.

Name: _____

Address:

_____

Phone: _____

Email: _____ (*Make sure your email address is one that you check daily and is appropriately named.*)

Objective

What type of position are you seeking? Include an objective if you have a clear direction or goal.

_____
_____
_____
_____

Use additional paper if needed

Education

List all the schools you have attended. Do not abbreviate.

Grade/High School:_____City/State:_____

Highest Grade Completed:_____

GED:_____City/State:_____

College:_____City/State:_____

Major/Degree:_____Years Attended:_____

Vocational/Trade
School:_____City/State:_____

Major/Degree: _____Years Attended: _____

Honors/Awards:
_____
_____
_____
_____

Research, Class Projects, Special Studies

Note research or class projects which are related to your field of interest if appropriate.
_____
_____
_____

Certifications & Licenses

1. **Examples might include CPR/First Aid, Microsoft, Teaching, etc.**

Name of Certificate/License:_____Date Rec'd/Expires:_____

Organization granting Certification/Licensure:_____

2. **Examples might include CPR/First Aid, Microsoft, Teaching, etc.**

Name of Certificate/License:_____Date Rec'd/Expires:_____

Organization granting Certification/Licensure:_____

Experience – Work, Internships and/or Related

List your experience, with the most recent information first (no more than 15 years of work history). When noting your responsibilities use action verbs to describe your skills and activities.

Position/Title (1):_____

Dates:_____to _____

Employer/Company:_____

City, State:_____

Responsibilities & Accomplishments:

_____
_____

Position/Title (2):_____

Dates:_____to _____

Employer/Company:_____

City, State:_____

Responsibilities & Accomplishments:

_____
_____

Position/Title (3):_____

Dates:_____to _____

Employer/Company:_____

City, State:_____

Responsibilities & Accomplishments:

_____
_____

Military Service

Include Branch, Rank, Dates, Jobs, and Duties.

_____
_____
_____

Honors & Awards

Include name of honor/award, date received & name of organization giving award.

_____
_____
_____

Skills

This section can help you demonstrate proficiency in areas not otherwise outlined in your academic or experience sections. Focus on skills relevant to your desired position/career field. Skills might include languages (note level of fluency), computer skills (list programs and languages you are able to use), or other field specific areas, such as techniques, methods, and tools/instruments used.

_____
_____
_____

Professional Associations

In this section, list the name of the organization and dates of membership. Note if you are a student member of a professional association/organization.

_____
_____
_____

Involvement

In this section, list Campus, Community, and Volunteer activities that demonstrate involvement in organizations and leadership roles.

_____
_____
_____

References

References are not included on your resume. Create a separate references page, listing at least 3 individuals who can attest to your work ethic, academic performance, skills, and abilities. Ask these individuals prior to including them.

Name:_____Title:_____

Organization:_____

Address: _____

Phone: _____ Email (optional):_____

Name:_____Title:_____

Organization:_____

Address:_____

Phone: _____ Email (optional):_____

Name:_____Title:_____

Organization:_____

Address:_____

Phone: _____ Email (optional):_____

Job Applications

Sometimes a company's policy may require you to fill out an application before being considered for a job. This allows an employer the opportunity to compare you to other applicants. You may be asked to complete a job application on paper or online. These days the chances are you will have to apply online.

Be Prepared

Make sure you come prepared for your interview. What are some things you should bring to the interview?

_____   _____

_____   _____

_____   _____

_____   _____

What are some questions you should expect from the employer?

_____
_____
_____

What are some questions you may ask an employer?

_____
_____
_____

How will you respond if you are asked about any history concerning your incarceration?

_____
_____
_____
_____
_____
_____
_____
_____

Use additional paper if needed

5. Clothing

You will need to wear appropriate clothing for job hunting and interviewing. You will also need clothing for everyday wear. Remember to dress for success whenever you will be out on potential employment-seeking activities, even if it is not an official job search event. You can make an impression with a potential employer at any public or private event you attend! There are community service and support organizations that may be able to assist with clothing. Find out and list possible options for clothing assistance in your area.

Clothing Provider: _____

Location: _____

Hours of Operation: _____

Requirements: _____

Clothing Provider: _____

Location: _____

Hours of Operation: _____

Requirements: _____

Notes on how you plan to Dress for Success:

_____
_____
_____
_____

What are some of the "*Do's*" and "*Don'ts*" when it comes to dressing and personal appearance in job seeking?

Do's   **Don'ts**

_____   _____

_____   _____

_____   _____

_____   _____

6. Transportation

One very important area for you to consider is your transportation plan. How you get to work, report to your Community Supervision Officer, and other important appointments can determine your success as you transition back into the community.

How do you plan to get around for interviews, appointments, work, reporting, etc.? List some transportation options for your area as well as community service providers that may be able to assist with transportation:

Public Transportations: _____

Carpool: _____

Community Assistance: _____

Medical Shuttle: _____

Taxi Services: _____

Drive: _____

Walk: _____

Bicycle: _____

Other: _____

Additionally, some community service providers will help with transportation by helping with public transportation (ORCA Cards, free bus passes, etc.), and shuttle services (medical). For example, HOM provides each participant with a public transportation voucher upon intake into the program and offers a transportation service for case management and clinical related appointments.

7. Food & Other Benefits

"Man (Nor Woman) Can Live by Bread (Or Ramen Noodles) Alone" So How Do You
Plan to Nutritionally Support Yourself?

If you are low-income (generally you are after being released): You may be eligible for Basic Food (i.e., food stamps/EBT) or the Emergency Food Assistance Program. You may also be eligible for Medicaid/Apple Health or public housing assistance; you can find more information about those programs in the Healthcare Benefits and Housing chapters of this Guide.

Many communities have Food Banks/Pantries, Soup Kitchens, and other meal assistance programs as well. Locate food options in your area in the resource directory.

What is your immediate plan to sign up for EBT:

_____
_____
_____
_____
_____
_____
_____

What are some food banks/pantries in the area you will be released to?

_____
_____
_____
_____
_____
_____

A New Beginning

Jake, a recently released individual, found himself alone and helpless in a world that had drastically changed during his incarceration. Desperate for shelter and sustenance, he ventured into the city, hoping for a glimmer of hope or kindness. Unfortunately, he encountered only cold stares and closed doors, feeling like an outcast and a threat. However, his curiosity was piqued when he noticed a church displaying a banner that read "Welcome Home". Despite his lack of religious affiliation, he recalled attending church as a child with his mother. Intrigued, he entered and was greeted by a compassionate woman named Mary, who was part of a ministry dedicated to aiding individuals like him. She invited him to join them for a meal and a meeting. In a hall filled with others who had experienced incarceration and were striving to rebuild their lives, Jake was warmly embraced. They shared their stories, offering him empathy, guidance, and encouragement. The ministry provided various resources such as counseling, mentoring, job training, and housing assistance. Overwhelmed with gratitude and newfound hope, Jake realized that he was not alone, that there were people who genuinely cared about his well-being and were eager to assist him. He felt a sense of belonging, purpose, and faith. Determined to transform his life, he decided to become a part of the ministry and follow their guidance. Expressing his appreciation to Mary and the others, Jake declared his readiness for a fresh start alongside them. They embraced him joyfully, declaring him a welcomed addition to their family. Overwhelmed with emotion, Jake gazed at the banner, its message resonating deep within his heart: "Welcome Home".

8. Money Management

Monthly Budget			
Income Source	Salary	Gross	Net
Job 1			
Job 2			
Other			
Total			
Fixed Expenses	Budgeted	Actual	Difference
Rent/Mortgage			
Homeowners/Renters Insurance			
Property Taxes			
Credit Card Payments			
Health Insurance			
Phone Bill			
Internet			
Utilities			
Child Support/ Childcare			
Supervision Fees/Restitution			
Variable Expenses			
Food/Groceries			
Food – Meals Out			
Toiletries/Household Items			
Clothing			
Medical Expenses			
Entertainment			
Transportation			
Car Payment			
Public Transportation (Orca, etc.)			
Gas			
Repairs and Maintenance			
Auto Insurance			
Parking			
Other			
Savings			
Total Expenses			
Balance (remaining)			

9. Medical/Health

Taking care of your physical health, including the continuation of medication you were taking while incarcerated, is a critical step in reentry. If you are on medication, you will only be given a limited supply of take-home meds and you will need to follow up with your private doctor or at one of the publicly funded clinics in your release area as soon as possible. There may be a medication assistance program you can find online or locally, which can assist with paying for some of the medication you currently take. For more information read our Health Chapter.

Medical Problems:

_____
_____
_____
_____

Medication List:

_____
_____

Immunizations:

_____
_____

Clinics in my area to visit:

_____
_____
_____
_____

10. Education

Education and Marketable Skills

Continuing your education will help you develop marketable skills. You may also be eligible for student financial aid and/or scholarships.

What are your educational plans upon release? Where will you pursue them?

List GED, College, or Vocational Training options available in your area.

_____
_____
_____
_____
_____
_____

How will you obtain funding (FASFA, Scholarships, etc.):

_____
_____
_____
_____

How will you obtain your school transcripts:

_____
_____

How will you obtain your immunization records:

_____
_____

11.   Selective Service

What is Selective Service Registration?

Registration with the Selective Service System is a civic and legal responsibility for all male U.S. Citizens within 30 days of their 18th birthday. Male, non-citizens living in the US, 18-25 yrs. old must register to remain eligible for citizenship. Failure to register can affect your ability to obtain certain services such as: obtaining driver's licenses, federal student aid and federal grants, federal job training, most federal jobs. If you are over 26 yrs old and have never registered, you can have your counselor assist you with applying for a Status of Information letter.

If you do not register, there can be a penalty of up to $250,000 and up to 5 years in prison.

Have you registered for Selective Service?

How Do You Register?

Under 25:

- Registration On-Line (https://www.sss.gov/)
- The U.S. Post Office
- Your counselor can help you register during your time in prison. Talk to them about getting this completed

Over 25:

Complete a request form for a status information letter (in the forms section of this guide). You will have to describe, in detail, the circumstances you believe prevented you from registering and provide copies of documents showing any periods when you were hospitalized, institutionalized, or incarcerated occurring between your 18th and 26th birthdays. If you are a non-citizen, you may be required to provide documents that show when you entered the United States. Please include your name, social security number, date of birth, and return address. Please note the following:

- Keep your SIL in your permanent files for future reference.
- Send a copy, not your original, SIL to submit with your application for state-based student financial aid, employment, security clearance, U.S. citizenship.
- Do not send your original documents. Only send copies of documents which you are required to send.

Please mail your form to:
Selective Service System
ATTN: SIL
P.O. Box 94638
Palatine, IL 60094-4638

Verification:

To verify registration status visit https://www.sss.gov/verify/, Required information: Last name, Social Security Number, Date of Birth.

12. Mental Health Services

List your Mental Health Diagnosis and MH Medication currently prescribed:

_____

_____

_____

_____

Where can you seek Mental Health Treatment and Assistance in your community (*use our resource directory to find potential resources in the community you will be released to*)?

_____

_____

_____

_____

Please speak with your mental health counselor about any questions you may have about your release from prison or anything in this section of the manual. He or she can be very helpful in preparing you for release and increasing your opportunity to remain in the community without returning to jail or prison.

13. Recovery

Has alcohol or substance use caused problems in your life? This self-assessment is designed to help you identify how an addiction or substance abuse problem can influence your life. Take this honestly and with an open mind. The results are for your own self-reflection and are not intended to replace the results of any assessment performed by a licensed clinician.

1. Do you ever use for something other than a medical reason?
2. When you use, do you use more than one drug at a time?
3. Do you use more than once per week?
4. Have you ever abused prescription medications?
5. Have you ever tried to stop using but couldn't stay stopped?
6. Do you ever feel ashamed or guilty after using?
7. Has your relationships with friends become distant?
8. Do you spend less time with your family and more time with friends who use?
9. Has your family or friends talked to you about your use?
10. Do your family members or friends every complain about your use?
11. While under the influence, have you gotten into fights with other people?
12. Have you ever lost a job due to coming in late, mistakes, or poor work performance due to your use?
13. Has your use caused problems or gotten you into trouble at your workplace?
14. Have you been arrested for illegal drug possession?
15. Do you participate in illegal activities in order to get your fix?
16. When you stop using, do you experience any withdrawal symptoms or feel sick?
17. Has your use ever resulted in blackouts?
18. Have you ever had medical problems such as memory loss, convulsions, bleeding, etc. as a result of your use?
19. Have you ever looked for or received help for your usage habits?
20. Have you participated or been in any type of treatment for your usage?

If you answered yes to more than five of the questions on the quiz, you may want to consider making changes in your life.

What is your plan for recovery immediately after being released (use our resource directory to find potential resources in the community you will be released to)?

_____

_____

_____

_____

We urge you to take your recovery seriously. As a reentry organization, we have witnessed many incarcerated individuals who died from overdoses after being released. This happens often because reentry is a difficult time, and many people cope with drugs when they face problems and stress. Another reason many people die is because they try to use the same amount of drugs as they did before being incarcerated and because most drugs are mixed with fentanyl which is a main cause of overdose deaths.

Use additional paper if needed

14. Family Reunification

Just as you had to adjust to life in prison, you will have to adjust to life as you return to the outside world. You cannot expect to feel immediately comfortable at first, but that does not mean it is time to give up. Be patient…with your family and with yourself as you re-integrate into the family, home and community.

Who are some positive people you plan to reconnect with when you get out of prison? Remember, you may need to "change your friends" and not hang around or associate with some of your past friends/family if they threaten you, your freedom, and your treatment

_____   _____

_____   _____

_____   _____

_____   _____

What and where are some family events you could go to with your loved ones as part of your re-integration? Look for events in your area that are free or low cost.

_____   _____

_____   _____

_____   _____

_____   _____

Here are some suggestions from others who have been through this that may help:

- Begin by appreciating the small things that others take for granted—such as privacy, being able to come and go as you please, etc.
- Avoid talking about life behind bars as your only conversation topic—practice making "small talk" about daily happenings instead. Begin visualizing positive ways to react to possible situations.
- Don't try to catch up on what you have missed; you cannot relive time lost.
- Be patient—know that you must take small steps toward a new way of living.
- Gradually you will begin to feel more like you belong here rather than there, back in prison.

Parental Accountability

What are/will be your responsibilities as a parent once you are released?

_____
_____
_____
_____

How do you plan to accomplish them?

_____
_____
_____
_____

Do you have Children? Will you need to start providing Child Support for anyone once you are released? Where can you get information and support concerning Child Support?

Child's Name	Age	Custody Situation	Pay Child Support	Mandated

Use additional paper if needed

15. Technology

Social Networking and the Internet

Social Media is a common part of everyday life and people engage in social networking for personal interactions and many other reasons. Many potential employers now require initial applications be made online and having an email account is a critical tool for reentry. Free "Wi-Fi" access is available at many places such as coffee shops, libraries and even McDonald's!

In most cases, you will be somewhat familiar with social media and its uses, but if you've been incarcerated 20+ years this may seem foreign to you. We suggest taking a digital basics class offered by many reentry organizations such as House of Mercy. For more information, read the technology chapter in this guide.

List some possible email address names you can establish once you are released. Remember, this will be seen by potential employers as well as friends and family and should be an appropriate name/address!

_____

_____

_____

You can create a free email address at: Yahoo Mail (___@yahoo.com) & Google Mail (___@gmail.com).

Social Network Site	Have you Heard of this Site	Have had/been on Account
Facebook		
Twitter		
Instagram		
Snapchat		
Tumbler		
Pinterest		
LinkedIn		

What is your plan for utilizing technology and social media for your benefit when you are released?

_____

_____

_____

_____

What will some potential pitfalls with technology/social media be for you that you can look out for?

_____

_____

_____

Use additional paper if needed

16. Living Under Supervision

What supervision are you under for your release? _____

How long will you be under community supervision (# of Years)? _____

Location of your Community Supervision Office: _____

Phone Number to Office: _____

What are some questions and/or issues you should talk to your supervisor officer about concerning your release and reentry?

_____
_____
_____
_____

Will you have fee(s) to pay?

Amount: _____

Other: _____
Use additional paper if needed

17. Appendix

Template for writing a S.M.A.R.T. Goal

Crafting S.M.A.R.T. Goals are designed to help you identify if what you want to achieve is realistic and determine a deadline. When writing S.M.A.R.T. Goals use concise language but include relevant information. These are designed to help you succeed, so be positive when answering the questions.

Initial Goal (Write the goal you have in mind):

_____

_____

1. **Specific** (What do you want to accomplish? Who needs to be included? When do you want to do this? Why is this a goal?)

_____

_____

_____

_____

2. **Measurable** (How can you measure progress and know if you've successfully met your goal?):

_____

_____

_____

_____

3. **Achievable** (Do you have the skills required to achieve the goal? If not, can you obtain them? What is the motivation for this goal? Is the amount of effort required on par with what the goal will achieve?):

_____

_____

_____

_____

4. **Relevant** (Why am I setting this goal now? Is it aligned with overall objectives?):

_____

_____

_____

_____

5. **Time-bound** (What's the deadline and is it realistic?):

_____

_____

_____

_____

S.M.A.R.T. Goal (Review what you have written, and craft a new goal statement based on what the answers to the questions above have revealed):

_____
_____
_____
_____
_____
_____
_____
_____
_____
_____
_____
_____
_____
_____
_____

Use additional paper if needed

SMART

SPECIFIC   MEASURABLE   ATTAINABLE   RELEVANT   TIME-BOUND

Part 3: After You Get Out

This main section is the longest in our guide and addresses the most common needs of a recently released person and how to go about meeting them. It includes the following chapters:

- Getting your ID
- Resources to Meet your Basic Needs
- Housing
- Employment
- Education
- Health
- Trauma and Mental Health
- Substance Use
- Technology
- Transportation
- Finances and Taxes
- Voting
- Veterans

1. Getting Your ID

Congratulations, you're out! If you couldn't get an ID while you were incarcerated, this will be your priority. Hopefully, you already have your birth certificate and Social Security card. If not, here's how you can get them:

- Call or go to the county clerk's office in the county where you were born. They can help you get your birth certificate.
- Go to a Social Security Administration Office to get your Social Security card. Call before you go to set up an appointment and find out what you need to bring.

 Note: You can get marriage licenses and divorce decrees at the county clerk's office in which you were married or divorced.

 ## State ID or Driver's License

Once you have your birth certificate and Social Security card, you can get a state ID or driver's license. These are the most common forms of ID. To get either a state ID or a driver's license, you'll need to visit the Department of Motor Vehicles. Make an appointment to visit a licensing office to start your application or to finish the application you started online. At the office you will:

- Provide proof of identity.
- Pay the driver licensing fee.
- Have your photo taken.
  - Before taking a photo, they'll ask you to remove anything that covers your face or head, like a hat or sunglasses.
  - They'll make exceptions for medical and religious reasons.

You'll get your temporary ID before you leave, but it won't be acceptable as ID because it doesn't include your photo and signature. Keep your temporary ID with you until you receive your permanent ID which should arrive in the mail within 7-10 days. If you haven't received it after 30 days, call 360-902-3900.

Do you plan to get a driver's license?

- Read Washington Driver Guide first. You can pick up a copy of this booklet at any public library or download the Washington State Driver Guide.
- If you've been incarcerated for a long time, we recommend getting a learner's permit. A learner's permit lets you practice driving until you feel comfortable taking the driver's test. To get a learner permit, you will need to pass a written test and a vision test. Once you get the permit, you can drive with another driver with at least 5 years of experience driving with a valid license in the front passenger seat.

- Pass the knowledge and drive test: If you are taking driver training or you have already passed the knowledge test, skip this step. Depending on your situation, you may or may not need to take a knowledge and drive test. Find what knowledge and drive tests you need to take.
- Decide if you want a standard driver license or an enhanced driver license (EDL): An EDL is an alternative to a passport card. You use it to re-enter the U.S. by land and sea after traveling to Canada, Mexico, Bermuda, and the Caribbean and to enter federal building. EDL complies with the Real ID Act and is an acceptable document for domestic air travel after May 3, 2023. See steps to getting your EDL/EID.
- Apply for a driver license: Make an appointment to visit a driver licensing office to apply for a license in person. If you have a Washington learner permit, you can apply for your license online. Make sure to review documents you should bring to your appointment. Be prepared to wait in line. At your appointment, you will:
  o Take a vision screening test.
  o Decide if you want to register to vote and be an organ donor.
  o Pay the driver license fees.

You'll get a temporary license before you leave your appointment. Keep your temporary license with you until you receive your permanent license.

- See tips for visiting a driver licensing office.

Visiting Driver Services can take a long time, so be sure to bring everything you need:

- *An original document with your written signature (credit card, court order, or Social Security card)*
- *An original document with your date of birth (birth certificate, passport, high school transcript, college transcript from classes you have taken at prison)*
- *An original document with your Social Security number (Social Security card, driver's license record, or military service record)*
- *Proof of address (bank statement, credit report, utility bills, medical record, HIV test)*
- *Payment*

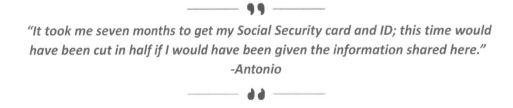

"It took me seven months to get my Social Security card and ID; this time would have been cut in half if I would have been given the information shared here."
-Antonio

Suspensions

Is your license suspended? A license can get suspended for many reasons:

- Not paying traffic tickets, parking tickets, or tolls.
- Driving while drunk or using drugs. This is called Driving Under the Influence, or DUI.
- If you do not make child support payments.
- If your license was suspended, you can get it back after the suspension period is over.

For a complete list, see: Types of driver license suspensions.

Revocations

Revoked means your driver's license is taken away. Driver's licenses are often revoked for more serious DUIs. For example, if someone was injured or killed because the driver was drunk or using drugs. If your license is revoked, you can get a new one. But you will have to wait for some time. The waiting periods for applying for a new license are:

- First offense. 90-day suspension (two days if enrolled in 90 days of the 24/7 sobriety program). If the driver's BAC is .15% or more, the suspension will be one year (four days if enrolled in 120 days of the 24/7 sobriety program).
- Second offense. Two-year suspension (one year if enrolled in six months of the 24/7 sobriety program). If the driver's BAC is .15% or more, the suspension will be 900 days.
- Second offense. Two-year suspension (one year if enrolled in six months of the 24/7 sobriety program). If the driver's BAC is .15% or more, the suspension will be 900 days.

If your license was revoked because someone was killed while you were driving your license will be revoked for two years.

Note: Driving with a suspended or revoked license is a criminal offense in Washington State, often called DWLS. It is a gross misdemeanor punishable by up to 364 days in jail and a $5,000 fine. If you are caught driving with a suspended or revoked license due to a DUI, you may face additional penalties, such as mandatory jail time, vehicle impoundment, and longer suspension or revocation periods.

How To Get Your License Back After the Suspension

It depends on several factors, including your blood alcohol content and whether you were involved in any previous DUI incidents, but, in general, to reinstate your suspended license in Washington State, you need to:

- Satisfy your court requirements and fines, if applicable.
- Register for a free and secure account with the DOL License eXpress at secure.dol.wa.gov/home. You will need an email address to activate your account. Don't have an email address? Call DOL's automated phone line at 360-902-3900
- Maintain proof of insurance for at least 3 years from your reinstatement with an SR22 from your insurance company, a deposit with the WA State Treasurer, or a security bond.
- Pay a licensing and reinstatement fee.
- File proof of financial responsibility (SR-22) for 3 years.
- Pay a $75 reissue fee and all required driver licensing fees.
- If your license was suspended due to a DUI, you will need to fill out an online request form for a hearing and pay a $375 fee or fill out an Application for DUI Indigent Waiver if your income is below the state's poverty level.

Links to further resources:

- My Driver License Was Suspended. Can I Get It Back?, http://www.washingtonlawhelp.org/resource/my-driver-license-was-suspended-can-i-get-it?ref=LhJ7K

- Got Unpaid Traffic Tickets? How To Avoid Getting Your Driver License Suspended, http://www.washingtonlawhelp.org/resource/got-unpaid-traffic-tickets-how-to-avoid-getti?ref=LhJ7K; or

- Child Support and License Suspension, http://www.washingtonlawhelp.org/resource/what-to-do-about-a-license-suspension-notice?ref=LhJ7K.

"If you go with the frame of mind that you are going to spend a hell of a lot of time in that place, it helps. Go with the right frame of mind, otherwise you're going to be miserable." -Anonymous

Signing up for the Selective Service

Did you know you may have to sign up for "the draft"? The draft is called the Selective Service. It is a program that lets the US military call men to serve in the military. You need to register for Selective Service if you are:

- Male
- Between 18-25
- Are a US citizen or an immigrant

Registering with the Selective Service does not mean you are in the military. It means you may be called to the military if there is a crisis.

If you are 18-25 you need to register for the Selective Service right away. If you don't, you could be fined or go to jail. You also cannot get a job with the government or get government training. You can register online at sss.gov/register/. Or pick up a form at any post office. You can send the form by mail to:

Selective Service System
Registration Information Office
PO Box 94739
Palatine, IL 60094-4739

You don't have to register if you were incarcerated the entire time you were 18 to 25. You will need to request a status information letter at https://www.sss.gov/verify/sil/.

What if you weren't incarcerated but you still didn't register? You can also request a status information letter. The letter should say that you did not "knowingly or willfully" fail to register for Selective Service. You could mention if you were incarcerated shortly after your 18th birthday, left school early, or any other things that might have made it hard to register.

2. Resources to Meet Your Basic Needs

Leaving prison is exciting, but not always easy. Many people have trouble finding a place to live or buying food after they leave prison. Other people struggle with drug or alcohol use or mental health issues. Be patient with yourself. Take your time as you figure things out. There are places you can go to for help.

This chapter has two main sections:

- How to apply for government benefits to meet your basic needs
- Other places to go to meet your basic needs

Apply for Benefits

Did you know that Washington State can help you with some basic needs? One of the first things you should do after release is apply for government assistance programs. You may complete an online application by using the WashingtonConnection.org website, applying by phone at 877-501-2233 or going to your local DSHS Office. Having been incarcerated, chances are you will be eligible for assistance such as:

- **Supplemental Nutrition Assistance Program (SNAP).** This used to be called food stamps. Each month, money is put onto a special debit card called an EBT "Quest" card. You can use the card to buy food from most grocery stores. See flyer.
- **Medicaid.** Medicaid is a program for people who make little or no money. It helps people pay for medicine, hospital visits, doctor appointments, and more. In many cases, you will have been signed up for this prior to release, but if this is not the case, go to Washington Health Plan Finder to learn more and apply. You can also call 1-855-923-4633 for help.
- **Temporary Assistance for Needy Families (TANF).** Provides money for families who need it. Click to learn more about TANF.

- **Aged Blind and Disabled Cash Assistance (ABD).** Provides money for people who have disabilities or who are blind. Click here to learn more about ABD.
- **Medicare Savings Program (MSP).** This program helps pay for the costs of Medicare for older people and people with disabilities. Click here to learn more about MSP.
- **The Housing and Essential Needs Referral (HEN)** program provides access to essential needs items and potential rental assistance for low-income individuals who are unable to work for at least 90 days due to a physical and/or mental incapacity. Click here to learn more about HEN.

1. On WashingtonConnection.org you can:

- Start a new application.
- Report a change, such as address, income, or family situation.
- Submit an eligibility review for continuing benefits.
- Ask "Do I Qualify?" or "Am I Eligible?"

Learn more about what you can do on WashingtonConnection.org in these FAQs.

2. Turn in your application.

You may complete an online application by clicking here, contacting the Customer Service Contact Center 877-501-2233 or going into your local Community Services Office.

- In some cases, a signed application is required.
- You can fax your application to 888-338-7410; or
- Mail your application to:

DSHS - CSD Customer Service Center
PO Box 11699, Tacoma, WA 98411-6699

Do you need to print the application? A printable version of the application is available in English and several other languages.

3. Have an interview.

Some programs don't require an interview; others do. At the end of your interview, you will be told whether additional information, or verification, is needed to make a decision on your case. If more information is needed, we will always request it in writing. If you need help, go to the Department of Social and Human Services (DSHS) office near you (Locator). You can also visit a hospital, non-profit organization, church, or other service provider and ask for help applying for benefits. Check the resource directory in the back of this guide for these resources in your county.

To get these benefits, you'll have to meet certain qualifications. For some programs, you must be a certain age. For most, you must meet income requirements (not make a lot of money).

When you sign up for benefits, ask if there are other services, too, like programs to help with rent and utilities including internet or childcare. Here are a few you may have access to:

- Low Income Home Energy Assistance Program (LIHEAP) - https://www.commerce.wa.gov/growing-the-economy/energy/low-income-home-energy-assistance/
- Internet bill assistance - https://www.affordableconnectivity.gov/
- Discount drug card - https://www.goodrx.com/discount-card
- Free and discount phones - https://www.lifelinesupport.org/ https://www.safelinkwireless.com/Enrollment

Social Security Programs

The Social Security Administration has other benefit programs that you may be able to use now that you are out of prison. These include:

Social Security Retirement Benefits. These payments are for people older than 62. To get the money, you must have worked or paid Social Security taxes for at least 10 years before you went to prison. Learn more here:

- The SSA's Retirement Calculator estimates your personal retirement benefits. Visit: www.ssa.gov/benefits/retirement/estimator.html
- The When to Start Receiving Retirement Benefits fact sheet can help you understand how Social Security fits into your retirement decision: http://www.socialsecurity.gov/pubs/EN-05-10147.pdf
- The SSA Retirement Planner gives information about your Social Security retirement benefits under current law: www.socialsecurity.gov/retire

Supplemental Security Income (SSI). This program provides income payments to people over 65 and adults and children who have a disability. You may be eligible if you are over 65, or you are blind or disabled and have little or no income and resources. You must also be a US citizen or national. SSI gives people money every month to help with things like food, clothing, and housing. Unlike Social Security Retirement

Benefits, SSI benefits are not based on your prior work or a family member's prior work history.

- For information about eligibility, visit: https://www.ssa.gov/ssi/
- For information on SSI benefits after incarceration, visit: https://www.ssa.gov/reentry/benefits.htm

Medicare. This program provides health insurance to people older than 65 and people with a disability. See http://www.ssa.gov/benefits/medicare/.

Social Security Disability Insurance (SSDI). This program gives money to adults and certain family members with disabilities. To use this program, you need to have worked for many years.

Social Security/SSI While Incarcerated

If you receive Social Security retirement, disability, or survivors' benefits, your benefits are suspended if you're convicted of a criminal offense and sent to jail or prison for more than 30 continuous days. Your benefits can start again the month following your release. Although you can't receive Social Security benefits while you're incarcerated, benefits to your spouse or children will continue as long as they remain eligible.

If you're receiving SSI, your payments also stop while you're incarcerated. Your payments can start again the month you're released, but if you are locked up more than 12 months, you are no longer eligible for SSI benefits. You must file a new application.

You are allowed to apply for Supplemental Security Income (SSI) a few months before your release so that benefits can begin quickly after your release. Speak to a reentry counselor at your facility for help.
- For information about the impact of incarceration on benefits, visit: www.ssa.gov/pubs/EN-05-10133.pdf
- For detailed information about eligibility for benefits after incarceration, visit: https://www.ssa.gov/reentry/%20benefits.htm

Learn more and apply at ssa.gov, or call (800) 722-1213 for help. Get in-person help by making an appointment with your local Social Security office. Go to https://secure.ssa.gov/ICON/main.jsp.

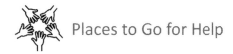 Places to Go for Help

There are many other places you can go for help – we've listed many others in our directory.

I need help with…	Where to get help	Website or phone number
Food	Food pantries, soup kitchens	Find one at https://foodlifeline.org/need-food/#map & https://2-harvest.org/food-near-me-wa/
Healthcare and dental care	Community health clinics and dental clinics are cheaper or even free. You can use them even if you don't have insurance.	Find one at https://nafcclinics.org/
Substance use treatment	Support group, treatment programs	• https://www.warecoveryhelpline.org/ • Call the SAMHSA National Helpline at (800) 662-4357. • For a support group, go to https://www.celebraterecovery.com/, aa.org (Alcoholics Anonymous) or na.org (Narcotics Anonymous).
Housing	Emergency housing, transitional housing	Go to • https://www.hud.gov/findshelter/, • https://deptofcommerce.app.box.com/v/CEAccessPoints, • https://publish.smartsheet.com/ebbc471a77e94778a2f105870aab5e91 • https://www.transitionalhousing.org/state/washington
Mental health (emergency)	Suicide hotline, hospital emergency room	• Call the National Suicide and Crisis Lifeline at 988. • Call 911 if you are having an emergency. • Call 1-866-789-1511 WA recovery helpline
Mental health (non-emergency)	Mental health clinics that offer free or low-cost services	Go to • https://findtreatment.gov/locator • https://www.hca.wa.gov/free-or-low-cost-health-care/i-need-behavioral-health-support/mental-health-services

———— 🙶 ————

"I came home after ten years; I went to a homeless shelter and three days later I had a job. A week and a half later, I had an apartment. My first paycheck, I got a cheap studio apartment. So you can do it. Don't let your feelings from being incarcerated judge who you are and what you can do. Because you can make it."
—Tony C.

"The advice I would give is to be patient. Things in the outside world move very quickly and I think that you have to be aware and accepting that you don't have to catch up." —Edmund B.

————  ————

3. Housing After Release

Finding a place to live is one of the most important parts of the reentry process. It can also be one of the hardest parts. The challenge is to find housing that is accessible, low cost, and stable.

This chapter covers the following topics:

- Transitional housing (halfway houses)
- Emergency housing
- Public & subsidized housing
- Private housing
- Help with rent
- Your legal rights
- Housing for people on the sex offense registry

Transitional Housing

Many people who leave prison go to a halfway house or transitional house. Some transitional houses allow people to stay three months, others up to two years. If you are looking for transitional housing, please see the Housing Chapter in Before You Leave and our list of housing options in our directory.

Emergency Shelters

If you find yourself without a place to stay, there are emergency shelters. Some shelters are safe houses for victims of domestic abuse. Some shelters may have certain restrictions—restrictions on pets, on genders, or for people convicted of sex and/or violent offenses. Many shelters offer food, laundry, and support services to help you find more permanent housing. Call 211 or look for emergency housing at https://www.shelterlistings.org/state/washington.html.

Subsidized and Public Housing

There are several different subsidized and public housing options. These options are supported by the government and have rent that is cheaper than in the private market. Space is often limited and there may be waitlists.

- **Public housing** is owned by the government. People who meet income requirements can live there. Contact your local Public Housing Authority (PHA) to find out about public housing in your area. Go to https://resources.hud.gov/# to find your PHA.
- **Section 8 housing** is a program where the government provides housing vouchers to help cover rent. You can live in a private apartment or house of your choice, and they will give you a voucher to help you pay for it. Section 8 housing is offered through your local Public Housing Authority (PHA). If you qualify, your PHA can provide a list of places where your voucher can be used.
- **Project-based subsidized housing**, or affordable housing, is housing that is owned by private property owners. They

receive subsidies from the government to make their housing cheaper for low-
- income people and families. Go to this website to find this type of housing: https://affordablehousingonline.com/public-housing-waiting-lists/Washington. Your local PHA may also have a list of project-based subsidized housing.
- **Permanent supportive housing.** If you are a senior, veteran, or if you have a disability, mental illness, or HIV/AIDS diagnosis, or if you have been homeless, you may be able to get permanent supportive housing. Permanent supportive housing includes support services, such as medical care and counseling. There is no limit to how long you can stay there. To find this type of housing check https://search.wa211.org/search, https://aptfinder.org/, https://deptofcommerce.app.box.com/v/CEAccessPoints.

Can I stay in public housing if I have a record?

Eligibility for these programs may be affected if you use illegal drugs, abuse alcohol, or have been evicted from federally assisted housing for drug crimes within the past three years. The Section 8 and public housing programs are administered by local organizations known as public housing authorities/agencies (PHAs). Your local PHA will determine additional eligibility criteria and rules specific to your area. While both programs primarily consider your family's income for eligibility, the criteria may vary across different cities. To find out if you qualify for Section 8 vouchers or public housing, please contact your local PHA (https://affordablehousingonline.com/housing-authorities/Washington). You can find information about PHAs in Washington at https://www.hud.gov/sites/dfiles/PIH/documents/PHA_Contact_Report_WA.pdf.

How much does subsidized or public housing cost?

How much you pay for housing depends on how much money you earn. Many places will require you to pay 30% of your income to rent.

How should I apply?

Public and subsidized housing programs often have long wait lists. You should apply as early as you can. Call your local Public Housing Authority and ask for instructions or apply online. To find your local housing authority visit https://www.hud.gov/sites/dfiles/PIH/documents/PHA_Contact_Report_WA.pdf. Once you have applied, they will let you know when there is a place available. You can call and check to see where you are on the waiting list.

Private Housing

Private housing can be easier to find than public housing because there is more of it. However, it also costs more. Private housing can be found online and in the classified section of newspapers. Some websites include:

- www.apartments.com
- www.zillow.com
- www.forrent.com
- www.craigslist.org
- www.trulia.com

You are likely to run into barriers because of your background. It may take a while to find a landlord who will rent to you. Large property management firms almost always conduct background checks, so you may have better luck with units in smaller complexes or in private homes.

Others who have come home from prison before you may be your best source of information. If you are part of a reentry program, use it as a resource. Use your network of friends and family. They may know of places where you can stay.

Renting an Apartment

Once you've found an apartment, call the landlord and set up a time to view it. Arrive on time and dress nicely. You want to give a good first impression.

On your visit, you may be asked to fill out an application and pay an application fee. The application will ask for information such as your employer, rent history, and current address. You may also be asked for references–people who can vouch for you, like employers or church leaders.

The application may also ask about your criminal history. Many landlords conduct background checks. You may worry that if you share your history, you may hurt your chance of getting the apartment. Even though this may be true, we suggest that you be up front if they ask. It may not disqualify you.

Questions you might ask a landlord:

- What is the rent?
- How much is the security deposit?
- Is there an application fee?
- Are utilities included?
- When is the rent due?
- What is the parking like?
- Are tenants able to make changes (e.g., paint the walls)?
- Is there an additional cost for pets/additional family members?
- Is there a background check, and if so, who would be excluded from eligibility?
- What are the terms of the lease?
- What is your timeline?

Warning:

 If anyone asks you for money before you have even seen the apartment, you are probably being scammed. **Do not pay anything before you have seen the apartment**.

If a landlord agrees to rent to you, you will sign a lease or a rental agreement.

- A **lease** is usually a year-long commitment, and you agree to pay a certain amount each month for the whole year.
- A **rental agreement** is typically month-by-month. After 30 days, both you or the landlord are free to back out or change the agreement.

Read it carefully before signing or paying any fees. It is legally binding. You won't be able to back out once you have signed. Keep a copy in a safe place.

Security deposits:

Many landlords require one to two month's rent as well as a security deposit before you move in. The security deposit shows that you are serious about renting the apartment. If you choose not to move into the apartment, the landlord keeps this money. Ask for a receipt for the security deposit and any other fees you pay.

When you move out, your security deposit will be used to cover any damage to the apartment that you caused. It's a good idea to take pictures of anything that is damaged when you move in so that you can show that you didn't cause it. Your landlord should not use your security deposit to pay for regular wear and tear of living in your apartment, but for items like a broken light fixture or carpet damage. You should receive a receipt for damages when you move out. Any leftover money from the security deposit should be mailed to you within 30 to 45 days.

2023 changes to Washington State's laws affecting renters:
https://www.washingtonlawhelp.org/resource/2023-changes-to-washington-renter-laws

Breaking a lease:

If you need to move out before your lease ends, you can do so, but you will have to pay a fee. The amount that you pay should be listed in the lease, so read it carefully. You may have to keep paying rent until they find someone else to rent the apartment.

Help with Rent

If you need help paying rent or utilities, there may be programs in your community that can help. Check with the Department of Human Services (DHS) to see if they offer rental assistance programs. Here's a link to a list of rental assistance programs across the state: https://publish.smartsheet.com/ebbc471a77e94778a2 f105870aab5e91. You can also get information on this type of resource and others by calling 211 (https://search.wa211.org/search).

Your Legal Rights

Important Housing Laws

Below we've listed some of the housing laws to be aware of. If a landlord breaks one of these laws, you can file a complaint. These laws apply if you are renting or buying a home, getting a mortgage, or seeking housing assistance.

Federal Fair Housing Act

Cannot discriminate based on race, color, national origin, religion, sex (including gender identity and sexual orientation), family status, and disability.

US Department of Housing and Urban Development Fair Housing Act Guidelines

In 2016, the US Department of Housing and Urban Development (HUD) released guidance for how the Fair Housing Act applies to people who have arrest or conviction records.

- Arrest records and convictions can be used to deny people housing, but landlords that automatically refuse someone with a criminal record may violate the law.
- In 2022, HUD released additional guidance for housing providers, encouraging them to not consider criminal history. If they do, they should consider everyone's circumstances instead of excluding all individuals with convictions.

State and City Specific Laws

Depending on where you live there may be additional laws that protect you from discrimination.

For example, due to a law passed in 2017, landlords in Seattle may not require that you talk about your criminal history, may not ask about your criminal history, and may not reject your application for housing because of your adult criminal history unless the landlord thinks there is reason to believe that you will be a danger to other tenants or to the property. A landlord cannot do any of these things at all, for any reason, based on your juvenile criminal history.

Eviction

Are you worried about getting kicked out of your apartment? Check out: https://www.washingtonlawhelp.org/resource/eviction#content. HUD offers information about eviction here: https://www.hud.gov/rent_relief and you can find your local office in their online directory here: https://www.hud.gov/program_offices/field_policy_mgt/localoffices#WA.

Housing Discrimination

If you have been discriminated against, there are several ways you can file a complaint:

- You can file a complaint through the Housing and Urban Development (HUD) agency. Submit the complaint as soon as possible. Call them toll-free at (800) 669-9777 or (800) 877-8339, or email ComplaintsOffice05@hud.gov.
- You can file a complaint in Washington state at https://www.hum.wa.gov/file-complaint.
- You can file a complaint in the city where you live. You may be able to file a grievance at your city's Human Relations Commission or similar agency.

Legal Assistance

Here are a few resources to help:

- Legal assistance for at-risk renters https://localhousingsolutions.org/housing-policy-library/legal-assistance-for-at-risk-renters/
- Eviction laws database: https://lsc.gov/initiatives/effect-state-local-laws-evictions/lsc-eviction-laws-database
- https://nwjustice.org/eviction-help

Housing for People on the Sex Offense Registry

Sadly, there are many housing restrictions for people on Sex Offense Registries, although specific laws vary by county. It can be very difficult to find housing that meets supervision requirements and has a landlord that will accept tenants who are on the registry. We wish we had better news, but the reality is it is hard for people on registries to find housing.

We know of many people who are required to register who have not been able to parole because they could not find housing. Some people have even stayed past the end of their prison sentence because they don't have a place to stay.

Still, there is hope. You may be able to live with family members, or there may be transitional houses that serve people on the registries. You also may be able to find private housing. Have patience and be in frequent communication with your community supervision officer as you navigate housing challenges. Whenever possible, seek support from local organizations that may be able to help.

Help and advocacy:

We encourage you to reach out to organizations in your community for people with sex offense convictions if they exist. Here are a few to get you started:

- Information and Tips on finding housing in Washington: https://sexoffenderonestopresource.com/search-by-state/washington-state-resources/
- "Registering With Dignity" handbook for people who are forced to register: https://narsol.org/wp-content/uploads/2017/12/RegisteringWithDignity-Handbook.pdf

4. Employment

You will hear a lot of discouraging talk about getting a job with a record. While it is hard, there are companies that are willing to hire people with records. Don't give up.

There is a lot involved with finding a job, so this is one of the longest chapters. It covers these topics:

- Employment resources
- Make a plan
- Popular job options
- Women and employment
- Look for jobs
- Apply for jobs
- Your legal rights
- Unemployment benefits

> 〝
> *"No matter what, don't stop persevering." –Anonymous*
> 〞

Employment Resources

Finding a job and building a career is hard, especially with a criminal record. We strongly suggest that you find people or programs to help you. Here are a few places to start.

- **American Job Centers** help people search for jobs and find training. Go to careeronestop.org to find a location of an American Job Center near you. This website has many resources to help you with your job search. Call (877) 872-5627 for help.
- **Goodwill**. Goodwill offers those with criminal backgrounds pre-release services, basic skills development, employment readiness training, occupational skill training, and job placement assistance (800) GOODWILL. https://www.goodwill.org/find-jobs-and-services/find-a-job/
- **People for People.** People for People provides several resources, including

employment training, for people in Eastern Washington, https://mypfp.org/services/employment-training/, (509) 248-6726, adminreception@pfp.org.

- **Honest Jobs:** You can set up a free profile on this job-search platform which has over 400,000 job openings from 1,300+ verified fair-chance employers, https://www.honestjobs.com/.
- **Indeed.com.** Not only can you search for jobs by type and location and also create accounts that recruiters use to contact you, but indeed.com has resources for justice-impacted individuals to get jobs: https://www.indeed.com/career-advice/finding-a-job/programs-for-felons-to-get-jobs.
- **Employment Security Dept.** www.esd.wa.gov/jobs-and-training.
- **Washington State Department of Labor & Industries**. The Department of Labor & Industries lists Apprenticeship Programs in Washington. Apprenticeships are generally

a mix of work and school that results in the apprentice being trained in a specific field (often, in the construction trades). https://www.lni.wa.gov/licensing-permits/apprenticeship/apprenticeship-preparation#

- **Reentry programs.** Reentry and transitional housing organizations in your community may offer employment services (see directory).
- Your **Community Corrections Officer** may have ideas about jobs and training you could apply for.
- Go to https://guides.loc.gov/reentry-resources/

employment for a list of helpful resources about employment for people who have been incarcerated.

Make a Plan

For many people who leave prison, the goal is to get any job that pays, even if it isn't ideal. The job may not be something you want to do forever, but it can help you get back on your feet. It can give you experience and lead you to a better job in the future.

Even as you look for jobs to meet your basic needs, it's good to explore different careers. Find out what careers match your interests and skills. Look for careers that are in demand where you can earn good money. Learn about the training that you will need.

Take time to make a plan. Talk to a career counselor about your skills and interests and the kind of job you are looking for. You can make use of the employment chapter on page 42 in the Personal Reentry Plan section of this guide to explore some of your career interests.

Here are a few of the many websites that can help you explore different careers:

- careeronestop.org. Explore careers, find training, check out their toolkit, search for jobs, and more.
- mynextmove.org. Explore careers and get information about what you can do to get a job.
- myskillsmyfuture.org. Find out how your skills, experience and interests can lead to a new career.

We also recommend reading *"Take Charge of Your Future."* This guide for formerly incarcerated people will help you take steps to get education and training for a career. It was developed by the US Department of Education. Request a FREE copy by calling (877) 433-7827 or emailing edpubs@edpubs.ed.gov. You can access it online here: https://www2.ed.gov/about/offices/list/ovae/pi/AdultEd/take-charge-your-future.pdf

Popular Career Options

In the next few pages, you will find information about popular career options for people with records. These options are just a few of the many options that are available.

 **Commercial Drivers**

Commercial drivers transport goods, people, and materials. They drive buses, delivery trucks, diesel trucks, and more.

Commercial Driver Job Facts at a Glance	
Wages	Earn $40,000 to $60,000 per year
Employment	Very large, with lots of openings
Education needed	High school diploma or GED (usually) Commercial Driver's License (CDL)
Other requirements	Have a good driving record, strong customer service skills for some positions

Prepare in prison: If you don't already have your GED, get it! Some reentry organizations offer programs to get your Commercial Driver's License (CDL).

Outside of prison: Here's how you can get started in this field:

1. **Apply for a temporary commercial learner's permit.** If you have had a CDL in the past or in a different state, speak with the Vehicle Services Department to find out what you need to do to get a license.
2. **Complete CDL training.** If you have not already had training, you may want to take a class at a commercial driver's training facility. Many community colleges offer this training. See "Registered CDL Training Schools."
3. **Take the road and written tests.** Find a copy of the "Commercial Driver Guide" in your prison's library or resource room or online through the DMV website.
4. **Get your CDL.** You will need to pay for the license, and it will need to be renewed regularly.
5. **For More Info. Visit:** https://www.dol.wa.gov/driver-licenses-and-permits/commercial-driver-licenses-cdl

Construction and Landscaping Jobs

There are many different construction and landscaping careers. People in these careers build and repair homes, buildings, roads and more. They maintain yards and parks. They install and service heating and cooling (HVAC) systems. They install solar panels. Jobs include:

- Road worker
- Painter
- Heating and air conditioning technician
- Welder
- Broadband installer

- Solar installer
- General laborer
- Landscaper
- Building maintenance jobs

Note: Some construction jobs (such as plumber, electrician, carpenter, or mason) often require an apprenticeship with a trade union. Some of these unions have restrictions about hiring people with criminal records. It's a good idea to check before applying for an apprenticeship. For more information check out the "*WSLC Directory of Labor Organizations in Washington State*."

Construction Job Facts at a Glance	
Wages	Earn $40,000 to $70,000 per year, depending on the job
Employment	Large occupation, lots of openings
Education needed	High school diploma or GED Some jobs require formal training, certificates, or an apprenticeship. Most jobs require on-the-job training.
Other requirements	Driver's license, OSHA certification

Prepare in prison: If you have the opportunity, take construction, building maintenance, or horticulture training while in prison. Many WADOC prisons have these programs. Talk to your counselor to find out what is available at your facility.

Outside of prison: There are lots of ways to get started in a construction field.

- **Some jobs don't require any training at all.** Look for entry level jobs. You'll get training on the job.
- **Look for community-based training programs** in the construction trades. For instance, ANEW is a pre-apprenticeship training program that helps individuals obtain careers in construction trades. Find out more here: https://anewcareer.org/programs/pre-apprenticeship-trades-rotation-training-program/
- **Community college certificate programs.** Many community colleges offer training in the construction trades. See this list for more information.
- **Women in trades** organizations may offer opportunities to women who are looking to enter either construction or welding. For more information visit: https://www.wawomenintrades.com/resources

 **Barbering and Cosmetology**

Barbering and Cosmetology Job Facts at a Glance	
Wages	$50,772/year
Employment	Large occupation, lots of openings
Education	To work for a company, you will likely need a GED or high school diploma and some training. Some jobs require a license. Others just want experience.
Other Requirements	Tools, if you're starting your own business, though you might be able to share these costs with a business partner.

Prepare in prison: If you can, get training while in prison.

Outside of prison: There are lots of ways to get started.

- **Training.** For more information click this link, and visit Washington State Department of Licensing.

- **Self-employment.** If you already have the skills and equipment, you can begin working for friends and build up a client base by word of mouth. Think about what you might be able to offer that others won't. Can you work outside of regular business hours? Are you willing to make house calls? Eventually, you may have to incorporate and pay taxes. You can read more about the process of starting your own business later in this chapter.

 **Computer or Information Technology Jobs**

There are many jobs for people who like to work with computers. Jobs include help desk technicians, computer network support specialists, computer programmers, computer systems analysts and more. This industry is constantly growing and well paid. Many of these jobs require only a small amount of training and are in great demand.

Technology Job Facts at a Glance	
Wages	Wages range widely, from about $35,000 for entry level jobs to $80,000+
Employment	Large occupation, lots of openings
Education needed	High school diploma or GED (associate or bachelor's degrees required for some jobs) Formal training program (such as CompTIA A+) On-the-job training
Other requirements	Strong computer skills, customer service skills

Prepare in prison: Take advantage of any opportunity to use computers while in prison and learn some basic skills, such as how to use Microsoft Office. Most prisons in Washington offer Information Technology (IT), digital media, and/or computer programming classes.

Outside of prison: There are many different training programs you can take.

- **Libraries, adult education, and community centers** often offer basic computer classes. Goodwill career centers offer training in computer and digital skills, and some classes are online.
- Go to **Northstar** at digitalliteracyassessment.org to test your digital literacy skills and build your skills. You can access classes online or find a Northstar location where you can attend classes. They offer certificates for skills you have mastered.
- Most **community colleges** offer IT certificate programs and degree programs. Many are very affordable.
- If you are a good self-learner, try taking computer and IT classes online. https://www.freecodecamp.org/ offers a free online course on Python (a popular programming language) and more. https://www.un-loop.org/ offers a 550-hour, full-stack software development bootcamp with professional and soft-skill curriculum primarily for the previously incarcerated in Washington state. If this is unfamiliar to you, don't worry, you will have the chance to learn. Programming languages create instructions to tell a website what you want it to look like and do. Edx and Coursera also have a lot of free courses for learning skills like coding or data entry.
- **Columbia University's** Justice Through Code program is a free semester-long intensive coding program for formerly incarcerated people. There are openings each semester, and you can complete the course online. The program helps people find jobs after they complete their training.

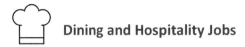 **Dining and Hospitality Jobs**

There are many good opportunities in the dining and hospitality industry, though entry level wages can be quite low. Right now, the industry is also seeing major shortages, which means that you might be able to move into a more advanced position more quickly.

There are many kinds of hospitality companies, and many kinds of roles within those companies. For a typical restaurant job, there is front of house, back of house, and bar. There are also positions in fast food chains, bars and clubs, hotels, and catering companies.

Many of these jobs require unconventional hours. This may put a strain on your personal relationships if you are gone most evenings and weekends. These hours can be good if you are available to provide childcare during the regular working day.

Dining and Hospitality Job Facts at a Glance	
Wages	Wages range widely, from about $22,000 for entry level jobs to $80,000+
Employment	Large occupation, lots of openings
Education needed	High school diploma or GED (associate or bachelor's degree required for some jobs) For some jobs, formal training, or on-the-job training
Other helpful skills	Customer service skills, ability to be calm under pressure, ability to do several things at once, ability to work well with a team

Prepare in prison: Many facilities have food service programs where you can get experience. Take advantage of those programs if they are available.

Outside of prison:

- Many community colleges and other training programs offer food services certificates, check out this list.

- **FareStart** offers paid culinary and Barista training for the previously incarcerated in combination with wrap-around support including counseling, housing, and referral services. Call FareStart at 206.607.7962 or email them at enroll@farestart.org.

- If you are passionate about food, wine, and hospitality, you might be interested in the Culinary, Hospitality, and Wine Area of Study at **South Seattle College**. This program will help you develop the skills and knowledge you need to succeed in the dynamic and diverse tourism and hospitality sectors. You will learn how to create, think critically, and serve customers with excellence. Moreover, if you have a history of justice involvement, you can benefit from the Justice Involved Solutions program, which provides support and guidance for reentry students who want to pursue an education and a career in this industry.

Human Services and Advocacy

Many of the formerly incarcerated work in human services to help people who have been incarcerated. They are caseworkers, counselors, educators, social workers, mediators, and program managers. They advocate for change and better policies.

We need people who have been incarcerated to help make our systems better. You have experience and wisdom that others can learn from! People will be able to relate to you because of your experience.

Social service careers can be a meaningful way of moving on and helping others. But they can also be stressful. Be aware that working with others who are struggling may be difficult as you cope with your own challenges and past trauma.

Human Services Job Facts at a Glance	
Wages	Wages range from about $30,000 for entry level jobs to $60,000+
Employment	Large occupation, lots of openings
Education needed	High school diploma or GED Some jobs require short-term, on-the-job training. Many positions require an associate or bachelor's degree or a license.
Other requirements	Strong people skills, ability to work in stressful situations. Most positions require basic computer skills.

Prepare in prison: Find ways to get involved in programs that help others. Can you help lead workshops? Tutor others? Be part of a peer support group? Help teach a reentry class? These opportunities will give you a taste of what it's like to work in human services. They can help you develop leadership skills.

Most jobs require some education. Get your GED and take some college classes if you can. Take some basic computer classes if they are available.

Outside of prison:

- **Get involved & volunteer.** We recommend that you get involved in reentry programs or other services that interest you. As you participate in these programs, ask the people who are helping you about their jobs and what they do. Then ask if there are things you can do to help. Volunteering is a great way to get your foot in the door. We know of people who got jobs after volunteering for a while. Even if you don't get a job at that organization, they may be able to help connect you to another similar job.
- **Take advantage of leadership/advocacy training.** Reentry organizations often offer training for formerly incarcerated people. Check out our directory of reentry organizations organized by county in the back of this guide.
- **Go to school.** Depending on what your career goal is, you may need an associate or bachelor's degree or an advanced degree. See our education chapter for advice.

Self-Employment

Being self-employed has its merits. You can set your own schedule and the money you make is yours (after you pay taxes). You might buy some equipment to do landscaping in your community. You might rent out a small booth to cut people's hair. You might repair people's homes. You might offer computer support. We interviewed David T., a formerly incarcerated individual who started his own business. He offered the following advice.

To get started, you'll need:

1. **A good idea.** Jot down a few ideas on paper first. Ask yourself, what am I good at? What services can I provide? Is there a clear need for this in the community?
2. **Training.** Get all the training you can. Take business or computer classes. You will need strong finance skills. You will need math skills, customer service skills, and more.
3. **Equipment**. Find out what equipment you will need.
4. **Space for work and storage.** Depending on your idea, you may be able to work at home or rent a storage shed. Maybe you can rent a small booth.
5. **Financial skills**. It can be challenging to manage finances and taxes.
6. **Feedback on your plan from others**. They might see a challenge or a good idea that you initially overlooked.

Growing Your Idea into a Business

Some people who are self-employed decide to grow their idea into a business or a 501c3 non-profit organization. You might start your own barbershop, a tutoring business, an HVAC business, a restaurant, or reentry organization.

Starting your own business takes a lot of work. Many of them fail. We recommend that you consult with others from the very beginning. Here are a few places you can go to for help.

.

- Legal services offices may offer free legal advice to people seeking to create their own business or 501c3.
- Some universities' business colleges offer advice, through student-run clinics, to people starting their own businesses.
- Local libraries or chambers of commerce may offer workshops for people starting their own business. They may have lists of resources in the area.

Build a business plan. Take time to jot down a few ideas on paper first, and then build out a solid business plan. A business plan is like a roadmap for starting your business. Start with the big picture:

- Who is my target customer?
- What problem am I solving?
- What is my timeline?
- What is my competition?

Next, map out the specifics:

- What are my startup costs?
- What is my pricing?
- How will I reach customers?

You can find many business plan questions and guides online, like this one from the Small Business Administration: https://www.sba.gov/business-guide/plan-your-business/write-your-business-plan

Anticipate challenges. Starting a business from scratch is hard. It can strain your relationships with friends, family, and partners. Communicate your plans with the people you care about. Take care to maintain your relationships and support networks. Anticipate challenges to your schedule and lifestyle.

Understand financial realities. Starting a small business requires a lot of money, or capital. Many have found success by working and saving while building their business plan. Getting loans may be an option for some. Take your business plan to a bank or a small business center to discuss financing and get feedback about your plan.

You may have heard that there are federal grants available for formerly incarcerated entrepreneurs. Unfortunately, this is somewhat misleading, since most of this funding goes to programs for entrepreneurs, and not to businesses directly. That being said, there may be programs, financial assistance, or grants you can access through nonprofit programs. There may be financial resources you can access from your local Small Business Development Center.

Seek professional business help. There will be lots of paperwork to manage. You'll have to do taxes and finances for your business. You will likely need to file with the state to make your business official. Talk with someone who understands the ins and outs of loans and taxes. Lawyers who advertise experience with incorporation can file your paperwork, but they also charge a fee.

Free resources do exist. Here are a few:

- Defy Ventures is an entrepreneurial training program for both incarcerated and previously incarcerated citizens who want to start or expand a business. See https://www.defyventures.org/ to find out more. They offer pre-release training and community training.
- Look for a small business accelerator. Seek out your local business association or Chamber of Commerce to get help.
- Additional resources may be found on https://inmatestoentrepreneurs.org/

such as a free online class on how to start and grow a business.

Women and Employment

It can be especially hard for women to find jobs after release. They are more likely than men to be unemployed. When they do find jobs, they often get paid less or work fewer hours. They are more likely to get hired in temp jobs and entry level jobs, even when they have skills and training for more advanced jobs.

As a woman, here are a few things you may face.

- Greater discrimination. People don't expect women to be locked up and often judge them more harshly.
- Difficulty balancing family and jobs. Perhaps you have young children, parents, or grandparents you are caring for. It's hard to work a job and care for your family at the same time. It's hard to find childcare.
- Many of the popular job options for those with criminal records hire mostly men. You may feel uncomfortable if you are the only woman on the crew.
- You may feel unsafe at your jobs, or unsafe getting to the job.

Despite these challenges, we recommend that you approach your job search with patience and hope. There are barriers that you will face, but many women have found jobs after prison. You can, too.

Here are a few suggestions:

- Get as much education and training as you can while in prison.

- Find reentry and job programs that serve women. They can help you access childcare and get the emotional support you need. We have listed a few in our directory.
- Be confident! Sometimes women think that they are not qualified. Don't pass up a chance to apply, even if you don't meet all the requirements.
- Don't be afraid to look for jobs in fields with mostly men, such as construction or IT. In fact, these fields need and want more women! There are free training programs to bring more women into these jobs, for example, ANEW offers the Trades Rotation Program (TRP) for women.

Look for Jobs

In general, you'll want to apply for jobs that you qualify for. What experience, education, and training do they require? Is the job a good fit for your skills?

Even if you don't meet all the requirements, you should still think about applying. Don't sell yourself short! Be confident in your skills and abilities. Sometimes, you can get the training you need on the job.

It's important to be realistic. You will probably have to apply for several jobs before you get hired. Be confident in your skills. You've already dealt with a lot of difficult things, so try to be patient and open-minded to the opportunities that arise.

Networking. Networking is the best way to find a job. Talk to family, friends, acquaintances, and professionals. They may not have a job for you right now, but they could give advice. Maybe they know someone else who is hiring.

Online. These days, many people find jobs through websites like monster.com, careerbuilder.com, and snagajob.com. Indeed.com is one of the largest sources of job

postings in the world. It collects job postings from employer websites, job boards, and more. These sites can be good if you want to work for a large employer. Lots of people submit online applications, especially to large companies. It may be hard to stand out among all the candidates. A newer job platform is now available specifically for those who have a criminal history called Honest Jobs that has thousands of verified fair-chance employers posting jobs on its website.

You may have better luck looking at company websites. Often, you will find a link to "Current Jobs," "Careers' or "Employment'' on the home page. The website "Jobs that Hire Felons'' has a long list of companies whose hiring policies include people with a background: jobsthathirefelons.org.

When searching for a job online, be careful to avoid scams. Scammers may request money or ask for information like your date of birth, Social Security number, or debit/credit card number. We recommend that you never give out this personal information on the internet.

 Don't have access to a computer to search for jobs or fill out job applications? You can use computers for free at your public library. They also often offer computer classes to get you started.

Attend a job fair to meet employers, recruiters, and schools. You may learn about a new field or opportunity that you didn't think of.

Keep a record of all the places you have applied to online applications, visits made in person, initial phone calls, follow-up phone calls, interviews.

Job application forms. The purpose of a job application is to get an interview. Employers use written job applications to decide who is worth talking to in person. Most hiring managers will review your application for 15 to 30 seconds. They'll want to see a form that's neat and complete.

Many job applications need to be filled out online these days. If you don't have access to a home computer, visit a local library, community center, or WorkSource site.

If you will be filling out a paper job application at a job site, bring notes about previous jobs and training: dates, job titles, former employer contact info. This is better than trying to remember the details and making mistakes. If you provide false information, you could be fired if they find out later.

Tips for filling out an application.

- List your past jobs and describe what you did. What skills did you develop? What were the important things you did during your shift?
- Focus on what you have to offer an employer. Downplay the negatives.
- List relevant work experience from your personal life. Were you a caregiver for your siblings, children, parents, or grandparents? What skills did you develop? Did you learn to communicate, resolve conflicts, manage people's health, take care of finances?
- Consider the skills they are looking for. If they want good customer service skills, explain how you worked with customers in your past jobs.
- Use examples from your personal life to explain your passion for this work. Maybe when you were a young child, you took care of your sick grandmother. This inspired you to become an excellent home health aide.
- Do not list your wages from past employment. Instead, write "will discuss at the interview."
- We suggest you list the jobs you held while incarcerated. You gained relevant experience and skills. For in-prison jobs, you can list your employer as the State of Washington.
- If they ask you for your "Reason for Leaving" give a positive reason, if

possible, even if you were fired or let go. Some examples of positive reasons for leaving are:
  - o You relocated (you left because you went to prison, or you were transferred).
  - o You wanted a career change.
  - o You became a full-time student.
  - o The work was seasonal.
  - o You wanted to advance or make more money.
- In some states, employers are not allowed to ask about felonies on job applications. Some still do. If they ask, "Have you ever been convicted of a felony?" we recommend that you check "Yes." Write, "Will discuss at interview." If you lie, you may get the job, but you could get fired later if they find out.
- The application may ask you for references, people who can vouch for you. These should not be family members or friends. Be sure to ask people if they are willing to be your reference before writing their names down. Good potential references include:
  - o Former or current employers
  - o Supervisors
  - o Teachers
  - o Social workers
  - o Religious leaders
  - o People you volunteer with

Resumes and cover letters. Many job applications require a resume and cover letter. A resume maps out past jobs, your skills, and your interests. Your cover letter is an actual letter from you to the employer. It tells a short story about who you are—why you want the job, your background, and what's important to you. Keep your letter to one page.

Writing good resumes and cover letters takes time. Examples of resumes and cover letters can be found in our forms section. Here are a few online resources:

- https://hbr.org/2014/02/how-to-write-a-cover-letter
- https://owl.purdue.edu/owl/purdue_owl.html
- https://www.indeed.com/career-advice/resume-samples?from=careerguidepromo-US

---- 🙶 ----

"I thought I'd be prepared because I had my resume in hand. As it turns out, you need several resumes, adjusted to different jobs, and the ability to write cover sheets on the fly." —Pablo

---- 🙷 ----

Interviews. Once you've submitted your job application, wait to be contacted. Hopefully, they will be interested in interviewing you. Most applications do not lead to interviews. Be patient. Continue to send out applications until you have a job offer.

Many job seekers are nervous about interviews. They want to say the right things and make a good impression. This is completely normal. Here are a few tips:

- **Practice**. Indeed.com has a list of common interview questions and answers that you can practice with a friend, counselor, or family member. https://www.indeed.com/career-advice/interviewing/top-interview-questions-and-answers
- **What to bring.** Bring your resume and contact information for your references. Bring copies of work licenses, your driving record, and your Social Security or immigration cards. Bring a pen and notebook to write down information.
- **Arrive 10 to 15 minutes early.** This shows you are responsible and eager to be there.

- **Wear appropriate clothes.** Wear something a bit more formal than what you would wear for the job.
- **Consider your body language.** Even when you are not speaking, you are sending a message. Make good eye contact, stand, and sit tall, and smile.
- **Test your equipment.** If your interview is online, test your video and internet connection beforehand. Make sure you're in a place without disruptions.
- **Come prepared to ask the employer questions.** Here are some examples:
  o What is the organization's plan for the next five years?
  o How will I be evaluated, and in what timeframes? By whom?
  o What are the day-to-day responsibilities of this job?
  o What computer equipment and software do you use?
  o When will a decision be made about this position?

---- 🙶 ----

"Interview tips? Look good, smell good, speak good."
David T.

---- 🙷 ----

Zoom Interviews. Since the pandemic, some employers prefer to use Zoom, or other online video conferencing platforms to conduct their interviews. If you are invited for a Zoom interview, you must create an account before your interview.

What you need:
- An active email (Gmail, AOL, Yahoo, etc.)
- A computer or electronic device with Wi-Fi

How to create a Free Zoom account:
- Sign up through https://zoom.us/freesignup/.
- Enter your email and follow the prompts.
- Be sure to use your legal name.
- Create a password that you will remember.

Before your interview, practice using the tools in the call. This will get you familiar with Zoom and allow you to focus on the interview itself rather than the technology.

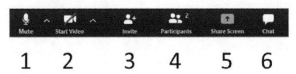

Zoom Controls

Common Zoom Features

1. **Mute/Unmute:** Used for your microphone. When in an interview, it is best to mute your microphone if there is a group of people or if there is background noise.
2. **Start/Stop Video:** Used for your camera. When joining a call, a good tip is to check your camera and surroundings before entering the call. For interviews, keep your camera on unless told otherwise.
3. **Invite:** This feature is used mostly for people who are hosting calls such as interviewers.
4. **Participants:** This shows you who is in the call with you.
5. **Share screen:** This button allows you to share your computer screen with other participants if needed.
6. **Chat:** Used to talk to others in the call.

Talking about your criminal record. You may have a hard time answering questions about your criminal record. Here are a few tips to increase your chance of getting hired:

- **Own It.** "At that time I was making some bad choices and I was convicted of...(state your offense)." Address any concerns an employer might have.
- **Redirect.** After addressing your background, steer the interview back to your skills and what you bring to the job. "I can see why that might concern you. But that was several years ago. Since then, I have had a solid work record. I come to work on time. I am a hard worker and quick learner."
- **Unrelated to job.** If your felony conviction is not related to the job you are applying for, you might say, "Yes, I was convicted of a felony, but it was not job related." Keep it positive. "I thought a lot about where my life was going, and I decided to make some changes." Talk about your current activities and future career goals. Mention education and job training, community work, and other activities.
- **Encourage the employer.** "I am a good worker and I want to work; I just need an opportunity to prove my skills to an employer." Tell them that you want the job!
- **Make a good first and last impression.** Employers are more likely to remember their first and last impression, so, if possible, try to address your criminal background history in the middle of the interview.

A note about background checks: If a company requires a background check, that may not mean a person with a conviction is automatically disqualified. It often depends on whether the circumstances of the conviction relate to the nature of employment. Many companies will set criteria for their background checks. The criteria to "pass" could be a certain amount of time since conviction, certain categories of charges, or charges in certain jurisdictions.

While you may choose not to apply to a company that requires a background check, be aware that the actual hiring policy may not disqualify you. If you're comfortable, you could inquire about the company's specific policy related to conviction history.

———— 99 ————

"If you're scared to tell an employer, hey, I've been to prison, just tell them. What's the worst thing they can do? Say no, we're not going to hire you. And you go to the next door. Knock on the next door. Say hey, are you hiring?" —Tony C.

———— 66 ————

Advice From an Employer

We reached out to Tanja, an employer who has hired many people who have been incarcerated. In the interview below, Tanja explains what employers are looking for. She gives advice about how to talk about your criminal history with employers.

———— 99 ————

"If you're scared to tell an employer, hey, I've been to prison, just tell them. What's the worst thing they can do? Say no, we're not going to hire you. And you go to the next door. Knock on the next door. Say hey, are you hiring?" — Tony C.

———— 66 ————

What are the most important qualities you look for in a job candidate? For me, the most important quality is reliability. I also appreciate it when people are eager to learn and respond well to constructive criticism. The fit between the person and the position is also critical.

How much do you need to say about your criminal background? I think it really depends on the position. It is a mistake to come in and tell me your whole life. That is too much too soon. But being super vague will make me wonder if you are trying to hide something. For me, honesty is critical. I let people know I am not here to judge and as far as I am concerned, they have done their time. What I care about is the present and the future. Can they do this job now? How much training and supervision will they need? What are their skills and how can these skills aid in job performance?

What impresses you about candidates? I am usually impressed when I see someone who has done their homework. They know what the position is, they Googled the company, and they know what we are looking for. It is ideal to tailor your history to the position and capitalize on your skills. Link these skills to the job announcement and tell me how these skills will be used to help me. Also demonstrate enthusiasm for what the company does. If it is the restaurant industry, tell me how much you enjoy the food and why.

What questions should the interviewee ask the employer? Do your homework about my company, the job description, and ask me questions as if you had the position. Ask for details about logistics: How many hours, what days and times do you need me? What qualities are you looking for in a worker? What would a typical day be like on the job? What are the opportunities for growth? Do you offer training, and if so, how does that work? Who will be my supervisor? What is their management style? These questions will make me believe you are serious about the job.

What questions can they expect in an interview, and how would you handle the tricky ones?

- Why are you applying for this job now?
- What is your availability? Convince me that you will be available and reliable. Make sure you can make the work schedule work.
- What are your best skills? What skills would you like to develop in the future?
- What were you doing before? This

question can be tricky if you have a big gap in your resume. If you were just released, be honest, but capitalize on the skills you have that make you right for this position even though you have been out of the market for a while. Emphasize how the situation has changed, point me to your references and how they will assure me that you are worth taking a chance on.

 Your Legal Rights

Equal Employment Laws

The Equal Employment Opportunity Commission (EEOC) is a federal agency that enforces federal laws that prohibit discrimination in the workplace. These laws apply to job applicants and employees across the country. The EEOC addresses the following issues that may be relevant to you:

Background check. Employers who wish to do a background check must:

- Get the applicant's or employee's written consent ahead of time.
- Tell the applicant if the content of the report will be used for employment decisions.
- Before taking adverse action (like not hiring an applicant or firing an employee) based on background information, give the applicant or employee a copy of the report.
- Inform the applicant or employee of their right to review and dispute the report.

Employment Denial. The EEOC cannot prohibit employers from obtaining or using arrest or conviction records. However, the EEOC does provide guidance to ensure that arrest and conviction records are not used in a way that discriminates against a person because of their race, color, religion, sex, national origin, age,

disability, or genetic information. EEOC guidance outlines best practices and suggests employers limit their questions about arrest or conviction records to records that are job related. Factors employers could include:

- The nature and gravity of the criminal offense or conduct.
- How much time has passed since the conduct or sentence.
- The nature of the job (where it is performed, supervision & interaction with others).

Employers can still choose candidates with more or better experience, but the EEOC discourages use of irrelevant criminal history when making employment decisions. If you believe you have been discriminated against, you can file a complaint by mail, telephone (800) 669-4000, or in person at an EEOC office: https://www.eeoc.gov/

Certificate of Rehabilitation

A criminal record can prevent you from getting a license in certain fields, including education, transit, and childcare. You may be able to get a Certificate of Restoration of Opportunity (CROP). This allows you to apply for jobs that require these licenses. It does not remove offenses from your record, but it may allow you to get a license.

For more information about a CROP, including how to get one, see "Certificate of Restoration of Opportunity (CROP)" by the Northwest Justice Project at https://www.washingtonlawhelp.org/resource/certificate-of-restoration-of-opportunity-crop. NJP has also put together a packet to help you file for a CROP, available at https://www.washingtonlawhelp.org/resource/filing-a-petition-for-certificate-of-restoration-of-opportunity-crop.

Work Opportunity Tax Credits

If employers seem reluctant to hire you, you may want to tell them about the Work Opportunity Tax Credit. Employers who hire people with convictions receive a tax credit of up to 40% of up to $6,000 of wages paid to eligible individuals with felonies who have left prison within the last year. It is only offered during their first year of employment.

Federal Bonding Program

When interviewing for a job, you may also want to tell the employer about the Federal Bonding Program. It is an insurance policy that protects employers against employee dishonesty or theft. It provides employers with no-cost insurance coverage for employees with past convictions. Coverage is free for 6 months and ranges from $5,000 to $25,000. Learn more here: https://bonds4jobs.com/, esd.wa.gov/about-employees/federal-bonding.

Ban the Box

Some states have laws that prevent employers from conducting criminal background checks until after an interview is conducted. This law is called "Ban the Box" because it prohibits employers from asking you to check a box on your application if you've had a criminal conviction. You may submit a complaint against an employer who violates this rule. Washington state is a "Ban the Box" state. For more information please review this flier from the Washington State Attorney General's Office.

Conflicts and Safety

If you are being harassed or discriminated against because of your race, gender identity, or sexual orientation, your civil rights are being violated. If you are comfortable enough where you are working, you can speak to Human Resources about what you have experienced. Sometimes it's better to seek help elsewhere.

There are resources that can support you. If you have been sexually harassed, you can contact **RAINN**, the National Sexual Assault Hotline at (800) 656-4673 for personal support. They can help you file a complaint.

It is a good idea to get a lawyer before starting a lawsuit (and there are pro bono lawyers who can help–see our Legal Matters section). If you are ready to file a complaint on your own, you may do so at the **US Department of Justice Civil Rights Division**.

If you are working in a place that is unsafe, you can file a complaint with the Occupational Safety and Health Administration (OSHA) by calling (800) 321-6742 or online at https://www.osha.gov/workers/file-complaint. If you think that something may be unsafe, but don't have proof, you may notify your employer in writing. If they do not resolve the issue, you may then file a complaint with OSHA. It is illegal for employers to retaliate against you for filing a complaint.

Of course, it is hard to address these problems if you are in an insecure position and need to keep your job. If you can talk to a pro bono lawyer, they might be able to give you advice so that you are not put in a worse situation.

Unemployment Benefits

Most people who leave prison are not eligible for unemployment benefits. To qualify, you must have made at least $1,600 in the last 12 months before you file your claim and lost your job through no fault of your own. You cannot receive unemployment directly after you return home if you lost your previous job due to your incarceration or if you were in prison for more than 12 months.

If you believe you may qualify, visit https://esd.wa.gov/unemployment.

5. Education

A lot of people think about going back to school after they leave prison. Going to school helps you learn more about the world. It can also help you meet new people and get better jobs.

This chapter has information about different education programs, like:

- ABE and GED programs
- Vocational training and apprenticeships
- College
- Paying for college

It is never too late to learn or go to school or college.
Learning can even make you feel happier and more fulfilled. You can go to school part-time or full-time. If you are still in prison, take classes before you leave.

ABE, GED, and High School Equivalency Programs

Adult Basic Education (ABE) programs can help you get better at reading, writing, math, listening, and speaking. Usually, you can find ABE programs at adult schools, career centers, libraries, and community colleges. They are free or cost only a little. For-profit agencies like Kaplan and ELS Language Centers also offer ABE, but they charge more money. ABE programs can also help you learn English or prepare for the GED. A list of ABE programs in Washington can be found at Providers of Basic Education for Adults | SBCTC.

The General Education Development (GED) test is like a high school diploma. The GED allows adults who have not completed high school to show they have mastered the knowledge and skills associated with a high school diploma, which is a requirement for many jobs. If you did not graduate from high school, you can take this test and it will count on your resume as a diploma. You can register online to take the GED test at ged.com. Most tests will be administered on the computer at a testing site, but some testing locations may offer paper tests. For more

information about getting a GED in Washington visit:https://www.sbctc.edu/becoming-a-student/basic-education/ged-students

The GED is not an easy test. You will probably need to study. A lot of places have free preparation programs that can help you get ready:

- Community colleges
- Adult learning centers (Find one using this directory: https://www.nld.org/programs?p=Washington&r=5#program-search-container
- Online study programs
- American Job Centers
- https://ged.com/study/ged_classes/

A lot of programs will let you sign up at any time. They can also give you a study plan to help you get better in harder subjects. For more info see https://bestaccreditedcolleges.org/articles/all-about-the-ged-washington.html

Do you need help learning how to use new technology? Go to Northstar at digitalliteracyassessment.org to get help. They have online classes and in-person ones at different locations. They will give you certificates when you gain new skills.

Vocational Training and Apprenticeships

Vocational programs help you learn how to do a job. They can teach you things like welding, car repair, plumbing and more. You can go to community and technical colleges, as well as trade schools to take vocational classes. Some community-based organizations also offer vocational training.

A lot of prisons have vocational classes. Take them if you can. Vocational classes help you get some experience and see if you like the work. Once you leave, you can get an entry-level position or an apprenticeship. Apprenticeships help you get training and experience. You'll also get paid through an apprenticeship. Apprenticeships are usually offered through trade unions.

For more information on apprenticeship programs, go to

- https://www.apprenticeship.gov/apprenticeship-job-finder
- https://wacareerpaths.com/apprenticeships/
- https://www.lni.wa.gov/licensing-permits/apprenticeship/apprenticeship-preparation

———— 99 ————

"Consider seeking simple certifications, like CDL, sanitation, limo driver, or forklift." —Earl W.

———— 66 ————

Degree Type	Information
Vocational certificates	Certificates that prepare you for specific jobs or tasks. Offered by community colleges, technical schools, or workforce programs.
Associate degree	2-year degree granted by a community college, university, or technical school.
Bachelor's degree	4-year degree granted by a college or university.
Master's degree	2+ years, after earning a bachelor's degree. Typically requires research.
Doctor of Philosophy (PhD)	4+ years, after earning a bachelor's or master's degree. The highest academic degree to earn.
Professional degrees (MD, JD, MBA)	Degrees required to practice in certain professions (doctors, lawyers, business), after earning a bachelor's degree.

College

Community college. If you haven't been in school for a while, you might want to start at community college. Community colleges are inexpensive and offer many different classes. A lot of them offer programs where you can get a GED and college credit at the same time. Community colleges usually offer associate degrees, certificate programs, and workforce training.

4-year college. Many people who want to earn a 4-year bachelor's degree start by attending community college for a year. Then they transfer to a 4-year college to finish. You'll save money for the first two years because community college costs less than 4-year schools.

You must earn a certain number of credits to get a 4-year degree. Some credits must be in general subjects like science, math, and history. If you finish these credits at a community college and then transfer to a four-year college, your credits can transfer over too. Make sure to check that your new school will count your transfer credits.

Check out the website of the Washington State Board for Community and Technical Colleges for information about planning for college, paying for college, and picking a college. Visit it at https://www.sbctc.edu/our-colleges/. To learn more, visit the websites of the schools or call, email, or visit an admissions counselor or academic advisor at these schools.

Where should you apply?

Deciding where to go may take some time. Think about what kind of degree you want and what kind of college you want to go to. Research colleges online or at the local library. Almost all colleges have websites where you can learn about their price, academic programs, non-academic activities, the town where they are located, and many other things.

Applying for College

Step 1: Get the Application. For almost all colleges, you will apply on their websites. If you need help with this a librarian at a public library will likely be able to help you.

Step 2: Gather Your Information. To apply for college, you will probably need:

- Your Social Security number.
- A state driver's license or identification card.
- The dates of high school and previous college attendance.
- Unopened transcripts from high school, GED, and/or college transcripts, whichever you completed most recently.
- Many four-year colleges will also ask for ACT or SAT test scores.

Some applications may ask about your criminal history. If you tell them you have been convicted of a felony, some schools will ask for more information. Just because they are asking for the information doesn't mean you will be rejected, but different schools have different policies about backgrounds. You can also ask to speak with an admissions counselor about this.

Step 3: Take the SAT or ACT exam. Is this your first time applying for college? Many four-year colleges require you to take the ACT or SAT college entrance exam. An admissions counselor can give you more information. It helps to study. You can buy study guides or get them from your public library. Khan Academy offers online SAT test prep for free at https://www.khanacademy.org/sat

Step 4: Complete the Essay. Most four-year colleges require a "statement of purpose" essay. This might be the hardest part of the application, but these essays let you shine. Make sure you put your goals in the essay. Ask a few people you trust to check your statement for mistakes. Ask them to also make sure you sound purposeful and confident.

Step 5: Submit the Application. You'll probably hear from a community college within a few weeks. They'll let you know by phone or letter if you've been accepted. Four-year colleges can take longer. If you have questions, contact the school's admissions office.

Paying for Your Education

Paying for your education can be hard. Below we describe how you can get money for college.

Free Tuition Programs

Some colleges offer free tuition if you meet certain income requirements. Check with the college you are interested in attending. Washington State offers the WA Grant, for more information visit https://wsac.wa.gov/wcg. Veterans can also get money for college. See studentaid.gov/understand-aid/types/military.

Even if you have tuition covered, you'll need to pay for living expenses, books, and fees.

Financial Aid: FAFSA

Do you need financial aid for college? The Free Application for Federal Student Aid (FAFSA) is the place to start. For more information, visit https://www.sbctc.edu/paying-for-college/.

How do I apply? You can find the FAFSA online at www.fafsa.gov, or you can request a paper copy from 800-4-FEDAID ((800) 433-3243). Applying for federal student aid is free. But it can be complicated. If you're worried or have questions, ask for help. College financial aid offices can help you over the phone or email or in person.

When is it due? Check on the form to see when it is due for your state. You should also ask your college when it is due. They might want it much earlier. Look at the school's website or call the financial aid office. Turn in your FAFSA as soon as you can because some financial aid runs out fast. If you can, turn in your FAFSA while you're in

prison. That way everything will be ready in time for you to start school.

What kind of aid will I get? The aid you get will depend on how much money you make and the cost of your school. Your aid package may include the following:

- **Pell Grants** are government grants that are based on financial need.
- **Scholarships** can come from the college or from other organizations. Ask your financial aid office about scholarships. Scholarship information can also be found at public libraries and online.
- **Loans** have a lower interest rate than banks, and you won't have to start paying it back until after you graduate. Be aware that if you take out student loans, you will have to pay them back. Think carefully how you will repay your loans. Your loans will impact your decisions about money and jobs.
- **Work study positions** allow you to pay for college by working for the school. You can say you are interested in work-study when you fill out the FAFSA. Work-study is a good way to make money and get more work experience. They are often offered first come, first served.

Your financial aid package may include several kinds of aid. You don't have to accept the whole package. You can choose the parts that work for you. For example, you could accept a grant but not a loan. Reach out to the office if you have questions or want help understanding your package.

Can I get federal student aid if I have a criminal record? In most cases, yes. You cannot get federal student aid if you were subject to an involuntary civil commitment after completing a period of incarceration for a forcible or non-forcible sexual offense.

For more information on federal financial aid for those inside prison, on parole, and for those with a felony conviction, see studentaid.gov/understand-aid/eligibility/require ments/criminal-convictions.

> *If a grant, loan, or scholarship offer sounds too good to be true, it probably is. There are many for-profit companies that take advantage of people who are looking to go to college. Applying for financial aid should be free, and you should research the agency or company before applying.*

Remember to keep copies of all applications and related paperwork in a safe space.

Defaulted student loans

If you have outstanding student loans that are currently in default, this will impact your eligibility for financial aid. Being in bad standing with old loans can be overwhelming, but you have options! You can even begin exploring these options in prison. Your priority will be to get out of default. You may not need to pay off the entire loan or even make a large payment. You may be able to rehabilitate or consolidate your loans at little to no cost—sometimes $5/month to get back in good standing. You can do this online, by phone, or by mail. See https://studentaid.gov/announcements-events/d efault-fresh-start.

Helpful Resources

- For useful information about how to get your education after incarceration, see Study.com's guide, *"How to Earn Your Degree and Get Hired After Incarceration."* You can access it here: https://bestaccreditedcolleges.org/resour ces/formerly-incarcerated-education-care er-guide

- The Formerly Incarcerated College Graduates Network is an amazing resource! Build community, find support from peers, share resources, find job openings, advocate for policy change, and share your story. Visit: www.ficgn.org

- The Prison Scholar Fund is committed to providing educational opportunities, professional development, transitional support, and advocacy for those impacted by incarceration. For more information visit: https://www.prisonscholars.org/

- The Freedom Education Project's (http://www.fepps.org/) mission is to provide a rigorous college program to incarcerated women in Washington and create pathways to higher education after women are released from prison. The Project believes that education reduces recidivism, teaches valuable employment skills, prepares people for life outside prison, and helps them to become providers, leaders, and examples for their families and communities.

6. Health

When you leave prison, you will need to manage your own health. This can be a welcome change, but it is also stressful. There are many different options for health insurance. There are many kinds of clinics, hospitals, and doctors to choose from. There is paperwork, applications, and bills to figure out. Don't be afraid to ask for help from family and friends as you figure things out.

In this section, we cover:

- Staying healthy during COVID-19
- Health insurance
- Regular and specialty doctor visits
- Dental and vision insurance
- Paying for medications
- HIV prevention, testing and treatment

See also our Trauma and Mental Health chapter and Substance Use Disorder chapter.

Health Insurance

Getting medical care is costly! Health insurance can help pay for doctor's visits, medications, vaccines, laboratory tests, and emergencies. Health insurance can also be expensive, but medical care can cost hundreds or thousands of dollars if you are not insured.

> ***Getting care if you are uninsured.*** *If you don't have health insurance but need care, there are public and community health programs and clinics that offer free or low-cost services.*

These community clinics provide:

- Vaccinations and immunizations
- Full physicals
- Nutrition and food stamp programs
- STD screening, cancer screening, HIV/AIDS services

Ways to Get Health Insurance

- Dental care
- Pregnancy and maternity assistance
- Programs to quit smoking
- Hearing tests and eye exams

Find a public health program or clinic at:

- https://freeclinicdirectory.org/

- https://www.wahealthcareaccessalliance.org/search-for-clinics

- https://www.freeclinics.com/sta/washington

"Go to a community medical center. You can get a free full physical when you get out of prison. We have to make sure there are no underlying conditions that we aren't aware of." —Joe Joe

There are several different ways to get health insurance. Here is a list of the most common ways:

- **Government health insurance**: Medicare and Medicaid are government health insurance programs for certain populations. For more information, see below.
- **Employer health insurance**: Some employers offer health insurance plans for their employees. The employer might cover some of the cost, and the rest will be taken out of the employee's paycheck.
- **Student health insurance**: If you're a full-time college student, you may be able to purchase health insurance through your college or university.
- **Through a parent**: People who are age 26 or younger and have a parent with health insurance are allowed to be added to their coverage as a dependent.
- **Healthcare Marketplace**: Created by the Affordable Care Act, the Marketplace offers health plans for purchase, and the cost may be discounted depending on your income.
- **Through a private agent**: You might be able to purchase personal health insurance directly from the company or through an insurance agent.

Medicaid and Medicare

Medicaid and Medicare are government programs that help with healthcare costs. Most hospitals and health clinics accept Medicaid payments.

- **Medicaid:** Called "Apple Health" in Washington State, is a government program for people who meet eligibility requirements (such as income requirements)
- **Medicare:** Program for those 65 years old or older

To see if you qualify, visit:

- https://www.hca.wa.gov/free-or-low-cost-health-care/i-need-medical-dental-or-vision-care/eligibility-overview

- https://www.wahealthplanfinder.org/us/en/health-coverage/enrollment-periods/steps-apply.html
- www.healthcare.gov
- First Timers' Guide to Washington Apple Health (Medicaid), Washington Health Care Authority Part 1: www.hca.wa.gov/assets/free-or-low-cost/19-024.pdf Part 2: www.hca.wa.gov/assets/free-or-low-cost/19-041.pdf

You can apply to Medicaid or Medicare one of four ways:

1. You may be able to apply in prison before you leave. Talk to your counselor or clinical services.
2. Apply online
3. You may be able to apply in person at a hospital or at a DSHS center or another place that offers case management.
4. Apply by mail or fax. You can call your state's DSHS to mail you an application. Complete the application and mail or fax it back in.

Before applying you need to have a few documents ready:

- Income verification. This could be pay stubs, a financial aid award letter, a written statement from your employer, or a copy of your check stub showing your total income before taxes.
- Your Social Security number.
- Proof of residency—any official document that shows your address and name together will work.

When you fill out your Medicaid application, you can also apply for other benefits, such as SNAP (Supplemental Nutrition Assistance Program) and TANF (Temporary Assistance for Needy Families). See Resources to Meet your Basic Needs for more information about these and other assistance programs.

If you are receiving Medicaid or benefits from any of these other programs, report any changes to your income or dependent status as soon as possible. If you begin making more money than is allowed, you may no longer qualify for these programs.

Applying for health insurance can be a complex process, and it is understandable if you feel overwhelmed and would like some assistance. Luckily, there are various options available to help you navigate through this process. Whether you prefer face-to-face interaction, telephone assistance, or online guidance, there are resources to cater to your preferred method.

Washington Healthplanfinder understands the need for guidance and has trained representatives who specialize in assisting individuals with filling out forms and comparing different insurance plans. These representatives are knowledgeable and can provide you with the necessary support to ensure a smooth application process. It is important to note that these services are completely free, so there is no need to hesitate in utilizing them.

If you require assistance, you can easily contact Washington Healthplanfinder's toll-free number at 1-855-923-4633. The advantage of this service is that it is available in a remarkable 175 languages, ensuring that language barriers do not hinder your ability to receive the necessary help. Additionally, if you are hard of hearing, there is a separate number, 1-855-627-9604, specifically designed to cater to your needs.

Another option available to you is to seek assistance from a Navigator. Navigators are certified representatives who have been trained to help individuals complete their health insurance applications. These Navigators can be found in various health clinics or through agencies that are listed on the Washington Healthplanfinder website. By visiting https://www.wahbexchange.org/partners/navigators/, you can easily find the nearest Navigator to your location.

Alternatively, you may choose to seek help from a licensed broker. These brokers are professionals who have undergone training provided by the state. They possess the knowledge and expertise to guide you through the application process and can also recommend suitable insurance plans based on your specific needs. It is important to note that only brokers are authorized to recommend plans. To find a broker near you, you can visit: www.wahealthplanfinder.org/HBEWeb/Annon_DisplayBrokerNavigatorSearch.action?brokerNavigator=BRK&request_locale=en.

Health Insurance Vocabulary

When thinking about getting health insurance, it helps to know the vocabulary. Ask questions and make sure you understand what you are getting.

- **Premiums**. The amount you pay for your health insurance every month.
- **Yearly deductible**. The amount you pay for covered health care services before your insurance plan starts to pay. With a $2,000 deductible, for example, you pay the first $2,000 of covered services yourself. Many plans cover the costs for certain services, like a checkup or disease management programs before you've met your deductible.
- **Copay**. A fixed amount ($20, for example) you pay for a covered health care service after you've paid your deductible.
- **Coinsurance**. The percentage of costs of a health care service that you pay (20% for example) after you've paid your deductible. In this example the insurance plan would pay the other 80%.
- **Out-of-pocket maximum**. The most you must pay for covered services in a plan year. After you spend this amount on deductibles, co-payments, and coinsurance for in-network care and services, your health plan pays 100%
- **Approved network or in-network**. The facilities, providers, and suppliers your health insurer has contracted with.
- **Out-of-network**. Health care providers who don't contract with your health insurance or plan. Out-of- network costs are usually higher than in-network.

These definitions and more can be found at: www.healthcare.gov/glossary/

Dental and Vision Care

Get your teeth cleaned and examined regularly. Oral health is important for your overall health. Teeth problems can lead to bigger health problems in the future.

Get your eyes checked regularly, too. If you have vision problems like glaucoma, cataracts, or retinal tears it is especially important to take care of your eyes.

You may be interested in a healthcare plan that covers dental or eye care. Some dentists will accept Medicaid payments—ask them to find out. Dental and vision are not always included in health insurance plans, so think about your needs and check each plan before you enroll. There may be separate dental or vision plans that you can get.

Some health insurance plans offer vision care, which covers yearly eye exams and some of the cost of glasses and contacts. Check your health insurance plan to see what is covered because you may have to buy a separate plan for eye care. Medicare does cover eye exams, and Medicaid covers vision care for children.

Low-Cost Dental and Eye Care.

Here are some options for dental care:

- https://www.nidcr.nih.gov/health-info/finding-dental-care to find low-cost dental care.
- https://search.wa211.org/search?query=dental&query_type=query&query_language=en
- https://www.freedentalcare.us/st/washington
- https://www.wahealthcareaccessalliance.org/search-for-clinics
- https://dentistlink.org/

There are several programs that offer free or low-cost eye exams and glasses:

- Eyecare America (eye exams) - www.aao.org/eyecare-america
- https://search.wa211.org/search?query=vision&query_type=query&query_language=en
- InfantSEE (free eye exams for babies 6-12 mo.) - www.infantsee.org
- https://www.wahealthcareaccessalliance.org/search-for-clinics
- New Eyes (free glasses program) - (973) 376-4903
- Purchasing glasses online for cheap: Zennioptical.com and www.goggles4u.com offer frames starting at around $10. You will need a prescription.

 Doctor Visits

It's a good idea to establish a regular relationship with your doctor. Most health insurance plans require you to pick a primary care provider. This person will serve as your "medical home" and is usually a family physician, nurse practitioner, physician's assistant, or internal medicine physician. Having regular visits with a primary care provider is the best way to manage your health. Go see this person instead of going to the emergency room or urgent care. This will save you money and time and keep you healthy.

A primary care physician can give you a full physical exam, perform lab work, and provide prescription renewals. It is recommended that you have a full physical at least once a year and complete routine exams. Below are age and sex-based recommendations for health screenings.

ROUTINE EXAMS THAT CAN KEEP YOU HEALTHY

Age	Men	Women
18-39	blood pressure, cholesterol, flu shot, syphilis screen, TDAP shot, HPV shot, chlamydia/gonorrhea, HIV, skin exam	blood pressure, cholesterol, flu shot, TDAP shot, HPV shot, breast exam, after 21 PAP smear, skin exam, chlamydia/gonorrhea, HIV
40-64	blood pressure, blood sugar, colonoscopy (over 50), stool test, flu shot, shingles shot (over 60), prostate screen (over 50), lung cancer screen only if you smoke, skin exam	blood pressure, blood sugar, colonoscopy (over 50), stool test, flu shot, shingles shot (over 60), breast screen, mammogram (over 40), lung cancer screen only if you smoke, postmenopausal bone screening, PAP, pelvic, HPV, skin exam
65+	blood pressure, blood sugar, cholesterol, colonoscopy until 75, hearing test, aneurysm screen if smoker, only prostate and lung screening if you have risk factors, pneumonia shot x2, skin exam	blood pressure, blood sugar, cholesterol, colonoscopy until 75, hearing test, mammogram until 75, bone screening, PAP until 65, pneumonia shot x2, skin exam

Your primary care provider can also refer you to specialists for some health concerns. One way to contact your primary care physician is by signing up through your hospital network's online portal. This will allow you to access your medical records, send messages to your doctor and schedule appointments.

"Going to the office of my primary care physician was actually a pleasant experience. It was nothing like it was on the inside." —Pablo

Pharmacy

Some insurance plans will help you pay for expensive medical prescriptions, while others do

not. If you are having trouble paying for your prescriptions, here are a few options:

- Ask your doctor or pharmacist if there is a generic version of the drugs you need. Generic drugs are much less expensive.
- Go to Goodrx.com to compare prices of prescription medications. It tells you where you can go for the best price. You can download their app on a smartphone.
- Stores like Target, Walmart, Costco, and Sam's Club often have special programs where you can purchase generic drugs for very cheap ($4 for 30-day quantity or $10 for a 90-day quantity).
- Go to www.rxassist.org to find out if the medication you need is offered for free to people who qualify.

HIV/AIDS and Other Diseases

Being in prison increases the risk of getting some diseases. After release from prison, consider getting tested for HIV, Hepatitis C (HCV), Hepatitis B (HBV) and tuberculosis. HIV, HBV and HCV can be detected by a blood test. Tuberculosis can be tested by blood or by a skin test; if these tests are positive, the disease is confirmed by a chest X-ray. Locations for HIV testing can be found by using the CDC's HIV Test Locator at: https://www.cdc.gov/std/hiv

If you test positive for HIV or another serious disease, know that you can still live a long and meaningful life. You should make an appointment to see a healthcare provider to stay healthy and possibly begin treatments.

You should still be cautious if the test comes back negative. It is possible that the tests cannot yet detect the virus in your body. You can request another test later.

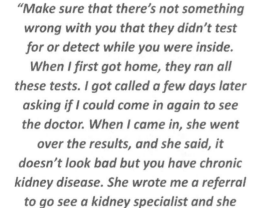

"Make sure that there's not something wrong with you that they didn't test for or detect while you were inside. When I first got home, they ran all these tests. I got called a few days later asking if I could come in again to see the doctor. When I came in, she went over the results, and she said, it doesn't look bad but you have chronic kidney disease. She wrote me a referral to go see a kidney specialist and she gave me some literature to read about the disease and how I could have gotten it." —Shaun W.

What Does Having HIV Mean?

HIV is a virus that spreads by attacking and killing healthy cells in the body. This happens all over the body, destroying cells or forcing them to create new infected cells.

HIV targets immune system cells, known as T-cells. T-cells fight off infection by killing cells that have been infected by germs. As more T-cells start dying, the immune system is open to attack. If the number of T-cells drops too low, the risk of infection increases and can lead to AIDS. When someone has AIDS, their immune system becomes too weak to fight off other infections. If untreated, people can die of AIDS.

Fortunately, people who have HIV today can live long and productive lives as long as they take steps to stay on top of their infection. HIV can be managed with daily medication, regular testing and doctor visits, and healthy lifestyle changes (exercise, stopping smoking, getting enough sleep, etc.).

Sometimes HIV testing is offered as part of the prison outtake process. We suggest you take advantage of this free testing, as knowing your status is very important to you and our loved ones.

Risk

The most common way for HIV to be transmitted is through sexual contact, but infected and untreated mothers can pass it on to their children. Avoid contact with blood, semen, or vaginal fluid of sexual partners who are HIV-positive. Do not share needles or syringes and make sure to use protection (condoms) for any sexual contact.

Know the risk of spreading HIV to a sexual partner who is not HIV positive. Being treated with antiretroviral medications can reduce your chances of transmitting HIV to a partner. Taking antiretroviral medications regularly lowers the levels of HIV in your blood. This does not mean that the virus is completely gone, so take precautions and use condoms even though the risk of transmission is low. If you do not have HIV but are in a relationship with someone who does, you can take PrEP (Pre-Exposure Prophylaxis), which reduces the risk of being infected.

There are also certain sexual activities that can increase your chances of transmitting HIV. For more information about HIV transmission and risk factors, visit: https://www.hiv.gov/hiv-basics/

7. Trauma and Mental Health

Know that if you are struggling with trauma or mental health issues, you are not alone. Most people who are incarcerated have experienced trauma. Many also have a mental health issue or have had one in the past. Being in prison can trigger mental health issues or make them worse. Your time in prison may cause trauma that affects your mental health long after you leave.

If you have mental health issues, **seek treatment as soon as you are released.** Reentry is hard. Mental health issues can make reentry much harder. Sadly, people who do not get treatment are more likely to return to prison.
There are mental health professionals who can help you.
They can provide talk therapy and medication, if needed. They can help you learn to better handle stress and life problems.

You matter! Make your mental health a priority. When you do, you will experience deep personal growth and be able to better help others. You can learn to become stronger so that you can bounce back from hard things.

This chapter covers the following topics:

- Trauma
- Bouncing back
- Treatment for mental health

- Types of treatment
- Attitudes about mental health

Trauma

Just about everyone who has been to prison has experienced trauma. Trauma is a mental health issue that many people face.

Trauma is the emotional response you have to a stressful and possibly life-changing event. It can also be the result of toxic stress that builds up over time. Trauma is more common than people think, and its effects can be very serious. Traumatic events in childhood can have effects throughout your life.

— 👣 —

"Trauma is something that all of us go through. You have to get to the point that you realize that what you've been going through is trauma. Nothing you went through is normal. It's not normal to be secluded. Even before prison, we were on the streets, experiencing trauma and violence to the point that it became a natural thing. We became desensitized to those things."
—Anonymous

"The residue of prison stays with you. Keys rattling means it's a guard coming. You wake up with a heightened sense of alertness. You are late and you worry you have missed your chance. You can't calm down. You have a pattern of sleeplessness. You are easily annoyed. Tense situations escalate into violence." -Kilroy

Trauma can come from lots of things, such as:

- Physical, sexual, or emotional abuse
- Neglect
- Witnessing violence
- Having a loved one with substance use or mental health issues
- Parent separation or divorce
- Poverty
- Being incarcerated or having a family member who is incarcerated
- Living in unsafe neighborhoods

People in prison, especially women, are more likely to have experienced trauma. There are strong connections between trauma, poor mental health, and incarceration.

Where to get help.

If you have experienced trauma at any point in your life, you may benefit from treatment or counseling. Counselors can help you understand the effects of trauma on your well-being, your emotions, and your behaviors.

Trauma-focused treatments provide you with skills to better understand what happened to you. You can learn to cope with the emotions and memories connected to these scary experiences. The goal is to help you reach a healthier new perspective on what took place in your life.

If you are enrolled in Apple Health, behavioral health is covered by your plan. You do not need a referral from your managed care plan, because this type of health care is funded directly by Medicaid. Instead, you should directly contact a mental health treatment agency to set up your care. To find a treatment agency, or if you are in a crisis, contact the Washington Recovery Helpline at 1-866-789-1511 or online at

https://www.warecoveryhelpline.org/mental-health/.

Here are a few places you can go for help:

- Go to this directory to find a mental health provider: https://www.samhsa.gov/data/sites/default/files/reports/rpt34657/National_Directory_MH_facilities_2021.pdf. When calling to set up an appointment, ask if they provide trauma-focused treatment.
- Your primary care provider may be able to connect you to a mental health consultant located in your clinic, so ask if one is available.
- Many reentry programs provide trauma-informed care. Ask what services they provide.

Bouncing Back

When you face trauma or stress and overcome it, you can strengthen your ability to bounce back from hard things. Being able to bounce back instead of getting stuck is called resilience.

Being resilient does not mean that stress is not hard for you. It means you have taught yourself to better cope with hard things. Resilience can be learned. It is not a trait that only some people have. It is something that everyone has the ability to strengthen, like when you build muscle. It takes time and work but it can be done. There is hope!

If you feel stuck or are not making progress, seek help from a mental health professional. Seeking help is an important part of building resilience.

According to the American Psychological Association, there are four main areas of resilience. Work to improve your resilience in these four areas.

Build your connections

Connect with people you trust and who understand you. Remind yourself that you are not alone. If you have experienced trauma, it is common to want to isolate yourself. Fight that urge. Find a group to join and get active in the community.

Foster wellness

Take care of your body. Your body needs food, sleep, water, and exercise to fight off stress. When you take care of your body, you will feel better. There is a big connection between your physical and mental health.

Avoid negative outlets. When things are stressful it is tempting to want to turn to drugs, alcohol, or other negative ways of coping. This is like putting a Band-Aid on a large wound. Instead, try to focus on healthy things you can give your body to help you cope.

---- 🙶 ----

"In prison I had ways to cope with trauma. I would exercise, draw. This allowed me to escape that mental state for a little while."
–Anonymous

"Having a support group provides you with a reminder that there are other ways to cope." –Kilroy

---- 🙷 ----

Find purpose

Help others. Find meaning and purpose by helping others. Get involved with a community organization, church, or help a friend who is struggling.

Be proactive. Ask yourself, *"What can I do about this problem*?" Set achievable goals and break

them down into smaller steps. Start working on these steps.

Look for opportunities for self-discovery. Self-awareness can help you grow. Think about how you have grown because of a struggle, like being locked up. How have you become a better person? You may find that thinking about your growth helps you increase self-worth and appreciate your path in life.

Embrace healthy thoughts

Keep things in perspective. You do not always have control of events in your life. But you do have control of how you make sense of things and respond to them. How you think about your situation impacts how you feel. Recognize that negative thoughts are just that, thoughts that can be acknowledged and set aside.

Accept change. Being able to accept change is a part of life. There may be some things that get in the way of your goals. It is ok to accept some things. Focus instead on the things that are in your power to change and control.

Maintain a hopeful outlook. It is not realistic to be positive all the time. Allow yourself to feel upset for a little bit, but then focus on what gives you hope. What do you want and how can you make that happen?

Learn from your past. Look back at what has helped you in the past during hard times. Remind yourself of what has helped you find strength before. What have you learned about yourself from your past experiences?

---- 🙶 ----

"Advice for socializing outside? Learning coping skills and anger management. Being less abrasive and open-minded."
– Ear

---- 🙷 ----

Reflect

1. What has helped you "bounce back" from hard things in the past?

2. What are some things you would like to try to strengthen your resilience muscles?

 ## Seeking Treatment for your Mental Health

Everyone can benefit from mental health support during reentry. Reentry is stressful. Even if you do not have mental health issues, you may benefit from talking to someone to help you adjust.

It is a good idea to schedule an appointment with a mental health provider *before your release*. Many community mental health centers have long waiting lists, so set up an appointment ahead of time. This will help you have the support you need when things are tough.

There are several different options for care, depending on what your needs are.

Crisis Care

Are you in a crisis? Are you worried about hurting yourself or others? Do you have suicidal thoughts? Are you seeing and hearing things that aren't there? Are your symptoms so bad that you are having trouble functioning? Get help right away.

If you are in crisis, you may need an emergency evaluation to see if you need to be hospitalized. The types of treatments you get during a crisis are very brief. They are meant to keep you safe and get you stable. You'll get connected to on-going treatment when you leave the hospital. Be sure to follow up with a mental health professional in your community after a crisis.

Here are a few places you can turn to:

- **National Suicide and Crisis Lifeline:** Call 988; available 24/7, online chat: 988lifeline.org
- **Crisis Text Line:** Text "HELLO" to 741741, available 24/7
- **Call 911** and **ask for a C.I.T. (Crisis Intervention Trained) officer** if you or someone you know is in immediate danger or go to the nearest emergency room.
- **Crisis Connections:** https://www.crisisconnections.org/24-hour-crisis-line/
- **Dept. of Health:** https://doh.wa.gov/you-and-your-family/injury-and-violence-prevention/suicide-prevention/hotlines-text-and-chat-resources

Non-Crisis Care

If you need help, but it's not an emergency, find a community provider for treatment. When you call, ask for a mental health assessment or intake with a therapist or counselor (for talk therapy) or psychiatrist or psychiatric nurse practitioner (for medication).

These resources will help you find a community provider near you:

- **Directory of mental health care providers:** https://www.samhsa.gov/data/sites/default/files/reports/rpt34657/National_Directory_MH_facilities_2021.pdf
- https://www.warecoveryhelpline.org/mental-health/
- **Washington State Behavioral Health Agencies Directory:** https://doh.wa.gov/sites/default/files/2022-02/606019-BHADirectory.pdf

- **Your primary care provider** may be able to connect you to a mental health consultant located in your clinic so ask if one is available.
- **Treatment Referral Helpline:** Call (800) 662-HELP (4357) Substance Abuse and Mental Health Services Administration
- **Behavioral Health Treatment Services Locator:** https://findtreatment.samhsa.gov

Who Provides Services?

There are different mental health professionals who can make a diagnosis and provide treatment.

- **Counselors, social workers, and family therapists** offer assessment, diagnosis, and treatment of mental health issues through talk therapy or counseling.
- **Clinical psychologists** diagnose and treat mental health issues through talk therapy. They also can also offer testing of behaviors, emotions, and thoughts. This testing can be helpful for making a diagnosis.
- **Psychiatrists or psychiatric nurse practitioners** also assess, diagnose, and treat mental health issues, but they take a medical approach and can prescribe medications.

Most mental health professionals have different specialties. If you are able, find someone who has training and experience working with the problems you face

Types of Treatment

Mental health professionals offer many types of treatment. Often, it's helpful to combine different types of treatment, like therapy and medication.

The most important part of treatment is not the type of treatment you choose but the relationship you have with your mental health provider. Make sure that you feel safe and connected to your provider so that you can benefit from treatment. If you do not feel safe and connected, seek out alternative care.

Individual therapy or counseling. Talk therapy involves working one-on-one with a mental health professional. Therapy can help you heal, grow, and move toward a more productive and healthy life. A therapist will help you learn to live your best life with mental health issues.

Group therapy or counseling. This is like individual treatment, but you will do therapy with other people. These are not self-help groups. A mental health professional will lead the group. You will likely attend weekly sessions. The power of group treatment comes from the group members. It can be helpful to have a support network of others who have similar challenges. Many groups target a specific problem, but some may be more general.

————— 🙶 —————

"I benefited a lot from [my support group]. Everybody in those meetings had a similar experience. We are at a place now where we can reflect on some of the things we went through. Maturity comes with age. They have been part of my unofficial therapy."
—Anonymous

————— 🙶 —————

Family therapy or counseling. The goal of family therapy is to improve relationships and resolve conflicts. It can include your romantic partner, children, and other family members. It is often used with other types of treatments.

————— 🙶 —————

"Many conflicts arise because your family has no idea what you've gone through in prison. Or they don't understand your diagnosis. Families need a guide for what it's like for those of us who have been through prison, who have experienced trauma." -Kilroy

————— 🙶 —————

Medication. Just as medication can treat heart disease and diabetes, medication can treat mental health issues. Medications are not always needed, but most people with moderate to severe mental health issues benefit from medication.

Some mental health issues are significant enough to require medication. Bipolar disorder and schizophrenia symptoms cannot be managed without the help of medication. If you have these disorders, make sure you take your medication every day. Don't skip doses. If you have severe anxiety or depression, you will also likely benefit from medication. Taking medication can help relieve symptoms so
that you feel better. Combined with talk therapy, medication can help you lead a healthy and productive life.

Medications are prescribed by a psychiatrist or psychiatric nurse practitioner after an evaluation. The evaluation will last between 30 and 60 minutes. After that, appointments will be brief (about 15 minutes). Your psychiatrist will monitor your medications and side effects. It takes time for your body to adjust to medications. It also takes time for your provider to find what works best for you. Many medications have side effects, especially when you first take them. Don't give up if the first medication isn't for you. It may take a couple of tries to find the right medicine and dosage.

Warning: Don't quit taking medication once you start feeling better. Feeling good may be a sign that the medication is working, not that you don't need it anymore! Always consult with a psychiatric practitioner before stopping your medications. Stopping medications all at once can be very dangerous. Your psychiatrist can help you decide if it's ok to stop. They can help you stop gradually and safely.

Paying for Treatment. Medicaid will cover mental health treatment. If you need to apply for Medicaid, the Health chapter tells you how you can apply for Medicaid. Not all mental health

treatment programs accept Medicaid. Make sure to ask if the program accepts Medicaid when you call to make your first appointment. Some programs will also offer services on a "sliding fee scale" so you can pay what you can afford if you do not have insurance. Keep in mind that most programs that do accept Medicaid may have long waiting lists, so plan ahead. If possible, make your appointments before your release.

If you are enrolling in private insurance, make sure to select a plan that includes mental health treatment. When you make an appointment, ask if they accept your insurance. You may be able to see a mental health professional in private practice. This may decrease your waiting time for an appointment.

Attitudes About Mental Health

Some people feel embarrassed or ashamed of having mental health issues. These attitudes may have come from your family, your community, or from the media. These attitudes can make it hard for you to get better.

Everyone has a role to fight against these negative attitudes! The National Alliance on Mental Illness (NAMI) offers some suggestions about what you can do to help:

- Compare physical and mental illness. Lots of people have mental health issues, just as lots of people have physical health issues like diabetes and heart disease. Getting treatment is a positive thing.
- Talk openly about mental health. Share your experience with people you trust.
- Educate yourself and others. Respond to negative comments by sharing facts and experiences.
- Be conscious of language. Remind people that words matter. Try to avoid words like *crazy* or *maddening* that are all too common in our daily language.
- Show compassion for those with mental health issues, including yourself.

- Be honest about treatment. Getting mental health treatment is normal, just like other health care treatments.
- Choose empowerment over shame.

———— 99 ————

"In prison, people tend to mock those who go through a mental health episode. Everyone knows who's taking pills. You condition yourself to not talk. You don't want to express your feelings or admit something is wrong." -Kilroy

———— 66 ————

———— 99 ————

"When I first met with the group, guys would just sit there. They wouldn't open up. So I opened myself up. I'd tell them, this is what's been bothering me. Break the ice. Then someone else would talk about their experience." –Kilroy

"It's all right to show your emotions. It's a natural thing to vent, to cry." –Anonymous

———— 66 ————

 Reflect

1. What negative attitudes do you have about mental health issues and treatment?

2. Where do these negative attitudes come from?

3. What are some things you can do to fight these negative attitudes?

Common Mental Health Issues

Several mental health issues are common in people who spend time in prison. We describe them here so that you can know what they are and when you may need to get help. If you think you might have one of these health issues, talk to a health professional who can evaluate you and provide a diagnosis.

Major depressive disorder. Everyone feels sad occasionally, but not everyone feels depressed. Symptoms include:

- Feeling sad or uninterested in things most of the time.
- Changes in eating and sleeping habits.
- Having low energy and/or a hard time focusing. Feeling tearful, empty, or hopeless.
- Feeling angry and irritable.

- Feeling miserable but not understanding why. Having chronic pain, headaches, fatigue, or digestive issues.

Do these symptoms last for at least two weeks? Do they get in the way of your everyday life? You may be depressed. Talk therapy or medicine can help.

If you are severely depressed, you may also have thoughts of wanting to hurt yourself or die (this is a big concern for women who are recently released). Severe depression may also cause you to hear or see things that are not there. **If you have these severe symptoms, go to the nearest emergency room right away or call the suicide and crisis lifeline: 988.**

Bipolar disorder. Most people have changes in mood at times. If you're stressed, you might feel angry or scared. If you lost someone you love, you might feel sad. Hormone changes can also affect moods.

If you have intense mood swings that last for several days, you may have bipolar disorder. People with bipolar disorder have extreme shifts in mood, energy, and ability to function. These mood shifts include episodes of depression (above) and mania. Signs of mania are:

Increased self-esteem and feeling like you are on top of the world.
Less need for sleep.
Talking a lot and often fast.
Having so many thoughts that you cannot keep up with them.
Being distracted easily.
Feeling restless. You might pace the room or bounce your leg.
Doing things that are risky and can cause harm: spending a lot of money, having unprotected sex with various partners, and using drugs or alcohol.

For some people, manic and depressive episodes can be very extreme. Symptoms can include seeing and hearing things that are not there. This can really impact your ability to function. If your symptoms are severe, get help right away. Less severe episodes of mania (known as hypomania) and depression may not impact your life as much.

Managing bipolar disorder requires help from medicine and talk therapy. Keep a record of your mood changes so that you know if you need to seek help.

Generalized anxiety disorder. Feeling anxious or stressed once in a while is a normal part of life. If your anxiety feels out of control, you might have an anxiety disorder. Generalized anxiety disorder is when you worry a lot and are nervous about everyday things, even things that you have no control over, for no apparent reason. You might feel like something really bad is going to happen. Anxiety leaves you feeling restless, tired, irritable, and tense. It can impact your ability to focus and sleep.

If these problems do not go away and begin to impact your relationships and responsibilities, get help. Talk therapy can help. Medication can help when symptoms are severe.

Schizophrenia. Some people can have a distorted sense of reality. This is known as schizophrenia. It is a severe mental health condition that requires medication to manage. Talk therapy can help you build life skills to cope. Schizophrenia involves a range of problems with thinking, behavior, and emotions. Signs of schizophrenia can vary, but it usually involves:

- Problems with thinking (having a hard time organizing your thoughts, forgetting things, not being able to focus, struggling to make decisions).
- Delusions (false beliefs that are not based in reality). Hallucinations (seeing or hearing things that aren't really there).
- Disorganized speech (not being able to put words or sentences together).
- Lacking skills that people usually have (the ability to express emotion, be part of activities, and engage with others)

These symptoms can have a big impact on your life. If these symptoms are present for at least a month, get help.

Post-traumatic stress disorder (PTSD). Some traumatic events are so shocking, scary, or dangerous that they can change the way we think and feel long after the event has passed. It's natural to feel scared, nervous, or depressed after something bad has happened. If these feelings last for over a month, you may have post-traumatic stress disorder (PTSD).

Common symptoms of PTSD include:

- Having nightmares or flashbacks.
- Avoiding people or situations that remind you of the event.
- Feeling on edge and anxious a lot. Feeling depressed.
- Trouble remembering things. Feeling

emotionally detached.

Medications and talk therapy can be useful in working through these symptoms.

Personality disorders. Your personality is the combination of characteristics or qualities that form your distinctive character. Sometimes people can develop personality disorders, which are patterns and traits that are harmful to themselves and others. For people in prison, the two most common personality disorders are:

- **Borderline personality disorder:** Having unstable moods, behavior, and relationships. Feeling emotionally unstable, worthless, insecure, or impulsive. These feelings or behaviors can hurt your relationships with others.
- **Antisocial personality disorder:** Acting in ways that show a lack of care about other people. For example, lying, breaking laws, or acting impulsively. Not caring about your own safety or the safety of others.

Since personality traits are pretty stable over our lifetime, these disorders can be hard to treat. Despite that, it is not impossible. Often treatment includes long- term therapy. Medications tend to not work as well for these disorders.

Multiple disorders. Many people who are in prison have more than one mental health disorder. People who have depression are more likely to have anxiety, too. Many people who have a mental health disorder also have a substance use problem. Some people have a mental health disorder, a personality disorder, and a substance use disorder.

If you have more than one of these disorders, let your providers know about everything you are struggling with. If you address one problem and not the other, you may find it difficult to fully recover.

—————— ❞ ——————

"What I felt was most difficult when I first got out was figuring out how to relate to other people. You have both the lack of 'normal' experiences that most people have as late-teenagers and young adults. Plus you have the negative effects of long-term imprisonment." —Greg A.

—————— ❞ ——————

8. Substance Use Disorders

Do you have difficulty controlling your use of alcohol, illegal drugs, or medications? If so, this is one of the most important chapters you will read. As you know, drug and alcohol problems can make it much harder to get a job, form healthy relationships, find housing, and stay out of prison.

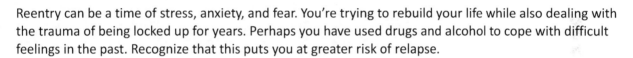

We urge you to get help. Your reentry success depends upon it! As you begin to recover, your mind will clear, and you will be better able to rebuild your life.

For many, prison is a time to get clean from drugs or alcohol. But just because you were clean in prison doesn't mean that you are fully recovered. Many people find that problems with drugs or alcohol return when they are released.

Reentry can be a time of stress, anxiety, and fear. You're trying to rebuild your life while also dealing with the trauma of being locked up for years. Perhaps you have used drugs and alcohol to cope with difficult feelings in the past. Recognize that this puts you at greater risk of relapse.

There is hope. Know that many people recover from substance use disorders, and you can, too. We honor your efforts. Recovery isn't easy and you may have setbacks. We believe in YOU and your ability to recover.

This chapter covers the following topics:

- Where to get help
- Safer drug use
- Treatment programs

- Peer support groups
- The road to recover

----------- 🙶 -----------

"What ends up happening is you get out and you realize your issues don't end. Now you have to deal with other issues. You get hit with all this stuff. You start to get into bad habits again, revert to old coping mechanisms. You have alcohol available, you have drugs. The bottle becomes more available than the gym."
—Anonymous

"Please create a plan and hit the ground running. If you know this is going to be a challenge for you, create a support group before you get out. Have a support group to go to the first day you are released. Tell them you need help! I recently lost a cellmate and friend of many years because of a relapse when the stress of reentry got to him. It only took one time and now he is gone. Please create a plan, don't try to wing it." – Jeremy

----------- 🙷 -----------

Where to Get Help

Let's be honest. The first few days, weeks, and months after release are really challenging. This is why it's a good idea to make plans to get help *before you are released*.

It's best if you can set up a time to meet with a treatment provider within 2-3 days of release. Join a support group, such as Alcoholics Anonymous, right away or make an appointment to see a counselor. Don't wait to get help.

If you are enrolled in Apple Health, substance abuse treatment is covered by your plan. You do not need a referral from your managed care plan, because this type of health care is funded directly by Medicaid. Instead, you should directly contact a treatment agency to set up your care. To find a treatment agency, or if you are in a crisis, contact the Washington Recovery Helpline at 1-866-789-1511 or online at www.warecoveryhelpline.org/.

Here are a few places you can go for help:

- **Call 911** if you have overdosed and need immediate help.
- **Call 211** or go to https://wa211.org/ to get connected to resources including substance use services and housing.
- **WA Recovery Helpline:** https://www.warecoveryhelpline.org/substance-abuse/
- **Washington State Behavioral Health Agencies Directory:** https://doh.wa.gov/sites/default/files/2022-02/606019-BHADirectory.pdf
- **Your primary care provider** may be able to connect you to an SUD consultant located in your clinic so ask if one is available.
- **Treatment Referral Helpline:** Call (800) 662-HELP (4357) Substance Abuse and Mental Health Services Administration
- **National Helpline:** Call (800) 662-4357 for the Substance Abuse and Mental Health Services Administration's national helpline. Get confidential free help from public health

agencies to find substance use treatment and information. See their website: https://findtreatment.samhsa.gov/
- **National sober house directory:** https://soberhousedirectory.com/
- **Peer support groups.** Find a Celebrate Recovery support group by going to https://locator.crgroups.info/. Find an Alcoholics Anonymous support group by calling 855-977-9213 or going to aa.org. Find a Narcotics Anonymous support group by calling 1-818-773-9999 or going to na.org. There are also non-religious support group options.
- Behavioral Health Treatment Services Locator: https://findtreatment.samhsa.gov

Safer Drug Use

Many substance use treatment programs focus on getting clean or sobering up. You may need to pass drug tests as a condition of your parole. Many jobs require drug testing.

Some people find that quitting completely is the only thing that works for them. If they start drinking a little, this quickly turns back into drinking a lot. Groups like Alcoholics Anonymous encourage quitting completely and provide peer support to reach this goal.

Quitting isn't easy. Many people are able to quit for a while, but then return to drug use on and off. If this is your experience, there are things you can do to **reduce the harm of drug use in your life**. There are ways to manage your drug use so that it doesn't take over your life. Moderating your use of drugs or alcohol is also a worthy goal. Work with a counselor or program that offers **substance use management**.

Here are a few safety tips:

- Learn how to inject safely and care for your veins to avoid getting HIV or another disease. https://anypositivechange.org/better-vein-care/

- Find out if there are organizations in your area that offer safer injecting equipment.
- Learn the signs of overdose and how to respond. Teach your friends and family to recognize these signs, too. Check for organizations in your area that can provide injectable naloxone, a drug that reverses opiate overdose.

Warning: Did you know that people who have recently returned from prison are at greater risk for overdose? If you stopped using drugs or alcohol while in prison, you may have a reduced tolerance for these drugs. This means that your body can't handle the same amount of drugs that you took before. This can lead to overdose or even death.

Signs of an Overdose:

- Unresponsive or unconscious
- Slow or stopped breathing
- Snoring or gurgling sounds
- Cold, clammy skin

- Blue lips, discolored fingernails

What to do: Try to wake the person up. Call 911 if you can't wake them. Start CPR if their breathing is slow or they have stopped breathing. Provide Naloxone (NARCAN®) if available.

*House of Mercy does not prescribe this line of thinking in recovery. As a faith-based organization, HOM believes that an individual can be free of addiction. Yet, as HOM is producing this reentry guide for a diverse population of ALL people in reentry, HOM has chosen to make this information available as to eliminate any real or perceived barrier to recovery. For a faith-based view on recovery please visit: https://www.celebraterecovery.com/how-do-i-know-cr-works, https://www.focusonthefamily.com/family-qa/finding-freedom-from-addiction-through-faith-in-god/

 Reflect

Whether your goal is safer drug use or quitting entirely, take time to reflect on your drug or alcohol use. Here are a few things you should reflect on, either alone or with a counselor:

1. Where do you use and when? Can you find ways to separate drug use from driving or working tasks?

2. Who do you use with? How are your relationships helping or hurting your recovery? How can you navigate these relationships to quit or be safer?

3. What are your personal rituals around drug use? Can you modify those rituals so that you use less or use in safer ways?

4. Think about your attitudes and emotions about drug use, such as shame and guilt. How are these emotions getting in the way of your recovery?

5. What are your emotional triggers? What are some more helpful ways to deal with difficult emotions?

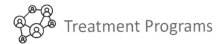

Treatment Programs

There are many kinds of treatment programs. You may need to enroll in an in-patient intensive treatment program or live in a recovery home. If your disorder is less severe, you may be able to receive outpatient services, therapy, or join a support group. Treatment should last long enough to change behaviors and thought patterns. For those with severe drug problems, at least three months of intensive treatment is recommended. After that, follow-up support can be helpful for months and even years.

There are four main types of treatment. Often, treatment programs combine all four.

- **Cognitive-behavioral therapy.** Meet with a therapist to learn how to manage stress and triggers that have led to drug use in the past. The therapist can help you find ways to motivate yourself.
- **Medication-assisted treatment.** Some medications can reduce your cravings and help you stop using. Doctors can prescribe medications such as methadone, buprenorphine, and naltrexone to help you overcome an addiction.
- **Faith-Based.** There are free faith-based treatment options in Washington including:
  o Salvation Army https://seattlearp.salvationarmy.org/seattle_adult_rehabilitation_program/
  o Union Gospel Mission: Seattle - https://www.ugm.org/what-we-do/recovery/, Yakima - https://yugm.org/recoveryservices/, Spokane - https://www.uniongospelmission.org/recovery
  o Adult & Teen Challenge https://teenchallengeusa.org/centers/?location=Washington
- **Peer support.** Many people find that a peer support group can help. Find a Celebrate Recovery support group by going to https://locator.crgroups.info/. Find an

Alcoholics Anonymous support group by calling 855-977-9213 or going to aa.org. Find a Narcotics Anonymous support group by calling 1-818-773-9999 or going to na.org. There are also non-religious support group options.

A good treatment program should also:

- **Empower you.** It should build upon your strengths. It shouldn't shame you. It should help you take an active role in your recovery.
- **Provide mental health treatment.** Many people who have substance use disorders also have mental health problems. It is essential to treat both mental health issues and substance use issues together.
- **Address past trauma.** Many people use drugs to cope with past trauma. A good treatment program will help you develop effective coping strategies and recover from the effects of trauma and violence.
- **Provide support services.** Recovery is about more than getting clean. Good treatment programs offer services to help you rebuild your life. They may help you find employment and safe housing.

Are you pregnant? Do you have children you are caring for?

For the sake of you and your children, reach out and get help. Many women are afraid their children will be taken away if their substance use becomes known. But continuing to use drugs or alcohol also puts you and your children at great risk.

As you are surely aware, society is not kind to mothers with substance use problems. You have likely sensed how harshly people judge you. You may have intense feelings of guilt and shame. We recommend that you seek out a treatment program that can help with the unique challenges women and mothers face. Always let your doctor know if you are pregnant or think you may be pregnant before starting medical treatment for a substance use disorder. Some medications are not safe to take while pregnant or nursing.

Paying for Treatment.

Medicaid covers the cost of many substance use treatment services, such as counseling, therapy, medication management, social work services, and peer support. Our Health chapter explains how to apply for Medicaid. Not all treatment programs accept Medicaid. Before starting services, ask if they accept Medicaid.

If you are enrolling in a private insurance plan, choose a plan that covers substance use treatment. When making an appointment with a service provider or clinic, check that they accept your insurance.

Even if you do not yet have insurance, there are affordable clinics and programs that you can go to for help. Look for "sliding scale" services where you pay reduced fees depending on your income. We have listed a few in our directory.

Finding a Peer Support Group

If you are struggling with drug or alcohol use, join a support group to get help and encouragement from others. These groups are usually free.

In *Becoming Ms. Burton*, Susan Burton describes how her first Alcoholics Anonymous group meeting gave her hope:

People stood up and shared their stories. . . . I rose, took a deep breath. "Look what drugs and alcohol have done to me," I said, my voice quivering. My hands were shaking so much the Styrofoam cup of coffee I held was wasting on me. But no one seemed to judge my piteous condition. The immediate compassion, the empathy, the love that rolled off these strangers was enough to put a sizable dent in my pain, my shame, my guilt, and all that sorrow. In that room, I found hope.

Celebrate Recovery (CR) Alcoholics Anonymous (AA) and Narcotics Anonymous (NA) are the

largest peer recovery organizations and have chapters throughout the country. Visit https://www.celebraterecovery.com/ aa.org or na.org to find a meeting or online group. CR, AA and NA use a religious approach, though they are not tied to a specific religion. Their 12-step process begins by asking members to admit that they no longer have control over their drug or alcohol use. Members are asked to turn themselves over to a higher power to find the strength to change.

There are non-religious support group options, too. These options focus on helping people find motivation within themselves. People learn to control themselves instead of looking to a higher power for help. Here are a few popular options, with in person and online meetings throughout the US:

- **Self-Management and Recovery Training (SMART)** peer support groups help participants resolve problems with any addiction. Go to smartrecovery.org or call 440-951-5357 to find a meeting or online community.
- **Women for Sobriety** is a peer-support program for women overcoming substance use disorders. Go to womenforsobriety.org or call 215-536-8026 to find an in-person or online meeting.
- **Secular Organizations for Sobriety** is a network of peer groups to help people maintain sobriety/abstinence from alcohol and drug addictions, food addiction and more. Go to sossobriety.org or call 314-353-3532 to find a meeting.
- **LifeRing Secular Recovery** is an organization of people who share practical experiences and sobriety support. They focus on empowering you to overcome your addiction. Go to https://lifering.org/ or call 800-811-4142 to find a meeting.

Ask your primary care provider for recommendations. Many community centers and churches also sponsor support groups or can direct you to others.

Approach your first meeting with an open mind and try to find out all you can. You may need to attend several meetings before you feel things are "clicking." If you don't feel you have found "your" group, keep trying. Chapters can be very different, and members come and go. Look for:

- Regularly scheduled meetings
- Warmth and friendliness
- Some focus and structure to meetings
- Some time to mingle informally

Reflect

1. What treatment (medication, therapy, peer support group) have you tried in the past?

2. How have these treatments helped you? What worked and what didn't work?

3. What kinds of treatment would you like to try?

4. Where can you go for help?

The Road to Recovery

The road to recovery can be a long one. Don't be too discouraged if you relapse. A relapse doesn't always mean that the treatment isn't working. Give it another chance. Recognize that if you stopped using once, you can again. You have developed skills that will help you next time. Ask if there is a different treatment that may work better for you. Sometimes multiple periods of treatment are needed.

Recovery isn't just about stopping using. It's about change. It's about improving your overall health and wellness. It's about living up to your full potential. The Substance Abuse and Mental Health Services Administration (SAMHSA) lists four main aspects of recovery:

1. **Health:** Overcome or manage one's disease or symptoms
2. **Home:** Find a stable and safe place to live
3. **Purpose:** Take part in meaningful daily activities (job, church, school, family caretaking, etc.)
4. **Community:** Build relationships and social networks that provide support, friendship, love, and hope

Reflect

1. What does recovery look like to you?

2. Where are you on your road towards recovery?

3. What are some good short-term goals you can work towards?

9. Transportation

How are you going to get around? Transportation is important for your job, for spending time with friends and family, and for living a meaningful life.

If you return to a large city you'll have many transportation options. In small towns, your choices may be more limited. Below we discuss the options you might have so that you can decide what will work best for you.

This chapter covers:

- Transportation options (buses, trains, taxis, bikes, cars, and more)
- Buying a car
- Driving legally

 Transportation Options

Buses and Metro

Save money by using public transportation. If you use the bus or metro often, you can buy a pass for a month or a year. This will make the cost of each ride cheaper. Students, older people, veterans, or persons with disabilities can get discounts. Here are a few ways to get started:

- Do a google search for "public transportation" with the name of your city or county. Many systems have route maps and discount programs for riders. For example, King, Snohomish, Pierce, and Kitsap Counties use the ORCA card which offers various discounts, flexibility, and convenience of use. To find out more visit https://www.myorca.com/.
- https://wa.gov/how-to-guides/use-public-transportation
- Visit the website www.google.com/maps. Enter where you plan to start your trip and where you'll end. The website will give step by step instructions of what public transportation you can use. Many counties offer phone apps to make planning trips easier, for example, King County Metro has a generous offering of mobile and web apps to assist you:

https://kingcounty.gov/en/dept/metro/rider-tools/mobile-and-web-apps.

Long-Distance Travel

Here are a few good options for longer trips:

- Buses are probably your cheapest option. Greyhound, FlixBus, and MegaBus are a few long-distance bus companies. Bus tickets can be purchased online or in person.
- Trains are a bit more expensive but can be a good way to travel long-distance. Go to amtrak.com for more information.
- Airplane tickets are more expensive but will get you where you need to go quickly. If you have never flown before or have questions about how flying has changed, check out FirstTimeFlyerHQ.com.

It is always a good idea to compare prices between buses, trains, and planes, as well as between companies. You can also use services such as Google Flights https://www.google.com/travel/flights/ to do so.

Ride-hailing Apps and Taxis

If you have a smartphone and a credit or debit card, you can get a ride-hailing app like Uber or Lyft. They can take you on short trips in your city.

118

Ride-hailing services are just like taxis, but the drivers use their own cars. Before you ride, read these tips on how to be safe at uber.com/us/en/ride/safety/tips

You can use taxis in all major cities. They usually cost more than ride-hailing apps.

Biking & Bike Sharing

Biking is a good way to save money and exercise while you get to places. In some cities you can rent bikes. In other places, look for second-hand bike stores. If you bike, make sure you know the rules of the road. Usually, bicycles follow the same rules as cars. They must stop at stop signs and stop lights. You must use hand signals to turn or switch lanes. And you must yield to pedestrians. Wear a helmet for safety.

Find out how to rent electric bikes and scooters to use in Seattle at: https://seattle.gov/transportation/projects-and-programs/programs/bike-program/how-to-use-scooter-share-and-bike-share#howtorentascooterorbike.

Most map apps, like Google Maps will provide bike routes as well. Just type in your destination and hit the bike icon to get directions for how to travel by bike.

Carpool, Rideshare, and Carshare Programs

Another option for saving money is to carpool. You can look up carpool programs online like https://www.rideshareonline.com/ to carpool with strangers. Or you can ask someone you know if you can carpool and share the cost of gas.

If you don't need a car very often, join a carsharing program like Zipcar. Zipcar lets you reserve a car when you need it. You won't have to pay for insurance, repairs, or any of the things that make owning a car so expensive.

 Buying a Car

If you do buy a car, buy one you can afford. A few tips:

- **Budget.** If you are taking out a loan to buy a car, make a budget. Decide how much you can spend on monthly payments. See the "Finances, Credit, and Taxes" chapter for more information on buying with credit and budgeting.
- **Research.** Do some research on the types of cars that will meet your needs. Think about what will be safe and reliable. Edmunds.com and Consumerreports.org are great places to start. You can look at how much the cars are worth by going to Kelley's Blue Book (kbb.com).
- **Buy from a place you can trust.** Don't go to car dealerships that say they sell to people with bad credit. Be suspicious of companies or people who push you into buying a vehicle before you are ready. Buying from a person can be cheaper, but it is also riskier than buying from a trustworthy dealer.
- **Check out the history.** Once you've found a car you like, ask the dealer if you can see its history report. Ask for the Vehicle Identification Number (VIN). You can check a car's history online at websites like autotrader.com or Carfax.com.
- **Mechanic.** If you are buying from a dealer, make sure that the car passes a mechanical evaluation. If you are buying from a person, ask a mechanic to look at it before you buy it.
- **Negotiate the price.** Check prices on cars like yours and go to more than one place to compare cars. This can help you negotiate a good deal.
- **Read the fine print.** Understand the contract before you sign anything. Remember, what counts is what is in the contract, not what the salesperson promised. Make sure that you fill out all the paperwork you need, especially if you are buying from an individual owner.
- **Title and registration.** Make sure to get the title and registration before you give them any money.

 Driving Legally

Car Insurance

In Washington you must have car insurance and a driver's license to drive. If you are pulled over and you don't have insurance, you may have to pay a fine. You can also get charged.

When you have car insurance, you pay a monthly fee, and then the insurance covers some of the costs if you get in an accident. In Washington State, the minimum insurance a driver needs is limited liability coverage limits of at least:

- $25,000 in bodily injury per person
- $50,000 in total bodily injury per accident
- $10,000 in property damage per accident

Some insurance plans cover most or all the costs if you are in an accident. Some do not. Some have different costs if you caused the accident or if someone else did. If you get in an accident, you may have to pay more money each month for insurance.

Buying insurance can be confusing. Here are a few tips:

- Talk to an agent by phone or in person. Don't sign up online.

- Find out what the maximum amount of coverage is for the plan. This is the amount they will pay if you hit a car, compared to the amount you must pay.
- Your state's DMV website may provide more information on insurance and prices.

Car Registration

In Washington you must register your car. You will have to renew this registration every year, for a fee. If you don't register your car or renew it, you can get a big ticket. You must register your vehicle in person at your local DMV, but you can renew it online. Check the WADOL website to find out what you need to bring:
https://www.dol.wa.gov/vehicles-and-boats/vehicle-registration
https://www.dol.wa.gov/vehicles-and-boats/vehicle-registration

Rules of the Road

Be safe when you drive! We care about you! Don't drink alcohol. Don't text or use your phone while driving. Pull over to make a call. Wear your seatbelt; it reduces your chance of death in the event of a serious accident by 50%!

 Reflect

1. What transportation options do I have right now?

2. What do I need to do to prepare to get a car?

3. What are some steps I can take to learn more about a transportation option new to me?

10. Technology

Technology has changed a lot in the last few years. If you have been inside a long time, you might feel stressed by all the new technology. Don't worry! You'll be able to figure it out.

You will need phones and computers for a lot of things after you leave prison. You will use them for work, banking, communicating with family, making appointments, meeting with parole officers, ordering pizza, watching TV shows, paying bills, shopping, applying for jobs, and much more.

Ask your family and friends to help you learn how to use a cellphone, smartphone, or computer.
Learning how to use them can be fun! Play around with games, news, sports or even watch cat videos! Playing can help you learn to use them. Take your time and get used to the technology that you use—soon it will feel like second nature.

This chapter covers the following topics:

- Getting a phone
- Technology basics
- Using the internet
- Email accounts, passwords, and security

- Smartphone apps
- Social media
- Video conferencing

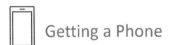 ## Getting a Phone

We recommend getting a cell phone when you get out. You will need a cell phone to keep in contact with family, friends, your employer, and your community corrections officer. There are three types of phones:

- **Basic cell phones** let you call people and send text messages. They are not so costly and easy to use.
- **Smartphones** can make calls and send text messages, and they can also get on the internet (more about the internet below). Smartphones have programs (called "apps") that can do things like play music, give driving directions, check the weather, take pictures, and go on social networks like Twitter and Facebook. A smartphone can help you find

jobs, look up services, find your way around, and more.
- **Landline phones** are phones connected to people's homes or businesses. They can't move around. Few people use landline phones these days.

Lifeline and SafeLink

Do you have Medicaid, SNAP, SSI, or Public Housing Assistance? If you do, you should also be able to get a free or discounted phone or internet. SafeLink will provide you with one of these for free:

- Smartphone
- SIM card. If you buy your own phone, they will give you a SIM card to put in it. A SIM

card is a memory chip that lets your phone connect to their mobile network.

- Phone plan. A phone plan lets you text, make calls and use data. Their basic phone plan limits how much you can do, but you can add more for a fee.

Lifeline is a program that works with SafeLink to lower the monthly cost of phone and internet. If you qualify, you can get up to $9.25 toward your monthly bill. Lifeline can be used for phone or internet, but not both.

How to apply. When you apply for public benefits (such as SNAP or Medicaid), ask if you can apply for SafeLink and Lifeline as well. Ask a friend, family member, case manager, or counselor to help you apply for SafeLink at safelinkwireless.com. You can also get help by calling (800) 723-3546. You can apply for Lifeline at lifelinesupport.org. To apply for these services, you will need your contact info, mailing/home address and Social Security number. You will also need proof that you meet the income requirements. These services are typically limited to one person per household.

Phone Services and Plans

What if you need to buy your own phone? HOM participants have suggested MetroPCS and Straight Talk Mobile (Walmart) as good, cheaper choices. They aren't the best phones, but they won't be too expensive. If you had a cellphone before you were incarcerated, ask your family if they still have the phone. It might still work, and you may want to use it again or change the number. Contact the phone service provider for help with this.

Cell phones come with service plans that you must pay every month. You have two basic options for service plans:

- **Prepaid phone plans or no-contract plans.** You pay at the start of each month. You can stop your service at the end of each month or

switch to a different service (MetroPCS, Straight Talk, Cricket).

- **Post-paid phone plan with a contract.** You enter a contract to pay a monthly fee for service. They add up your costs at the end of each billing cycle and charge you (T-Mobile, Verizon, AT&T).

Phone plans have different options. Generally, the services will cover the following:

- **Talk:** How many minutes you can talk on the phone each month. Many plans these days have unlimited talk time.
- **Text:** How many text messages you can send each month. Many plans these days have unlimited text.
- **Data:** Data lets your phone go on the internet when you don't have access to Wi-Fi (see Technology Basics below). If you only need a phone for calls, you may not need to purchase a data plan. You can use the internet on your phone for free at the library and many other public places and restaurants. If you do need data, start with a small amount, like 1 or 2 GB, and use your data carefully. You can always get more if you need it.

Phone service companies like T-Mobile and MetroPCS have different plans and rates. Some offer deals for sharing a cell phone plan with family members. Think about what you will use your phone for and how much you can afford to spend on it. Some phone or internet service providers may also offer discounts.

 Technology Basics

Here are some technology basics to help you get started.

Internet or world wide web. A network that connects computers and phones all over the world. Through an internet connection, people can share information, access resources, and communicate. Sometimes people call the internet the world wide web, or they will say, "you need web access," which means you need to be able to connect to the internet.

Online. When you are "online" you are connected to the internet. People might say, "Get online to access this resource." This means that you can access the resource on a computer or smartphone through the internet.

Smartphone. A phone that does a lot of the things a computer can do. It usually has a touchscreen surface, internet access, and you can download **applications (apps).** Apps have different tools to help with work, entertainment, money and more. Most people these days have a smartphone.

Wi-Fi. To access the internet, you need to be connected to it. One way to do that is through Wi-Fi access. Wi-Fi access allows you to connect to the internet without using wires. You can access Wi-Fi for free at public libraries and some restaurants (McDonalds, Starbucks), or you can buy Wi-Fi access for your home.

Data. Another way to connect to the internet is through a smartphone data plan. Data allows you to connect to the internet on your smartphone if you are in a place that doesn't have Wi-Fi. Data plans can be expensive, and they usually have limits to how much data you can use every month.

Web browser. A web browser is a program that allows you to access the internet on your phone or computer. Examples of web browsers are Google Chrome, Firefox, Internet Explorer, and Safari.

Search engine. A search engine is what you use when you are trying to find information on the internet. First, you will open a web browser. You should see a bar at the top with a little magnifying glass. This is how you can use the search engine. You can type a question or web address into the bar, and it will search for the

information you need. Google, Yahoo, and Bing are examples of search engines.

Website. All types of organizations have "websites" where you can find information, resources, entertainment and more.

Web address or URL. This is the "address" or location of the website or resource on the internet. You type this address into the search engine bar to go to the website or resource. We have included many web addresses to websites in this guide and in the directory. Web addresses usually look like this: http://example.com. When you type in a web address, you can leave out the http:// or www.

———— 🙶 ————

"I need assistance with the most basic things. That does make me somewhat defensive, and I'll end up trying to do things on my own and then I crash and burn." –Pablo

———— 🙷 ————

 Using the Internet

Make sure you have a way to get on the internet when you need to. Until you have your own device, you can borrow one from a family member or use a computer at the public library (*make sure to check with your CCO to see if you will have any internet restrictions before going online or using a smart phone*).

Do you have a smartphone, laptop, or tablet? Free wireless internet is available at the library, as well as many restaurants, coffee shops, hotel lobbies, chain technology stores, and even parks! You may have to ask what the password is before you can log on with your device.

Most things on the internet are found using a search engine like Google. Open a web browser such as Google Chrome, Microsoft Edge, Firefox, or Safari. The home page will have a search box where you can type in what you are looking for. Here are some tips for good searches:

- Start with the basics. Start with a simple search like "*Where's the closest Amtrak?*" or "*Best burgers in Seattle.*" You can always add more words if you need.
- Don't worry about the little things. Even if you spell things wrong, it should still work.

Getting help
- Ask a librarian to help you figure out the basics. They are there to help.
- Go to Northstar at digitalliteracyassessment.org to test your skills and learn more. You can access classes online or find a Northstar location where you can attend classes. They offer certificates for skills you have mastered.
- GCF global has a lot of free courses on how to use technology. Type this address in your search engine and click on a topic: https://edu.gcfglobal.org/en/topics/
- Wikihow also has lots of resources to help you figure out how to use technology. Type "wikihow" in your web browser, and then enter your question in the search box at the top of the page.
- Many community colleges, libraries, and adult basic education programs offer lessons on everything from basic word processing to programming code.

 Email Accounts, Passwords and Security

You will need your own email address. Email is now used more than paper mail. One way to do this is through Gmail, because Gmail accounts are free. Type gmail.com into the web browser and click "Create account."

You will select your own email username. It should be something easy for you to remember, like your own name, or some combination of your name, initials, and numbers. You will probably use your email to apply for jobs, so make sure your email address is professional (e.g., *j.doe1999@gmail.com*).

Your password should also be something easy for you to remember, but hard for other people to figure out. The best passwords use capital letters (ABCD), small letters (abcd), numbers (1234), and symbols (#$%^) in a combination of at least 8 characters (e.g., *IdK7246j!*).

You will probably use the internet to set up accounts for things like paying bills or accessing files for school or work. Protect your information by keeping your password secret and changing it every so often. Don't use the same password for every account you have. If you forget a password, you can usually change it by following instructions on the website. If you had email and other online accounts before you were incarcerated, you may want to reactivate them or close them. Change the passwords to keep everything safe.

If possible, do not put in sensitive personal information (like your Social Security Number or credit card information) at a public computer or over public internet.

 Smartphone Apps

Most smartphones come with these basic apps:

- Text messaging
- App to make phone calls
- A camera
- A clock
- A map service
- A browser (for example, Safari or Chrome)
- A calendar
- A calculator
- An address book (sometimes called "contacts")

You can also download more apps. They can be found in your phone's store (the app store or play store). Many useful apps are free. You will need to have either data or a Wi-Fi connection to download apps. You may have to enter your phone's password to buy it. It should show up on your home screen in just a few minutes. If an app costs money, your phone should give you the option to enter your credit or debit card information and will ask you to confirm the purchase before downloading.

Here are some apps you may want to use:

- Facebook Messenger is a text or video messaging app where you can communicate with family and friends.
- Facebook, Instagram, and Twitter are social media apps that let you share and view photos and comments.
- Spotify lets you listen to music. It will shuffle the music and play advertisements, like a radio (you can pay to eliminate the ads and create your own.
- Banking apps help you manage your money and pay bills.
- Transportation apps, like Citymapper and Seattle Transit, can help you use public transportation or find your way around.

Be careful with apps. Use careful judgment about what you'd like to keep private. Be aware that apps can use up your phone data.

 Social Media

Many people stay in touch with others and get news through social media. Social media are websites that allow people to talk and share photos. Some social media sites are used mostly for friends and family while others are used for jobs. Here are two popular social media platforms:

- **Facebook** is the most popular social media company in the US. People use this site to share photos, updates, and news. It helps people stay in touch with family and friends; others use it for work. You can comment publicly on posts created by others or message users individually. You can also join

Facebook groups to meet other people and get support. Signing up for Facebook is free. To sign up, type facebook.com into the search bar and click "Create Account."
- **LinkedIn** is a social network created for finding jobs. You can use it to talk with employers and share your resume. To create an account, type linkedin.com into your web browser and click "Join Now." Search "How to Create a LinkedIn Account Wikihow" to learn more.

Staying Safe on Social Media

Be careful when sharing information on Facebook or other social media apps. You can change the privacy settings so that only your friends see your posts. Public posts can be accessed by parole officers and employers. Social media sites track what you do, and they can use that to try to sell you things. Sometimes scam artists use social media to trick people into giving away money. Remember, the information that you see on social media may not be trustworthy. It's a good idea to check with other sources.

To learn more, check out this article on the National Cyberspace Alliance https://staysafeonline.org/resources/social-media/.

Video Conferencing

Many people use video conferencing to talk to family, friends, and co-workers. With video conferencing, you can talk to multiple people at the same time and see people's faces. Video conferencing apps can be a great way to stay connected to family members and friends. Lots of meetings these days aren't in person; instead, they use video conferencing. Many job interviews also use video conferencing.

Here are a few video conferencing options:

- Facetime (on all Apple products)
- Google Chat
- Skype

- Zoom (usually for professional use like meetings)

If you have a computer or phone, you can download an app for these video conferencing services. Some are free.

In most cases, you will be a guest in a video conferencing meeting. This means you will get an invitation to your email with the link that says, "Click to Join." When the webpage opens, you may join via the app or your web browser.

There may also be an option to call in with your phone.

Video conferencing etiquette tips:
- *If you are in a group, mute yourself when you're not talking (click on the microphone).*
- *Be aware of your backdrop. It's nice to turn your camera on so people can see you, but you can also turn your camera off (click on the camera icon) or use a virtual backdrop if you don't want people to see you or your living space.*

 Digital Literacy Resources

Learning technology is a lot like learning a new language. There are many free resources to help you learn. Fortunately, in Washington State, there has been a big push to provide digital literacy services to those in reentry. The State has invested a lot of money into organizations around the State to provide these services. There are many organizations that provide free training, digital navigation, free devices, and even free internet service in many cases.

- House of Mercy Digital Training Program – DigNav.com
- Equity in Education Coalition – https://eec-wa.org/
  - TechConnect - https://techconnectwa.org/

- Prison Scholar Fund - https://www.prisonscholars.org/what-we-do/transition/digital-services/
- Link Care to WA – Learn how to use tech to manage your healthcare https://www.prisonscholars.org/what-we-do/transition/digital-services/
- Techboomers.com is a free website that teaches people basic computer skills to help them improve their quality of life. You can learn about helpful websites, social media, online shopping, and technology basics.
- netliteracy.org has a huge amount of digital literacy resources. Visit their site for resources and training on everything from basic email and social media to artificial intelligence.

Additional Resources

Get A Phone And/or Internet Discount

Lifeline Program How to apply online, by mail, or through a phone or internet company videos

Affordable Connectivity Program How to apply online, by mail, or through a phone or internet company

Use Your Phone

- "Set-up," "Calling," and "Accessing Wireless Internet" how-to flyers by Telehealth Access for Seniors
- "Getting started with your Android device" guide by GCFLearnFree.org
- "Getting started with your iPhone device" guide by GCFLearnFree.org
- "Getting started with mobile devices" video by Chinook Arch Libraries

Use The Internet

- "Intro: what is the internet?" guide and video by GCFLearnFree.org
- "Browser basics" [and tips for visiting websites] video by GCFLearnFree.org

- "Connecting to the internet" [at home] video by GCFLearnFree.org
- "Accessing free Wi-Fi [wireless internet]" guide by Telehealth for Seniors
- "Introduction to internet safety" series of guides and videos by GCFLearnFree.org
- "WA Broadband Speed Test" Access and speed survey

Set Up Email

- "Get a free email address" video by the National Library of Medicine
- "Signing up for email" guide by DigitalLearn.org
- "Intro to email" video series and guides by DigitalLearn.org

Get Ready For A Phone Or Video Appointment

- "Telehealth: What is it? And how to make it work for you" video series by AT Lab Community Vision
- "How to make the most of your child's telehealth visit" guide by Harvard Medical School
- "Common features of video doctor visits" tips by the Health Resources and Service Administration
- "Calling" guide by Telehealth for Seniors
- "Using telehealth counseling" [for mental health] guide by CHPW & Healthwise

 Reflect

1. What technologies do I know how to use?

2. What do I need help with?

3. Where can I go for help?

11.   Legal Matters

After you are released, there may be times when you need to go to court or get legal help. For example, you might want to get your record sealed so you can get a better job. Maybe you want to get back custody of a child, or address LFO concerns.

This chapter covers the following topics:

- Getting legal help
- Responding to Family Law Actions While Incarcerated
- Fees and fines
- Sealing records
- Certificates of rehabilitation
- Executive clemency

Please note that we are not lawyers and do not provide legal advice. We try our best to help you understand your legal options. Ask a lawyer if you need more help.

Getting Legal Help

Pro Bono:

Figuring out the courts can be frustrating. It is best to get the help of a lawyer. Lawyers understand the rules and know how local judges and courtrooms work. Lawyers are often expensive, but there are lawyers who will work on your case for free (pro bono). These services are available through legal aid programs.

Some cases can be handled without lawyers. These are called pro se cases. Things like sealing criminal records, family law, and small claims matters often don't use lawyers. This is cheaper, but it is almost always better to hire a lawyer or find one who will work for free. You can also look at Legal Voice's publication on how to find a lawyer in Washington, available at http://www.legalvoice.org/how-to-find-a-lawyer.

Pro Se Help Desks:

If you decide to file pro se, most counties offer pro se help desks. The service is free. There are workers who can help you with pro se forms, courthouse directions, and legal consultations. Call your county circuit clerk's office for information.

Responding to Family Law Actions While Incarcerated

Divorce (Dissolution)

A summons is a document issued by the court that notifies an individual that their spouse has filed for divorce. The summons includes a petition for dissolution, which outlines the details of the divorce, such as child custody and property division. It is important to carefully read the petition to understand what your spouse is asking for. You have 20 days to respond to the summons and petition.

If you choose to respond to the summons, you have the right to participate in the divorce proceedings. Your opinion on matters such as child custody and property division will be taken into consideration by the court.

If you do not respond to the summons within the given time frame, the court may enter a default judgment. This means that the court will agree to everything your spouse has asked for in the petition. If you disagree with any aspect of the petition, it is crucial to file a written response within 20 days.

To respond to the petition, you can use a Do-It-Yourself packet called Responding to a Divorce, which is available from Washington LawHelp. This packet provides information on other packets you may need, such as those for parenting plans and child support. The court forms can also be found on the Washington Courts website or purchased at courthouses.

It is important to note that court forms are often updated or changed. You should try to contact the county court's family law facilitator or check the court website to make sure that the form you are using is the most current version. For more information on preparing your court papers and forms, you can refer to the memo "How to Format Court Documents"

In some cases, you may be able to request maintenance, also known as alimony or spousal support. However, if you are incarcerated, the court may not order your spouse to pay maintenance. You can ask the court to delay the decision on maintenance until you are released.

Parentage (Paternity/Legal Parent)

A Petition to Decide Parentage is a court action that determines the legal parent of a child. This petition can be used to establish or disestablish parentage, and it is often filed in response to a child support notice or order. The current legal parent or someone who believes they should or should not be the child's other legal parent can

file this petition. A prosecuting attorney can also file a petition to obtain child support from the other parent.

Being a legal parent grants you certain rights and responsibilities, including physical and legal custody of the child. Even if you are incarcerated, you can file for a parenting plan, residential schedule, and child support, as well as modifications to these orders if there is a parentage case pending. However, you are also obligated to provide for the child's care and upbringing, such as paying child support.

If you are served with a Petition to Decide Parentage, you have 20 days to respond. By filing a response, you have the right to participate in the proceedings and present your opinion and information regarding your legal parentage.

If you do not respond to the petition, the court may enter a default judgment, meaning they will agree to everything the other parent asked for. It is important to carefully read the documents and file a written response within 20 days if you disagree with anything in the petition.

To respond to the petition, you can use a Do-It-Yourself packet called Responding to a Petition to Decide Parentage, available from Washington LawHelp. The court forms can also be found on the Washington Courts website or purchased at courthouses.

Modification of Parenting Plan

If you are served with a Petition for Modification, you have 20 days to respond. By filing a response, you have the right to participate in the proceedings and can ask the court to deny the modification or propose your own changes to the parenting plan. You can also request changes specifically for the time you are incarcerated or for when you are released.

If you do not respond to the petition, the court may enter a default judgment, meaning they will approve the proposed changes to the parenting plan.

To respond to the petition, you can hire a lawyer or use a Do-It-Yourself packet called Responding to a Petition to Change Your Parenting Plan, Residential Schedule or Custody Order, available from Washington LawHelp. The court forms can also be found on the Washington Courts website or purchased at courthouses.

Child Support

If you do not have physical custody of your child while incarcerated, you will not receive court-ordered child support payments. The child support payments will likely go to the person caring for your child.

If you had a child support order before incarceration, you are still responsible for making the payments as directed by that order. Failure to pay child support while incarcerated can result in an increase in your child support debt. For more information, see the DSHS brochure "Do I Still Have to Pay Child Support?".

If you are served with a child support notice or proposed order, you have 20 days to respond. You can arrange to pay child support while incarcerated or appeal the order. If you have no source of income while incarcerated, you can state this in your response. If you believe you should not be considered the other legal parent of the child, you can contest paternity by filing a Petition to Decide Parentage.

To respond to the petition or notice, you can use a Do-It-Yourself packet called Responding to a Petition for a Parenting Plan, Residential Schedule and/or Child Support: Parentage Cases, available from Washington LawHelp. The court forms can also be found on the Washington Courts website or purchased at courthouses.

If the other parent files a petition to modify child support, you have 20 days to respond. By filing a response, you have the right to participate in the proceeding and can ask the court to deny the modification or propose your own changes for the time you are incarcerated and for when you are released.

To respond to the petition, you can use a Do-It-Yourself packet called Responding to a Petition to Modify Your Child Support Court Order, available from Washington LawHelp. The court forms can also be found on the Washington Courts website or purchased at courthouses.

You can try to change your child support order while incarcerated by sending a request for review to the Division of Child Support (DCS). DCS will determine if you qualify for a modification of your child support order. If DCS cannot change your child support, you can still ask the court to modify the order using a Do-It-Yourself packet called Filing a Petition to Modify Your Child Support Court Order, available from Washington LawHelp.

Custody

Whether or not you can have custody of your child while incarcerated depends on various factors, such as your custody arrangement before incarceration and the age of your child. If you are pregnant and will give birth while incarcerated, there may be a Residential Parenting Program (RPP) available where you can live with and raise your newborn while serving your sentence.

If you already have primary care of your child through a parenting plan, you can make decisions about who will care for your child while incarcerated and stay involved as a parent see https://legalvoice.org/options-grandparents. You may also be eligible for the Community Parenting Alternative (CPA), which allows you to spend the last 12 months of your sentence under electronic monitoring surveillance instead of incarceration.

If the other parent asks the court to change the parenting plan, you have the right to be notified and respond. You can also try to change the parenting plan once you are released, but it can be challenging and requires showing good reasons or substantial changes in circumstances.

You can request visitation with your children by including it in your response to the proposed parenting plan or child support order. You can ask the court for a specific visitation plan, such as phone calls, video calls, letters, and in-person visits. It is important to consider the best interests of the child when requesting visitation.

Dependency Actions

A dependency action is initiated by Child Protective Services (CPS) when they investigate allegations of child abandonment, abuse, or neglect within the family. If the investigation reveals concerns for the child's safety and well-being, CPS may file a petition in juvenile court to make the child a dependent of the state.

If a dependency petition is filed for your child, you have the right to be notified and to attend all dependency hearings. You also have the right to a lawyer at public expense. The court will hold hearings to determine where the child will live and who will be their guardian during the dependency. The goal of the dependency is to provide temporary care for the child while giving the parents the opportunity to address and resolve the issues that led to the dependency. If the parents fail to correct these issues, the state may file a petition to permanently terminate their parental rights.

If you are asked to sign a relinquishment or surrender agreement, it is important to consult with a lawyer before doing so. These agreements permanently give up your parental rights and place your child up for adoption. You have the right to be at the hearings in person and to have a lawyer. There are two main hearings: the preliminary hearing (this happens after you object to the termination), and the fact-finding hearing (trial). For more information, see Child Protective Services (CPS) and Dependency Actions as well as Options for Grandparents and Other Nonparental Caregivers and the Incarcerated Parent's Project

webpage about child welfare cases. You can request that your child be adopted by a specific person and include an open adoption agreement to maintain contact with your child after adoption.

Hearings

You **Do** have the right to attend hearings in actions that may terminate your parental rights or declare your child dependent. It is important to be present and have a lawyer representing you at these hearings. In other family law hearings, such as divorce or child support, you may not have the right to attend in person, but you have the right to meaningful access to these hearings. You can file a motion to request your presence at the hearings or ask to attend by phone. If you have served the minimum time required for a furlough, you can request temporary release to attend a hearing.

Where to Get Help

If you cannot afford a lawyer, you may be eligible for a free lawyer in dependency and termination cases. The Washington State Office of Public Defense is responsible for providing lawyers in these cases. Another resource you can explore is Legal Voice's publication on how to find a lawyer in Washington, which can be accessed at http://www.legalvoice.org/how-to-find-a-lawyer.

For other family law cases, you may need to hire a private lawyer or seek assistance from volunteer lawyers. Family law facilitators, located in the Superior Courts, can help you find the correct forms and guide you in filing them. The cost of their services may vary by county.

There are resources available for information, forms, and do-it-yourself packets. Washington LawHelp and Legal Voice offer free legal information and publications on various family law issues. The court forms can also be found on the Washington Courts website or purchased at courthouses. Legal Voice offers free legal information on a variety of legal issues, including family law. Translations available for many publications. Call or write for free copies or download from their website. By mail: 907 Pine Street, Suite 500, Seattle, WA 98101

If you are incarcerated, there are contract attorneys available at some correctional facilities. If a law library is not available, you may request a temporary transfer to use the library or borrow materials.

Parenting programs such as the Community Parenting Alternative (CPA) and Residential Parenting Program (RPP) may be available for incarcerated parents. These programs provide opportunities for parenting and maintaining a relationship with your child.

Washington Law Help has put together some guides that may be useful; you can find them at http://www.washingtonlawhelp.org/resource/parentage-and-parenting-plans-for-unmarried-p, http://www.washingtonlawhelp.org/issues/family-law/parenting-plans-residential-time.

Remember that this publication provides general information and is not a substitute for specific legal advice.

Fees and Fines

There are many different fees and fines you may have to pay. You might have court fees or fines, like:

- Traffic tickets
- DUI fees
- Payments to the victims of the crime you were convicted of and other fines related to the crime (Legal Financial Obligations)
- Fines and debt for failing to pay child support
- Parole or probation fines, such as fees for anger management or parenting classes, and fees for any required registration

Even small fees can make it hard to get back on your feet. Still, it's important to plan how you will pay them. Not paying your fees or fines can get you in more trouble.

- Officials can hold those fees against you if you return to jail.
- Sometimes people are returned to jail for not paying fees, especially if they "willfully" do not pay them.
- Sometimes fees have a high interest rate, meaning the amount you owe will get larger the longer you wait to pay.

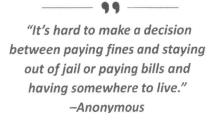

"It's hard to make a decision between paying fines and staying out of jail or paying bills and having somewhere to live."
–Anonymous

But there is good news. The new LFO (Legal Financial Obligations) legislation in 2023 in Washington State is aimed at providing relief for low-income people who are unable to pay their legal financial obligations. Legal financial obligations are fines, fees, costs, and restitution that people with criminal convictions must pay as part of their sentence.

The new legislation would allow judges to waive these obligations for those who are unable to pay them. This would provide relief for low-income individuals who may struggle to pay these obligations and could help reduce the burden of debt on these individuals.

For information on LFO relief please see:

- Washington LawHelp
https://www.washingtonlawhelp.org/resource/filing-a-motion-to-remit-remove-financial-legal-obligations-in-district-or-municipal-court
- Living with Conviction
https://livingwithconviction.org/lfo-help

Child Support Abatement

An eligible incarcerated parent (confined for, or sentenced to, at least six months) may have their child support temporarily reduced to $10 per month per child support order regardless of the number of children on that order.

For child support orders that include abatement language, the child support amount will gradually increase back to the full-ordered amount over the first year after release from confinement.

If the support order does not contain the language needed to qualify for reduced child support payments, the order may be modified to include abatement language. For more information, please call us at 1-800-442-KIDS, or visit https://www.dshs.wa.gov/esa/division-child-support/child-support-abatement#:~:text=To%20qualify%20to%20receive%20a%20reduction%20in%20child,support%20order%20that%20contains%20a%20section%20referencing%20abatement.

Expunging or Sealing Records

Sealing your record means employers can't ask about your record. This could make it easier to find a job. Ask your parole officer or reentry organization to see if this is an option for you. You may be able to get your record sealed once you are off community custody/parole, depending on the charge.

Sometimes it is also possible to get a record expunged. An expunged record is erased. This

means nobody can see it anymore. This usually only happens if your charges were dismissed.

Visit for more info:
https://www.washingtonlawhelp.org/issues/criminal/record-expungement-sealing-records

Certificates of Restoration of Opportunity

These are official documents that can restore rights you lost because of your conviction, for example, the right to earn an occupational license or serve on a jury. Certificates of rehabilitation allow you to apply for jobs that require licenses issued by the state. These jobs include ones in childcare, education, and transit.

Visit for more info:
https://www.washingtonlawhelp.org/resource/certificate-of-restoration-of-opportunity-crop

Executive Clemency

In Washington State, the Governor has the power to grant executive clemency to individuals convicted of a crime. The Washington State Clemency and Pardons Board is responsible for reviewing applications for clemency and making recommendations to the Governor. The Board is composed of five members appointed by the Governor and confirmed by the Senate.

The Board considers applications for clemency from individuals who have been convicted of a crime in Washington State. The Board reviews each application on a case-by-case basis and makes a recommendation to the Governor.

If you are interested in applying for clemency, you can request an application from https://governor.wa.gov/boards-commissions/clemency-pardons-board. You can also find more information about the clemency and pardons process on their website

Additional Resource

For a more exhaustive view into "Legal Matters" in Washington State, please reference "The Washington Appleseed Reentry Guide", which is a more legal-focused type reentry guide.

12. Finances, Credit, and Taxes

Thinking about money can be stressful. Take small steps toward managing your money, especially if you're doing it on your own for the first time. Making smart decisions about your money can help have control over your life. Having control over your finances will help you avoid money troubles in the long run and feel more secure about the future.

In this section, we cover banking basics and how to open a banking account. Then we address budgeting, financial planning, and credit. At the end of this section, we go over filing taxes.

 Financial Literacy

Financial literacy refers to the knowledge and skills needed to make informed and effective decisions regarding the management of personal finances. It includes understanding how to budget, save, invest, and manage debt, as well as being aware of financial risks and opportunities. Building up one's financial intelligence is important because it can help individuals achieve their financial goals, avoid financial pitfalls, and ultimately achieve greater financial security and stability. By being financially literate, individuals can make informed decisions about their money and take control of their financial future.

If you want to improve your financial skills, you have many options in Washington State. You can find programs that teach you how to budget, save, invest, and more. These programs are either free or low-cost, depending on your income level. You can pay what you can afford and learn how to manage your money better.

The Financial Empowerment Network maintains a Financial Wellness Provider Directory. Please visit https://www.fenwa.org/financial-wellness-providers to find a provider near you.

 Banking

It's a good idea to open a bank account so that you have a safe place to put your money. A bank account also helps you avoid the fees that come with check cashing and money transfer services.

There are two basic types of bank accounts: checking and savings accounts. A **checking account** keeps your money safe. It also gives you easy access to your money so you can buy things and pay bills. When you open a checking account, you get checks and a debit card. You can use these to buy things, pay bills, or get cash from your account using ATMs. Some checking accounts have monthly fees while others do not, so make sure you ask about fees.

There are many good reasons to have a bank account:

- Putting your paychecks in a bank account is cheaper than paying fees for check cashing services.
- Some employers put your earnings directly in your account.
- A debit card means you don't have to carry lots of cash. Your money is better protected against being lost or stolen.
- Many banks offer free access to online banking services, which you can use to keep

- track of your money, pay bills automatically, and transfer money between accounts.
- Apps like Venmo let you transfer and receive money without any fees. You can get Venmo on your phone and use it if you have a bank account. Most banks also use Zelle as a free money transfer service.
- You can work with banks to get car or mortgage loans, develop a retirement investment plan, and invest in stocks.

 You don't have to be a U.S. citizen or have a Social Security number to open a bank account. You can open an account using the Individual Taxpayer Identification Number (ITIN) assigned to you by the IRS, regardless of immigration status. Visit IRS.gov for more information about ITINs.

Opening a Bank Account

Banks and credit unions offer different products to choose from, like checking and savings accounts, loans, rewards programs, and credit cards. Before choosing a bank, think about what you need. When you first go to the bank, ask to speak to someone who can help you understand their services and how they can meet your needs.

Here are a few things to consider:

- Will you travel a lot for work, fun, or visiting family? You may want to choose a bank that has many branches and ATM locations. Online banks are also an option.
- What fees does the bank have? Some fees might be an overdraft fee (when you take out more money than you have), fees for closing accounts, fees for foreign transactions, and monthly maintenance fees.
- Has a bank ever shut down your checking account? If so, banks might reject your account application. Don't worry, though, because some banks offer second chance checking accounts. Call and ask smaller local

banks and credit unions about their account policies. Smaller companies tend to be more open to people who have had financial trouble.

- Is your bank or credit union backed by the government? If it is, that means that if the bank closes or has other problems, your money is protected. Make sure your bank is a member of the FDIC or NCUA.
- Does your employer, school, or community have a credit union? Credit unions are better in some ways than banks. See the chart on the following page comparing banks and credit unions.
- Are you a veteran? If so, you qualify for a USAA account. USAA members and their families can often get good rates on loans. Visit usaa.com for more information.
- Do you have bad credit? Many banks use a database called ChexSystems to check your bank customer history, but they don't always pull your credit report when you apply. Ask them what their policies are.

To open a bank account, you will need:

- A valid government ID
- A social security number (or Individual Taxpayer ID for non-US citizens)
- Money to make an initial deposit.

Banks may also require a second form of ID and/or proof of address, like a utility bill. Visit the Consumer Financial Protection Bureau's detailed Checklist for Opening a Bank or Credit Union Account for more information: Consumerfinance.gov/consumer-tools/

	Banks	Credit Unions
Pros	• Easier to open an account. • Many branches and ATM locations. • More options for types of accounts, loans, and credit cards. • Online banking and services.	• Credit Unions are non-for-profit institutions. They are owned by their members. • Because credit unions are smaller companies, they have better customer service. • Higher interest on savings accounts. • Lower rates for loans. • More flexibility.
Cons	• May have more restrictions or are less flexible when you make errors. • Higher interest rates on loans and credit cards. • Banks are owned by investors who may not care as much about the bank's customers.	• Membership is more exclusive in credit unions than banks. • Fewer locations. • Fewer product options. • Poorer online services.

Prior Banking History. When you apply for an account, the bank may pull a checking account report through a screening agency. This report shows history from the bank accounts you've had in the past, up to seven years. If your report shows certain high-risk behavior, like unpaid fees or fraud, your application may be denied.

If you are denied, you can take steps to address the problem, or find another bank or credit union that has a more flexible application process. Every bank is required to provide a notice of the reason for a denial. If your checking report is the cause, you can request a free copy. Every person is also allowed to pull their report for free at least once per year. Request yours by visiting: www.chexsystems.com or downloading and mailing a request form to:

> Chex Systems Inc., Attn: Consumer Relations
> 805 Hudson Road, Suite 100
> Woodbury, MN 55125

If you have negative banking history, you may be a candidate for "Second Chance Checking", which has fewer eligibility requirements. Find a list of banks that offer second chance checking here:

Second Chance Checking Accounts Across the U.S. - NerdWallet.

Consumer Finance Protection Bureau Resources

The Consumer Finance Protection Bureau (CFPB) has a variety of resources to help you navigate banking. These tools can be accessed here: https://www.consumerfinance.gov/

• The Guide to Consumer Reporting Companies explains how each type of consumer reporting works (banking history, credit reports, criminal background checks and more), plus how you can request or dispute your reports: Guide to Consumer Reporting Companies.
• The CFPB shows the pros and cons of various methods to receive paychecks, based on your needs and preferences. It compares prepaid cards, direct deposit, cashing checks, and more.
• If you are uncomfortable when it comes to banking or if you have never had an account before, you might appreciate the CFPB's: Guide to Selecting a Low Risk Account
• Visit the CFPB's Financial Resource Guides on:

Using Bank Cards for Purchases

If you've been in prison for a long time, buying things at the store may be very different. Perhaps you carried around cash in the past or wrote paper checks. Most people these days use debit cards or credit cards rather than paying with cash.

Here are some card options:

- **Debit cards** look just like credit cards but are different. Most debit cards are linked to a checking account, and you can only spend money that you have in your account. Debit cards can be used anywhere that you use a credit card. You can also use your debit card to get money from an ATM.

- With **prepaid debit cards,** you can load money onto the card when you get it, then use it to make purchases until the money runs out. Prepaid debit cards are often used by people who can't get a bank account. You might use one if you haven't been able to get your ID yet. Bluebird by American Express and Chime are prepaid debit cards with no monthly fee.

- Your **EBT (Electronic Benefits Transfer) card** for food stamps and/or cash benefits. Washington offers a card (Quest Card) that you can use just like a debit card at stores that accept EBT.

- With a **credit card**, you are borrowing money and will need to pay it back. We talk more about credit cards in the next section.

- There are also **gift cards** where people can put money on the card and then give it to someone to use like a debit card. Some cards--like a Visa Gift Card--can be used at any store, while other gift cards only work for specific stores.

For debit cards you will need to make a 4-digit PIN number, which is like a password. Before you use your card, make sure you have your PIN number set up. Usually, there is a number on the back of the card that you can call to set up the PIN number. When using a debit card or EBT card, make sure you know how much money you have. If you don't have enough money your card may not work.

Here's a brief guide (summarized from Wikihow) about what to expect when you check out at a store.

1. After the cashier scans your things, they will ask you to pay.
2. There will likely be a card reader on the counter. Card readers look a little bit like calculators. They usually have a screen with instructions to follow.
3. The screen on the card reader may ask if you agree to pay the amount on the screen. You may have to press "enter" or "yes" to continue.
4. Next, the screen may ask you to swipe your card. Other times, the cashier will let you know when the machine is ready for you to swipe your card.
5. For some card readers you'll swipe your card on the right side. For others you'll stick the card in the bottom of the machine and leave it there until the screen lets you know that you can take it out. Don't worry if you don't get it right the first time. Turn the card around and try again. Lots of people make mistakes and have to swipe their cards a few times or get help from a cashier.
6. The card reader may ask whether you want to pay by "debit" or "credit." If you hit debit, it may ask you to enter your 4-digit PIN number. Once the screen says "Approved" you should get a receipt. You can take your items and your receipt and leave.
7. Some debit cards allow you to get cash back with your purchase. The card reader screen will ask if you want cash, and you will enter the dollar amount you would like. The cashier will then give you the cash. The amount will come out of your bank account.
8. If you are using a credit card, you may be asked to sign a paper receipt or sign the screen with a special pen. It will ask you to press "enter" or "accept" when you are finished. Once you have finished signing and get your receipt, you should be ready to go.

 Remember: When using a credit or debit card, it's OK to ask for help! Lots of people have problems using their cards. The cashiers are there to help you.

Learn more about how to use a debit card here: wikihow.life/Use-a-Debit-Card.
Learn about how to use an ATM here: wikihow.com/Use-an-ATM.

"The first time I went to the store by myself, I got up to the front of the line and didn't know how to pay for my groceries. I saw this contraption for a card that looked real complicated and didn't know how to use it. A long line of people were behind me and getting restless when I was just standing there looking dumbfounded. I didn't want to tell anyone I had been locked up and didn't know how to use a link or debit card. I was embarrassed and panicked!" –Michael

 Financial Resources

One of the best things you can do to manage your money is to make a budget. Budgeting can help you know where your money is going so you do not spend more than you make. There are thousands of different budget forms you can download online for free. Or you can make your own. To make your own, add up how much money you make every month. Then, make a list of everything you spend money on in a month and compare the two numbers.

You can find information online about banks, credit unions, account options, and strategies for saving your money. Some financial planning websites have a "chat" where you can ask an advisor a question and get an answer right away. Here are some resources for help with money:

- Learnvest.com and Mint.com: financial planning.
- Thesimpledollar.com: understanding money and budgeting.
- Nerdwallet.com: budgeting, banking, credit, financial planning, investments, mortgages, car, and health insurance.
- Annuity.org: budgeting, personal finance, credit and more. Two resources that may be especially helpful are: annuity.org/financial-literacy and annuity.org/annuities/types/income.
- Business Insider Magazine has a list of some top-rated money advice websites: businessinsider.com/best-websites-money-advice-2014-12 .

The resources listed here are just suggestions. It is important to think on your own about any advice you are given. Feel free to do your own looking online.

 ## Avoid Scams

You don't want to become a victim of a scam. Visit this website for a list of common scams and their warning signs: fbi.gov/scams-and-safety/common-scams-and-crimes.

Here are a few scams to avoid:
- Be suspicious of emails or calls that offer you lots of money or "free gifts" if you pay a small fee. If the reward sounds too good to be true, avoid it.
- Beware of companies that try to push you into signing up for something immediately. Only sign up for services you understand. You can always ask them for more information if you are confused.
- Only give personal information (such as account numbers and Social Security numbers) to companies you know to be trustworthy.
- Never pay for a letter of credit.

 ## Credit

You may be considering getting a credit card so that you can buy things with credit. Buying on credit means that you buy things now and pay for them later. A bank loans you the money, and you agree to repay the bank later. Usually, this means that you buy something with your credit card, and then you make monthly payments to the bank until the loan is repaid.

Keep in mind that when you buy with credit, you must pay interest. Interest is a fee to the bank for borrowing the money. Interest rates can be very high. Think hard before you get any credit card, and make sure you do not sign up for too many. The more cards you have, the more payments you will have to make. Also, too many credit cards will have a negative effect on your credit score. Credit card companies make money when people get deeper and deeper into debt. You do not want to be that customer!

A credit counselor at a nonprofit organization can give you good advice about getting a credit card. One example is credit.org, which offers free telephone counseling sessions.

Sometimes, credit cards can lead to a lot of trouble. If you buy too much with credit cards, it can be hard to pay your monthly payments. A service like credit.org can help you figure things out if you get overwhelmed. A good practice is to only buy things with your credit card that you can pay back within a month. Be very careful: it is easy to slip into the bad habit of making purchases that you can't afford, which can lead to debt.

For some big purchases, such as buying a car, a house, or paying for college tuition, buying on credit makes a lot of sense. You may be unable to pay for a car all at once, but the cost becomes easier if you can spread it out over many months. Make sure to choose a car that is affordable so that you can manage the monthly payments. Try to get an interest rate that is as low as possible.

Again, be cautious and talk to a credit counselor before going into debt.

If you decide to get a credit card or buy something using credit, your bank will look at your credit score first. A credit score is a number that tells them whether they think you will repay a loan. If you have a good credit score, it will be easier to get loans and lower interest rates. If you were in debt before you went to prison, you will need to take steps to improve your credit score. Credit scores range from 300 (bad credit) to 850 (excellent credit).

Here are some guidelines for managing credit:

Get educated. Being uninformed can lead to costly mistakes. For a good primer on your credit score, check out this website: https://www.consumerfinance.gov/consumer-tools/credit-reports-and-scores/

Be smart. Avoid businesses (such as car dealerships and payday loan offices) that advertise directly to people with bad credit. They often have extremely high interest rates. They are counting on your not being able to pay your debts. Do not support any company whose business model depends on your lack of money.

Be cautious. Read the fine print carefully and understand the rules before you sign anything. Remember, what counts is what is in the contract, not what the salesperson promised.

Pay your debts. If you've gotten behind on any of your debts—or have had debts fall into collections—pay them or make a plan for starting to pay them. For information about managing debt, see this website: consumer.ftc.gov/articles/coping-debt.

Pay your bills on time. Paying on time is a good habit and can improve your credit score. The easiest way to do that is by setting up an automatic payment with your bank on your bills' due dates. Marking the dates on a calendar is fine, too.

Use credit cards wisely. If you choose to have a credit card, don't charge what you can't pay back at the end of the month. If you must borrow money with a credit card to pay your credit card bills, it's time to talk with a credit counselor.

"If possible I would suggest you have a loved one that you trust and who believes in you to add you to some line of credit much like parents do for their children. Trust me, you will need it."—Shaun

"Open a bank account. Work on building up your credit. If you get a credit card, use less than 30% of the credit limit, buy things with your credit card, and then use the 30-day grace period to pay the bill in its entirety. That's the slow way to build credit."
—Joe Joe

Tax Basics

Once you start earning money, you will have to pay federal income taxes. The amount you pay depends on how much you make and who lives with you. Things like childcare, disability, and healthcare costs will also change how much you pay. Taxes are taken out of your paycheck.

Every year, you must file your taxes. When you file taxes, you let the government know how much you have earned and how much you have paid in taxes. You can also tell them things like if you have children, disability, or healthcare costs. The government decides whether you have paid too much or too little in taxes. In many cases, you will find that you have paid too much, and you get a tax refund. If you have paid too little, you have to pay the amount you owe. If you do not file your taxes, you have to pay a fee and you will owe back taxes for the money you didn't pay.

W-4 Form: Claiming Incoming and Exemptions.
When you start a new job, you are asked to fill out an IRS Form W-4. This form helps your employer know how much of your paycheck should be withheld in taxes. It is important to fill out this form so that you can arrange to pay taxes month by month. If you don't fill it out, you'll have to pay them all at once at the end of the year. To learn how to fill out a W-4 form, visit the following website: wikihow.com/Fill-Out-a-W-4.

Filing Taxes. Every year, you will need to file your federal and taxes by *April 15*. Many people choose to file their taxes in January so that they can get a tax refund sooner. To file taxes, you will need a W-2 form from your employer(s). Employers will usually give you W-2 forms in January.

Do you work as an independent contractor or freelancer for different businesses or people? You may not be on a business's payroll, but you still do work for them. This is called "non-employment income." Unlike a W-2 form, which reports the wages you have earned from an employer, the 1099 form records your non-employment income. Usually, if a business pays you $600 or more in non-employment income, they should send you a 1099 form. Keep good track of the 1099 forms you get. If you haven't received a 1099, contact the employer or payer to request one. Whether you receive all your 1099 forms or not, you must report any non-employment income when you file your taxes.

Next, you will need to decide which type of tax return to complete. Some of the more common forms are:

- Form 1040 (U.S. Individual Income Tax Return)
- Form 1040A (U.S. Individual Income Tax Return)
- Form 1040EZ (Income Tax Return for Single and Joint Filers with No Dependents)
- Form 1040NR (U.S. Nonresident Alien Income Tax Return)

- Form 1040NR-EZ (U.S. Income Tax Return for Certain Nonresident Aliens with No Dependents).

Simply bring your W-2s and any 1099 or other IRS forms to their office. For a fee, they will file your taxes for you. This means you won't have to worry about mistakes or spending a lot of time on your taxes. This is a good idea for people who have multiple jobs or other complicated tax situations. If you are looking for a CPA, ask someone you trust to recommend one.

"I went in at 14, so when I got out at 37, I had no clue about how taxes worked. The first year I tried to use a fee tax filing program to do it myself, but I completely jacked it all up. I went to a professional and she fixed all my mistakes and got me a lot of extra money." – Jeremy

There are also online websites that can help you file your taxes. These websites cost less than a tax professional. If you have a simple tax situation you might want to use a website. The website will guide you through your return using a series of questions and automatic calculations. Remember to read all instructions and offers carefully. It should be free to file your federal tax return, but most online services charge to file your state tax return. Some of the most used online tax filing websites are:

- e-file.com
- turbotax.intuit.com
- hrblock.com
- taxact.com
- jacksonhewitt.com

Some places offer free tax help for people. See this website to check if there is a program near you:
irs.gov/individuals/free-tax-return-preparation-for-qualifying-taxpayers

13.   Voting

If you can vote, you should! Your vote matters. Less than half of the people in the US vote. This means that only a small number of people choose the people who make the laws that apply to all of us. Your vote can make a difference, especially at the local and state levels.

US federal elections (for US President, US Senators, and US Congress Representatives) happen every two or four years, on the first Tuesday in November. State and local elections can take place in any year, at any time. During any federal, state, or local elections, you may be voting for state leaders, county state attorneys, local officials, and sometimes judges. There may be other important offices and issues on the ballot.

 Step 1: Restore Voting Rights.

Effective January 1st, 2022, if you were convicted of a felony in Washington State, another state, or in federal court, your right to vote will be restored automatically unless you are currently serving a prison sentence. If you were convicted of a felony in another state or in federal court, your right to vote is restored automatically if you are not currently incarcerated for that felony. Misdemeanor convictions and convictions in juvenile court do not result in a loss of voting rights. A certificate of discharge (COD) is not required for voting rights restoration.

For more info, view this brochure: Felony Conviction and Voting Rights Restoration.

 Step 2: Register to Vote.

Once your right to vote is restored, you must register to vote if you want to vote. If you were previously registered to vote, you must re-register to vote.

- To register to vote in the state of Washington, you must be:
- A citizen of the United States
- A legal resident of Washington state for at least 30 days prior to election day
- At least 18 years old
- If you are 16 or 17, you can sign up as a Future Voter and be automatically registered to vote when you qualify
- Not disqualified from voting due to a court order
- Not currently serving a sentence of total confinement in prison under the jurisdiction of the department of corrections for a Washington felony conviction
- Not currently incarcerated for a federal or out-of-state felony conviction

It's easy and secure to register online, by mail with a paper form, or at a county elections office. Check your registration at VoteWA.gov.

What do I need to bring to register? It depends. At a minimum, you will need to write down your name, mailing address, date of birth, telephone number, and state ID or driver's license number or last four of your social security number.

When should you register? You can register at any time, but if you want to vote in an upcoming election, eight days prior to the election.

What if I have a disability? You can view the following link for voters with disabilities.

 Step 3: Learn about the Candidates and Issues.

This guide cannot tell you how to vote. But you can learn about candidates and issues by listening to the news, talking with people you trust, and looking up candidates and issues online. You can also find voter guides and ratings for judges online.

 Step 4: Vote!

Depending on your state, you may be required to show your ID to vote. Bring your voter registration card and ID with you just in case. Normally, there are two ways that you can vote:

- In person, on election day or during an early voting period.
- By mail-in ballot. Contact your election authority or (866) OUR-VOTE if you need help requesting a mail-in ballot.

You can take notes, voting guides, and this voter information into the voting booth. It's a good idea to do this because there can be a lot to remember.

Take your time. Do not let anyone rush you. If you need help, ask a poll worker. They cannot tell you who or what to vote for, but they can answer questions about the process. They can help you mark a ballot if you have difficulty reading or if your English is limited. You can also request a ballot in other languages.

Call (866) OUR-VOTE if you run into any problems while voting.

14. Veterans

This section covers VA (Veterans Administration) benefits and services. Although you can't get your VA pension while incarcerated, there are many veteran programs and benefits on the outside that can help you once you are released.

For assistance with VA benefits and services, contact a VA representative by calling (800) 393-0865 or going to the website:
https://www.dva.wa.gov/veterans-service-mem bers-and-their-families/veterans-benefits

Veterans who are in prison can use a Kiosk to contact a special inbox that is managed by DOC staff and WDVA staff. The inbox can help veterans with their questions and issues.

Veterans should also sign a waiver letter from WDVA that reduces their benefits after 60 days in prison. This will prevent them from owing money to the VA. Veterans should also update their address and payment details with the VA.

They can also request changes or new claims for their benefits or ask to receive their checks by mail.

If you have an injury or disability that is 80 to 100% related to your military service, you can receive 10% of your pension while incarcerated.

You cannot receive any of your pension for injuries or disabilities that happened after your service.

The 10% disability benefit for incarcerated veterans is not always fixed. If you have a 20% disability rating, you can still get the 10% benefit while in prison. But if you have only a 10% rating, your benefit will be reduced to 5%.

You cannot access VA healthcare while you are locked up, according to the rules. You can still file for disability claims and get exams for

Compensation and Pension.

When you are released from prison, you may qualify for these services again, depending on your situation. You need to meet the criteria for each benefit, which usually includes an Honorable discharge.

Transferring Benefits to Your Family

While you can't get your benefits in prison, you can transfer your pension to your family. This includes a spouse, children, or parents who rely on you for money. They must have financial need to get the benefits. This is called apportionment. You (or an adult you are giving your benefits to) should apply for apportionment within one year of the day you were incarcerated.

To apply, mail a letter to the Seattle VA Regional Office (VARO) 915 2nd Ave, Seattle, WA 98174.

Your letter should say who you are and whom you want to transfer your benefits to. You must also complete and mail VA Form 21-0788. There are three ways you can get this form:

- Ask a prison counselor for assistance. They may be able to get the form for you.
- Ask someone on the outside to download the form from the website below:

https://www.vba.va.gov/pubs/forms/VBA-21-0788-ARE.pdf

- Tear out and use the form in the back of this book.

If you have questions about the process, ask someone you trust to call the Washington State Department of Veterans Affairs at (800) 562-2308.

Once they get your application, the VA will review it. They may ask your spouse or children's guardian to fill out the same form. They will let you know if the apportionment is approved, and your family will retroactively receive your benefits. That means that your benefits will be saved and given to them, starting 60 days after your incarceration.

 Female Veterans. VA Medical Centers have program managers who help female veterans. They offer help with VA benefits and healthcare. Contact the closest VA Medical Center to find a program manager who specializes in female veterans.

Reinstating Benefits After Release

You can have your benefits start again 30 days before your scheduled release date. If you are in prison, ask your counselor or someone on the outside to help you contact the WDVA to get your benefits restored. They can call (800) 562-2308or go to https://www.dva.wa.gov/veterans-service-members-and-their-families/veterans-benefits for help.

This is all true, however WADOC offers incarcerated veterans a chance to agree to Reentry Services. This is where the counselor, navigators, and VA team will hold a Reentry Team Meeting to discuss all issues of reentering into the community to include having VA benefits reinstated. This may be the best route for you to go. We suggest discussing this with your counselor.

The VA has a reentry program called Health Care for Reentry Veterans (HCRV) Program. They offer:

- Post-release assessments
- Referrals to medical, psychiatric, and social services, including employment services and housing assistance
- Short-term case management after reentry. All VA Medical Centers have reentry staff. Contact the closest VA Medical Center to begin receiving services

You can find VA hospitals and clinics in your state here: https://www.va.gov/directory/guide/state.asp?dnum=ALL&STATE=WA

Filing Disability Claims

Do you have a disability related to your military service? You can file a disability claim online or in-person. You can get disability benefits in prison and once you are released to work release, a half-way house, or community custody.

You will need your medical records and any other proof of disability for your claim. You can also apply for a disability claim by filling out a paper application at a VA facility or mailing the claim to: Claims Intake Center, PO BOX 4444. Janesville, WI 53547-4444.

You can find VA facility in Washington by visiting: https://www.va.gov/find-locations/ Check out this website to learn how to file a claim: https://www.va.gov/disability/how-to-file-claim/

The VA accepts all claims filed on the proper form and that are complete. They do not reject all first-time claims. Yes, do keep a claim active by appealing it if you feel you have been inappropriately denied. Use the appeal process and seek help from a Veterans Service Organization (VSO) which is a free service, https://www.dva.wa.gov/resources/county-map. Some veterans hire a claims agent or an attorney.

Health

After you leave prison, you can get care at VA medical centers. You can enroll in their system by visiting a VA medical center, or by phone at: (877) 222- VETS. You can only receive care if you were honorably (or generally) discharged. You can receive treatment for injuries unconnected to your military service.

Not all VA healthcare is free. Your insurance will be billed for care, and you will have to pay part of your bill inpatient, outpatient, extended care (nursing home care), and medication costs. Some of these services may be free if your income is below a certain limit or if your illness is connected to your service. For more on eligibility, go to https://www.va.gov/health-care/eligibility/

The VA also offers mental health and substance use treatment at VA medical centers or at Vet Centers (depending on the treatment). Visit https://www.va.gov/health/vamc/ for a list of VA Medical Centers in your state.

Housing

Most Veterans who are in jail or prison will eventually reenter the community. VA's HCRV program is designed to promote success and prevent homelessness among Veterans returning home after incarceration. HCRV services include:

- Outreach and pre-release assessments services for Veterans in prison;
- Referrals and linkages to medical, mental health and social services, including employment services on release;
- Short-term case management assistance on release.

Washington HCRV Specialist: Anthony Sparber / anthony.sparber@va.gov

Veterans Transitional Housing Program

The Veterans Transitional Housing Program are located in Port Orchard and Orting, WA. Transitional housing facilities in Port Orchard and Orting help those in need with stable housing, vocational rehabilitation, and employment. Veterans are surrounded with staff and wrap-around services that lead to successful program completion and return to the community. See Brochure.

How to Apply

Request a referral from the Federal VA Medical Center Homeless Liaison Officer at (253) 583-2825.

To Apply fill out both of the following:
- Program Application and
- VA Request for and Authorization to Release Health Information

Contact

Monday - Friday 8:30-4:30
360-895-4382

Orting:
Delena Josephsen,
Cell: (253) 263-0735
Evening: (253)259-0581
1301 Orting Kapowsin Hwy.
Orting, WA 98360

Port Orchard:
William Brown
(360) 895-4371
thp@dva.wa.gov

Mailing Address:
Transitional Housing Program
PO BOX 8175
Port Orchard, WA 98366

Orting Veterans Village

The Veterans Village is not operated by WDVA. It is operated by Quixote Communities. Please visit: http://www.quixotecommunities.org/. Or contact: 360-872-0079 or info@quixotecommunities.org

Employment

The VA has employment help for honorably (or generally) discharged people. Local Veterans Employment Representatives (LVER) and Disabled Veterans Outreach Program Representatives (DVOP) help veterans find jobs. They also provide job training. You can get help here:

- https://www.va.gov/careers-employment/

- Washington State Pathways to Employment

- King County Veterans Program

The Homeless Veterans' Reintegration Project (HVRP) helps veterans with:

- Searching for jobs.
- Vocational counseling.
- Occupational skills training.
- On-the-job training.
- Trade skills certification and licensing.
- Job placement assistance.
- Referral to supportive services.

Vocational Rehabilitation and Employment services help veterans with disabilities related to military service. They offer help finding a job, job training, and advice. To connect with this program, call (800) 827-1000 or visit https://www.benefits.gov/benefit/296

Veterans Industries and Compensated Work Therapy programs help homeless and near homeless veterans with physical, mental health, or addiction problems. These programs contract with businesses to provide paid work for these veterans. They also have therapeutic housing. Veterans Industries Programs are sometimes housed within VA Medical Centers. For more information go to https://www.va.gov/health/cwt/

Additional Resources

Please visit https://www.dva.wa.gov/resources and view the county-specific resource directory to find additional veteran resources in your community.

15.   Deportation After Release

If you were born outside the US and do not have documentation, you may be subject to deportation after your release from prison. This can be true even if you were a child when you were brought over or had a legal permanent resident status before incarceration. Having a felony conviction may mean that status was stripped from you.

An immigration lawyer or non-profit that works to defend the rights of immigrants may be able to help you figure out your status. There may still be options for you to fight the removal proceedings if ICE intends to deport you. View the resource directory for more information.

The consulate of your country may also be able to help. In many prisons, representatives of the consulates of various countries like Mexico visit regularly. Ask if you can schedule an appointment with them if you think they can help. It's your right to speak to your country's consulate.

If you are taken into ICE (Immigration and Customs Enforcement) custody after you are released, you can ask a family member or trusted friend to look you up on ICE's Detainee Locator System: https://locator.ice.gov/odls/. They can see where you are detained and visit you there, bringing a bag that you can take with you as you are deported. If you know your "Alien registration number" this will help to locate you.

There is much more to know about your rights as an immigrant, what to expect with deportation and reentry in your home country. The Education Justice Project publishes a guide on this topic called *A New Path: A Guide to the Challenges and Opportunities After Deportation*, available in Spanish as well. You can write to the address below to request a free copy:

Education Justice Project

1001 S. Wright St.

Champaign, IL 61820

Part 4: Healing and Moving Forward

- Beginning to Heal
- Building Healthy Relationships
- Connecting With Your Community

16.   Beginning to Heal

Prison hurts in a lot of ways. People who are incarcerated sometimes push others away to protect themselves from that pain. Some people stay away from relationships, grieving, and emotional self-care to stop themselves from feeling helpless. Or they may want to protect themselves from being vulnerable with distance and indifference.

Healing is a part of moving forward and reconnecting the pieces of your life. It is a process, and it requires you to be both vulnerable and strong. It might sound hard to be vulnerable. You need to let yourself feel the pain of incarceration. Opening up to yourself and being open to trusting others is a big step toward getting your life back.

> ❞
> *"My family thinks that because I'm free, all my problems are over, but really we carry all this baggage with us. The coping mechanisms we had on the inside are still with us, and they create barriers on the outside."- Pablo*
> ❝

Prison is often traumatic. Recovery will take time. The work towards recovery is a form of healing. Vulnerability is not weakness. It is not weak to ask for help. Getting help from a professional is a good option. Support groups and individual counseling can help you deal with trauma that may have happened while you were in prison. See the Mental Health section for information on finding support.

This section addresses several aspects of wellness that can help you heal and move forward. It is based on suggestions given to us by formerly incarcerated people.

What is wellness? Wellness is a complicated subject. It means something different for everyone. After you leave prison, wellness is about making meaning out of your experiences. It also means making these experiences a part of who you are and who you want to be in the world. It is about forgiveness, healing, caring for yourself, and reconnecting with others.

Emotional wellness means being respectful of yourself and others. It means you are aware of your good or bad feelings and accept them. You express your feelings to others in healthy and constructive ways. It also means you think about other people's feelings and perspectives. People may think differently than you. Knowing how to disagree respectfully is key to healthy relationships. You may have other unresolved issues you're dealing with, such as grief, anger, or depression. Be patient and realize the path to emotional wellness can be a long one.

> ❞
> *"Reach out to somebody. One of our coping mechanisms that's prevalent with individuals who are incarcerated is that we retract ourselves, isolate ourselves to try to deal with it, with the psychological hurdles we're going through." --Pablo*
> ❝

Physical wellness is taking care of your body. It is important to stay active and healthy. Consider finding a gym, jogging, walking, biking, or looking up free at-home exercise videos online. It's good to eat healthy and drink plenty of water. Practice safe sex by using condoms. For those with addiction issues, getting help through counseling or recovery programs can be a positive step. You can read more about healthcare in our Health chapter.

Social wellness means you look for healthy relationships with many kinds of people. As we will discuss in our Building Healthy Relationships chapter, reentry is a time when you will strengthen old relationships and build new ones. While it can be difficult to put yourself out there, it can also lead to meaningful, healthy relationships.

> *"Advice for socializing outside? Learning coping skills and anger management. Being less abrasive and open-minded."*
> *– Earl*

Spiritual wellness is thinking about a larger meaning or purpose to life. This can, but does not have to, involve religion. You may decide to join a church, synagogue, or mosque. You may also decide to join a support group to find community and purpose. Set aside some time each day to be open, listen, and think about what's going on inside. Practice mindfulness or meditation. A description of some ways of doing so can be found in our Mindfulness chapter.

> *"Take a breath. You're going to be in for a ride, and you better pack your patience."--Pablo*

Occupational wellness is contributing meaningfully and respectfully in your job. Your job may not be your perfect job. But how you do it is entirely up to you. What strengths do you bring to the table? Bring those to your work. Invest in yourself by investing in what you do. Find ways to do a little extra and try new things if you are able. Take the time to realize the value of the work you do, and honor that. Also, beware of toxic work environments. Some jobs can be unhealthy, physically, emotionally, or otherwise.

Environmental wellness means being aware of Earth's resources and trying to create a healthy environment. There are many ways to contribute. You can grow vegetables in a community garden or volunteer to help with community clean up. Spend time in nature, even if it's at a local park, to help you feel healthy.

> *"What I felt was most difficult when I first got out is figuring out how to relate to other people. You have both the lack of 'normal' experiences that most people have as late-teenagers and young adults. Plus you have the negative effects of long-term imprisonment."*
> *--Greg A.*

17. Building Healthy Relationships

Prison makes it hard to stay connected with family, friends, and loved ones. Reentry removes some of these barriers, but it introduces new challenges, too. Rebuilding healthy, positive relationships will require time, patience, and openness. You've changed while in prison, and so have your loved ones. It's going to take time to get to know each other again.

Since you've been gone a long time, you may struggle to feel like you belong. You and your loved ones may feel uncertain about each other. You may wonder if you can trust each other.

Your relationship with loved ones may go through different stages when you return home. Things might start out great (the "honeymoon" stage) but get harder as you spend more time together. This is a common experience and you're not alone!

Four common relationship stages during reentry

Stage 1: Honeymoon. You and your loved ones are excited to be back together. Everyone's at their best, but anxiety is under the surface.	Stage 2: Uncertainty and suspicion. You and your loved ones might feel uncertain about your relationship and question motives. Are you going to stick around? Do you still want to be together?	Stage 3: Testing and learning to share. You and your loved ones may test each other to see if it's OK to share feelings and be yourself. Can you trust each other?	Stage 4: Belonging. You may struggle with how to get involved in family routines. What roles will you play? How can you be part of family life again?

You don't have to face relationship challenges alone! Here are a few places you can go for help:

- **Look for a family-oriented reentry program.** Divine Alternatives for Dads Services D.A.D.S. based in Seattle and Tacoma, for instance, offers programs to help people and their families reunite after prison. Learn more at https://www.aboutdads.org/services. Look for a similar program in your community.
- **Take a class.** Anger management, parenting, communication, or marriage and family classes can help you develop skills that will make your relationships stronger.
- **Get counseling or therapy**, either alone or with your partner or family. See our Mental Health chapter.
- **Join a returning resident support group.** Many community organizations offer supportive circles where you can share your struggles with others who share a similar background. They can provide advice and support.

> If you are in an abusive relationship, **call the National Domestic Violence Hotline: (877) 863-6338**

There is no "one-size-fits-all" solution to the challenges people face when reuniting with loved ones. Below, we share advice about common challenges that people face when reuniting with loved ones. We cover the following topics:

- Sharing (self-disclosure)
- Parenting after release
- Dealing with difficult emotions
- Anger management
- Institutionalization
- Domestic violence

Sharing (Self-disclosure)

Many people survive prison by becoming closed off and guarded. They seldom share things with others. But being closed off can hurt your relationships. Family members can also become closed off. They might only share positive things during their visits or visit rarely because it's too painful.

Tony explains why many people are closed off from their family members in prison:

> *You keep [your family] at an arm's length because you know you could lose them. A lot of us watched family members die. Family members get sick. Family members move away. You're watching the world go past you, and to keep that family interested in your life and to keep yourself interested in their life is really hard because you can't experience that life with them.*

Isolation helps people cope in prison, but it's not always helpful on the outside.

> *The coping mechanisms we had on the inside are still with us, and they create barriers on the outside. When you retract and people are not knowing the reason for your isolation, they think it's having to do with them. –Pablo*

So how do you open up when you're used to being closed off? How do you learn to share?

Self-disclosure is sharing information about ourselves that is truthful. It is being honest with your loved ones. It is one of the most important parts of a healthy relationship.

- It builds trust
- It provides emotional release
- When you share, your loved ones are more likely to share, too

There are risks to sharing. You may worry that your loved ones will reject you if they know how you feel. You may worry that you will hurt others if you share what you have experienced. You may feel embarrassed to admit that you need help.

You may feel that your family members won't be able to understand what you have gone through. All this can make you afraid to share.

Keep in mind that closeness doesn't happen overnight. You can choose what to share and when. When building relationships, most people share slowly. They take small steps and wait to see how people respond. Here are some tips for learning to open up to loved ones again:

- **Start with the easy stuff.** Share what you like to do for fun. Ask them what they like to do. What movies do they love? What do they do to relax?
- **Spend time together.** Take long walks. As you do, share some of your feelings, fears, and goals. Invite them to open up, too. Start small and see how they respond.
- **Learn to text.** Send short, friendly messages about your day to your family and friends. Ask how they are doing.
- **Avoid criticizing or trying to offer advice** when your loved ones share things with you. Just listen. Be positive and supportive.
- **Be willing to talk about your relationship**. How has your relationship changed? How can you perform your share of the work?

Keke describes the small ways he shares his life with his children and invites them to share their lives with him:

> *I take time out of my day, even five minutes, to call them and see what's going on. I text them every day, every morning. . . . I talk to them and get their point of view and see what's going on, try to spend time. I tell them I love them, how you are doing, how your day is going, what you got planned. Little simple stuff. I let them talk.*

David notes that if you want your children to open up to you, it helps to not be critical. He shares this advice:

> *In prison I became more educated, more aware. My relationships with my children became complicated because I had the tendency to correct them in their behavior. I was bombarding them with advice, and the more I did this, the more they were pushing me away. I had to learn to relax, to not be overbearing.*

Pablo also notes the importance of listening:

> *Be ready to hear some truths. Listen attentively. There is a lot of lived life in your absence. Everybody was in a bad situation. As we were surviving, so were they. Don't approach it with judgment. Try to be understanding with your family and with yourself.*

Keke notes the importance of being open and honest with your partner.

— 〞 —

The most challenging thing is [to] be honest with [your partner]. If she's taking time out of her life to stand by you, give her your life. [Don't] feed her a fairy tale. . . Don't come out trying to feed nobody no dream and definitely don't feed yourself a dream.

— 〝 —

Sharing your Past with Others

If you are in the habit of closing yourself off, it can be hard to make new friends. We offer a few methods for doing so below, and you can choose what you think would work best for you. Tony explains:

— 〞 —

You spend so much time keeping people at arm's distance. You never let anybody get close. [When you go into prison] you're so young, you're so vibrant, it's so easy to have friends, to have relationships, to have people that are close to you. But when you come home, you've gotten so used to keeping people at a distance that you just continue to do it. It's hard to make new friends.

— 〝 —

When meeting new people, it can be hard to know how much to share about your past. Not everyone will be accepting of who you are. Roberto talks about the challenge of getting to know people and deciding how much to share.

— 〞 —

How do I get to know people? How do you create a personal brand so that all the good things you offer are not eclipsed by the fact that you spent a significant amount of time in prison? How do you open a conversation with someone when you're trying to remain private, and also take into account all of the negative stigma that's attached to being incarcerated? You're just meeting people and you don't want to share too much about yourself. There's so much negative stigma. You have to break through that wall. On the other hand, if you do, it's still no guarantee that they are going to relate to you and understand what you're going through.

— 〝 —

Keke prefers telling people right away about his past. "I tell them in the door," he says.

— 〞 —

I learned from my experience that if you lay your cards out in the open, you get a better understanding. Nowadays, people google so much. Both of you have to be honest with each other. So that's what I do. I let them know right in the door. This is me. I've been to prison twice. I'm doing this, I'm doing that, trying to get myself together.

— 〝 —

Tony also prefers being open:

———— 99 ————

It's a little weird, a little awkward, to just come out and say, hey, I just spent ten years in prison. But I've never been one to be shy. I've always been real open about what I went through because it lets other people know that, look, just because I was in there doesn't mean I have to keep going back and forth, back and forth.

———— 66 ————

Heather, on the other hand, is more reserved:

———— 99 ————

I don't really mention [that I was in prison] to people. But, I guess it helps to have moved away to a different state, so really not that many people know me. They just know what they see of me now. They don't know . . . I made mistakes in the past. And I'm kind of comfortable with it. So, if I was to meet a guy or something and start dating, I wouldn't just throw all my dirty laundry out front. I'd get to know him. But if things were working out really good, I'd tell him all about it, and if he didn't accept it, then he probably wouldn't be the guy for me anyway.

———— 66 ————

Tony concludes,

———— 99 ————

"When you meet somebody, if it scares them that you've been to prison, then you know what? That's not the person that you need to be with."

———— 66 ————

> **When you are deciding how to share your past with people, consider these guidelines:**
>
> - Is the other person important to you? If so, sharing may help you be closer.
> - Is there a risk to sharing this information? Could they tell others or make it more difficult for you to get a job? Could they use it against you in other ways?
> - Is it appropriate to share? Sometimes it's wise to not share too much with strangers. What do they need to know about your past?
> - Will the other person be willing to share, too? Good relationships are built on reciprocity (a willingness to share on both sides).
> - Is sharing going to help or hurt? Think about the effect your sharing will have on the other person.

Asking for Help and Setting Boundaries

If you're used to being closed off, it may be especially hard to ask for help from loved ones. Pablo notes:

———— 99 ————

My family thinks that because I'm free, all my problems are over, but I need assistance with the most basic things. That does make me somewhat defensive, and I'll end up trying to do things on my own and then I crash and burn.

———— 66 ————

His advice?

———— 99 ————

"Ditch that machismo and ask for help. It's not a bad thing."

———— 66 ————

It can be embarrassing to have to ask for help. As Joe Joe explains:

> What we're competing with is not feeling like a helpless infant all the time. We're so used to being rejected that we don't reach out much for help.

Lee, whose partner was incarcerated, argues that:

> ...healthy adult relationships aren't about putting your needs in the back seat.
> ....You want to be considerate and not wear out your welcome. The effect of that is that maybe you're not expressing the things that you need. It's OK to say, "Hey, I need you to do this thing for me." Learn to communicate what you need.

Joe Joe offers this final piece of advice regarding asking for help:

> If you strive to lighten someone's load rather than adding to it, they are going to be more receptive to helping you. This is what really wins people over and will help get you where you need to go.

Some people going through reentry struggle to set boundaries with their loved ones. Your loved ones are happy to have you back. They may pressure you to get involved or do things you aren't ready for yet. They may ask you to do too many things at once.

It's OK to step back and take things slow. It's OK to say no to things and let them know that you aren't ready yet.

> You have to take things slow. All these new experiences, it can be extremely overwhelming. All those people tugging at you – those are extra stressors. Listen, take care of yourself. – Ricky

> I love a good challenge. I was pulled into a monkey bar contest, into diving off the high board. But these old bones are not the same as they were. You don't want to injure yourself. – Kilroy

> We're coming out feeling beholden to people for what they've done for us while we're inside, or for our loved ones. That clouds our judgment, our best interest. Realize you can't help anybody if you're not helping yourself. Being selfish is not a bad thing. If love is directed inwards, it can radiate outwards. You can't help anybody if you're not helping yourself. – Pablo

Parenting After Release

If you are a parent, you may be nervous about reuniting with your kids. You may feel guilt for what your kids have gone through while you were locked up. Some parents need or want time to get their feet on the ground before getting their kids back. These feelings are normal.

You may feel pressure to make up for lost time with your kids or to be a super parent. No matter what, resist the urge to parent out of guilt.

Lots of people have unrealistic expectations of parents, especially mothers.

- They are expected to spend lots of time and money on their kids.
- They should be there emotionally for their kids at all times.
- They should place the needs of their children above their own needs at all times.
- They should have a clean house and money to put their kids in good programs.

Parents who cannot or do not meet this ideal are often seen as bad.

These "super parent" ideals are impossible to live up to. And that's OK. Resist the urge to parent out of guilt.

Don't be too hard on yourself. You are going to make mistakes. We all do. Take mistakes as an opportunity to learn. Be willing to learn from your children, too. Building a healthy relationship with your children will take hard work, love, and compassion. It will take time and patience, but it is definitely worth it.

Some relationships may never entirely heal. Accept that your children and loved ones may not want the same kind of relationship you once had.

Here are a few things you can do to make the process easier to reunite with your family:
- **Educate yourself.** Read books and attend classes about parenting. Raising a child is always hard, so get all the tools you can.
- **Get counseling or therapy.** It can help you heal and provide tools for you to be a better parent. See our mental health chapter.
- **Do things you enjoy.** Meditate. Take some time to do things for yourself if you can. See our meditation chapter.
- **Talk to other parents,** especially those who have spent time in prison. Join a mother's group or a parent's group. Share your experiences, fears, and dreams.

———— 99 ————

Always remember that reconciliation and restoration are two different things. You may reconcile, but the relationship may never be restored. Just grieve properly. Be OK with that. Don't walk around forever with the grief on your back. If you've done all you can, it will be OK. – Josephine

There will be people in your life who will remain after such a long journey, and there will be some that fall to the wayside. Don't look back. Keep looking forward, looking inward. Seek inward happiness. – Pablo

You can't recapture time that has been lost. You have to start fresh. Don't be too gung-ho. Trust has to be reestablished. If they're angry, don't try to invalidate their anger. Talk about it. Don't pretend that the separation never happened, because it did. Try to seek counseling. – Josephine

When you're locked up, you have all this time to sit and think. You have ideas of how you want things to go, and then you get out and, of course, those are just ideas. . . . Take care of yourself and everything else will fall into place. . . . You can't stress out over everything that you have no control over. Don't give up hope. There's always hope... – Heather

———— 👣 ————

Reflect

1. What feelings do you have about reuniting with your kids?

2. How can you practice self-care during this time?

3. Where can you go for help? Who is in your support network?

Dealing with Difficult Emotions

In prison, you may have bottled up difficult emotions instead of working through them. Maybe you pushed aside feelings of fear, guilt, or anger and instead told family members that everything is going to be OK. Your family members may have done the same.

Here are a few of the emotions you might feel as you reunite with your loved ones.

- **Fear** is your body's reaction to danger or uncertainty. You may fear that nobody will love you because of the things you've done. You may be afraid that your children won't accept you. This fear can cause you to withdraw from them even more.
- **Sadness** is feeling unhappy or discouraged. You might feel discouraged that your children don't know you or that your sister doesn't want to talk to you.
- **Grief** is a profound feeling of loss. You might feel a sense of loss for the years you spent in prison, away from your family.
- **Guilt** is feeling bad about yourself, often for something you've done or haven't done that makes others suffer. You might feel guilt for not being around for your partner or kids.
- **Anger** is something you feel when someone or something has done you wrong. You might feel angry about what prison has done to you, or angry about something a loved one has said.

People experience emotions through their mind and body. For instance, fear can tighten your chest. You might feel sick to your stomach or start sweating. Some emotions can help you change and grow. Others can keep you from growing and harm your relationships.

Expect some of your repressed emotions to surface. Sounds, tastes, and smells can trigger memories from the past. You've lost partners, friends, and parents. Expect to feel rage, sorrow, frustration, and grief.

———— 🗨 ————

If you have any emotions at all, you're going to have guilt about making your family suffer. . . . They suffer with you while you're in there. To them, you're kind of dead because you're not around any longer. There is guilt. And we don't like to show it because, hey, we're tough guys. –Tony.

———— 🗨 ————

———— 🗨 ————

I was looking at videos with a friend and a song came on. I found myself crying for no apparent reason. I lost my father when I was locked up. That was one of his favorite songs. I had never had the opportunity to mourn. All of the pain came forward. – Pablo

———— 🗨 ————

It's normal to feel these emotions. It's what you do with these emotions that matters. Pushing aside difficult emotions instead of facing them can harm your relationships. Learning to recognize, express, and manage emotions can help you have healthier relationships. Here are some tips for managing emotions in healthier ways:

- **Identify your feelings. Let them wash over you.** They won't last forever. Give yourself time to feel them. Don't bury them. Doing so can cause these feelings to build up even more.
- **Express your feelings in helpful ways**. Separate people from actions. "I'm angry about something you have done," not "I am angry with you."
- **Recognize the difference between feeling and acting**. Just because you feel a certain way doesn't mean you have to act on it.
- **Accept responsibility for your feelings.** Try not to blame others for the way you feel. Instead of saying, "You're making me angry," say "I'm feeling angry."
- **Change your perception.** Think about what caused you to feel that way. Are there different ways to think about what happened that are more helpful?

Therapists or counselors can help you work through and manage your emotions. It may help to go to family or couple's therapy. Some organizations offer support for families working through the challenges of reentry.

In prison, you may have walked away from difficult emotions and conflicts. Perhaps you had space to think through difficult issues before facing them. On the outside, you may be expected to directly address issues with your loved ones rather than walking away. You may feel pressure to respond right away when you'd rather take your time.

Pablo explains what happens when you retreat instead of talking about how you are feeling with loved ones:

—— 🙶 ——

When you retreat, it telegraphs to the other person that you don't care. When you remain silent, people may think you're brushing them off.

—— 🙶 ——

It's OK to take some time to think before talking through a problem. As Lee explains,

—— 🙶 ——

"It's OK to say, 'I need time to think about this, I can't give you an answer right away.'"

—— 🙶 ——

But too often when people retreat, they never come back to it. If you need some space, commit to talking about it later.

Anger Management

As with other emotions, it's normal to feel and express anger. It gets to be a problem if it is out of control, aggressive or constant. It's a problem if it hurts the people around you.

Anger is a secondary emotion. For example, "He embarrassed me, then I got angry." Getting to the root of why you were embarrassed can help the anger subside.

You may have to take an anger management class as a condition of your parole. These classes can help you learn some basic skills for managing your anger. A therapist or counselor can also help. Anger management classes or therapy may cover topics such as:

- Causes behind your anger and triggers
- Expressing anger in better ways
- Time out and reflection
- Understanding how your anger affects you and others

Need to find an anger management class? If it's required for parole, you will need to make sure that it offers a certificate. Often there is a small fee for this certificate. Ask questions to make sure. You can take online or in person classes. To find a low or no-cost class, try the following resources:

- For a list of anger management providers in Washington State visit 211 Washington.
- Ask your CCO or your healthcare provider for some suggestions.
- Local universities and colleges sometimes offer anger management classes for the public.
- Local community centers and nonprofits often offer anger management classes as well.

Here are some anger management tips, modified from experts at the Mayo Clinic:

- **Think before you speak.** In the heat of the moment, it's easy to say something you'll later regret. Take a few moments to collect your thoughts. Allow others to do the same.
- **Once you're calm, express your anger.** As soon as you're thinking clearly, express your anger, concerns, and needs clearly and directly. Do so without hurting others or trying to control them.
- **Get some exercise.** Exercise can help reduce stress that can cause you to become angry. If you feel your anger building, go for a run.
- **Take a timeout.** Give yourself a short break when things get stressful. A few moments of quiet time might help you handle things better.
- **Identify possible solutions.** Instead of focusing on what made you mad, work on resolving the issue. Does your child's messy room stress you out? Close the door. Is your partner late for dinner every night? Schedule meals later in the evening or agree to eat on your own sometimes.
- **Stick with 'I' statements.** To avoid placing blame, use "I" statements. Be respectful and specific. For example, say, "I'm upset that you left the table without asking to help with the dishes" instead of "You never do any housework."

- **Use humor to release tension.** Humor can help you face what's making you angry without getting out of control.
- **Relax.** When your temper flares, put relaxation skills to work. Take deep breaths. Imagine a calm place or repeat a calming phrase, such as "Take it easy." Listen to music or go for a walk. Practice mindfulness (see our Mindfulness chapter).
- **Know when to seek help.** Learning to control anger is hard for everyone at times. Seek help if your anger seems out of control, causes you to do things you regret or hurts those around you.

 Reflect

1. Think about a time when you felt angry, and it got out of control. What happened? Why did it get out of control?
2. Now think about how you could have managed your anger better. What are some things you can try next time you get angry?

Institutionalization

Many people who have left prison continue to suffer the mental effects of being locked up long after they leave. **Institutionalization** is how your thoughts, speech, and actions are influenced by being locked up. You and your loved ones may not be aware of all the many ways prison has impacted you. This can cause all sorts of conflicts and misunderstandings.

Some people who leave prison suffer from **Post-Incarceration Syndrome (PIS);** a syndrome like Post-Traumatic Stress Syndrome (PTSD)**.** Time in prison can make mental health problems worse. It can make people more isolated and more violent. It can lead some people to feel that they have no purpose. It can make people fearful and hypervigilant.
Here are just a few of the many ways that time in prison may have impacted you and your relationships.

"I closed myself off as a way of coping."

"I have these defense mechanisms. I've learned to telegraph assertiveness and square up when faced with conflict." – *Pablo*

"I had hangups about talking to regular, free people. I didn't feel comfortable." – *Ricky*

"When I get upset, my posture says I'm ready for a fight." – *Pablo*

"In prison, we got up early. I'm up in the middle of the night. Up early in the morning."

"In prison, you have to watch your back. Now on the outside, I can't sit with my back to people. I have to be at the back of the room so I can see everyone." – *Kilroy*

"I'm loud because in jail, people tend to scream. Everyone has to speak over each other if they want to be heard." – *Antonio*

The tools you used to survive in prison were "blunt tools," as Pablo describes. You may have survived by being closed off, aggressive, and hypervigilant, by being loud and watching your back. These tools can drive your loved ones away on the outside.

You will need to add new tools to your toolbox — tools that are more delicate. They include listening, communicating, and being patient with each other. Have honest talks with loved ones. Invite them to help you recognize when you are acting in an aggressive way. Practice adjusting your body language.

It will take time for you and your loved ones to understand just how much your time in prison has impacted you. You may need counseling or help from a support group to work through these issues.

Domestic Violence

Domestic violence isn't just an anger problem. It's about control. Domestic violence is when one person exerts power or control over another person in a dating, family or household relationship.

It can take many forms, including:
- Verbal abuse (threats, name-calling, intimidation)
- Physical abuse (pushing, slapping, choking, destroying property)
- Controlling behavior (keeping you from seeing people, going places, or spending money)
- Emotional abuse (making you feel like you are worthless)
- Sexual abuse (unwanted sexual activity, often using force)

In some families or cultures, these behaviors are not seen as wrong. It's hard to break away from domestic violence when the attitudes about relationships around you are not healthy. It may take some time to change your way of thinking. It may take some time to realize that what you are doing or experiencing is wrong.

If you are in an abusive relationship, seek help. Making the decision to leave is hard. It can be risky. It takes courage to leave, especially if you fear for your own safety or the safety of your children. It's hard to leave if you depend on the other person for money.

Begin by calling the National Domestic Violence hotline: (877) 863-6338 or (877) TO-END-DV. This confidential, free 24-hour hotline provides support, information, and referrals. It can put you in touch with resources in your area. Even if you are not ready to leave the relationship, the hotline can help you get through hard times. It can help you take the next step.

Additional resources for survivors of domestic violence can be found at https://ncadv.org/resources.

For a list of places where you can go for help in your community do a search at 211 Washington or a county-specific search at https://wscadv.org/washington-domestic-violence-programs/

If money is keeping you from leaving a partner who is abusing you, there may be an emergency crisis fund for survivors of domestic violence in your community. Search online at https://wscadv.org/resources/financial-assistance/.

We have listed transitional housing and emergency shelter options in our Resource Directory. Many of these shelters serve people who are leaving an abusive relationship. Some provide protection if you fear for your safety. In addition, we have listed a few counseling resources available to people who are facing domestic violence.

If You are the Abusive Partner

If you have been abusive to a partner or family member, reach out to get help. The first important step is to acknowledge you have a problem. You can change, but it will take work. You may be required to stay away from your partner until you are in a better place, or you may choose to stay away for a while to keep them safe and give them some space.

To get help, consider attending a program for those who have been abusive. Programs like these will help you:
- See that it is NOT ok to abuse a partner
- Learn to take blame and credit for actions
- Learn nonviolent and non-controlling ways of communicating and behaving

In Washington you can look for state certified DVIT programs by county by clicking here. You could enroll in a DVIT program for people who control their partners with physical abuse, emotional abuse, sexual abuse, or economic abuse (withholding money).

 Reflect

1. What does a healthy relationship look like to you?

2. Think back on your relationships with your family or loved ones. In what ways were they healthy? In what ways were they unhealthy?

3. Where are the places you can go to for help if you are in an abusive relationship?

18.   Connecting With Your Community

Connecting with others is hard for many people after being released from prison. You were separated from your family and friends. Now you may feel loneliness and isolation, especially if the people you were close to are no longer around.

Getting involved in your community and making new friends may help you begin to heal. This might mean working to make a difference through politics, organizing, and volunteering. This may mean writing letters to elected officials, campaigning, voting, participating in government events, talking to people in your community, and volunteering.

Community Organizing and Advocacy

Community organizing is when community members join and push for their needs and rights. A community can be people who live in the same area, or people who have something in common. Community organizing can look like:

- Going door-to-door
- Public speeches
- Organizing meetings
- Gathering information about the community needs
- Sharing information to educate the public
- Developing community leadership
- Organizing fundraisers

Community organizing is a tool for making your voice heard and creating positive change. You would be surprised by what you can do when you join with others to make sure your community's voice is being heard.

There are many organizations that do community organizing online and on the ground. Now that you are out of prison, you can help them in important ways. You can help change the laws that affect people who have been in prison. HOM

alumni have volunteered with, coordinated, and been employed by groups including:

- Formerly Incarcerated College Graduates Network https://ficgn.org/
- Smart Justice Spokane (a broad coalition of over 30 organizations working together to end mass incarceration and eliminate racial disparities in our local criminal justice system) http://smartjusticespokane.org/about-us/
- Washington Statewide Reentry Council (council meetings open to all) https://www.commerce.wa.gov/about-us/boards-and-commissions/statewide-reentry-council/
- Restorative Community Coalition https://therestorativecommunity.org/
- Filthy Rags Outreach (former gang members advocacy) https://www.filthyragsoutreach.org/

You can contact these groups and many others to find out how you can get involved in your community. See the Resources Directory for more ideas.

"Get involved in advocacy work. If we want to change the process, we have to lead the process." --Marlon C.

Getting Involved in Your Community

Religious Organizations—Churches, synagogues, mosques, or other religious communities can help you find meaning, purpose, and fellowship. Many religious organizations have classes, support groups, and volunteer opportunities. Don't worry if it takes a while for you to find the place that feels right for you.

Libraries— Public libraries organize events and classes. They have book clubs, social gatherings, and concerts. Many also have a space where people can post information about community events, group meetings, and even job openings. Visit your local library's website or stop by in-person to find out what your library has to offer.

Reentry Programs—If you live in a town with a reentry program, consider volunteering your time there. Even if you didn't use this program, you could help people who are getting out now. Let them know you are happy to help. With some luck, you may even be able to turn your volunteer work into a paid job.

City and County Park Districts and Forest Preserves—Your town or city probably has a park district, and its website will include information about the parks in your area. Take time to visit these parks and spend time in nature. Many park districts offer sports programs and leagues, as well as other recreational programs.

Events and Activities—In many cities you can get free alternative papers weekly. They usually have information on concerts and local events and classes. The same information should also be found on the paper's website. A simple Google search can also help you find events in your area.

Serving Your Community

Volunteer work gives you the chance to make friends, solve problems, and do some good for your community. It is also good for your health.

Making new friends can prevent feelings of sadness and make you feel less alone. Watching how your work makes your community better can give you a sense of pride and fulfillment.

If you are out of work, volunteering can also help you get new skills to add to your resume. You may also meet new people who can help you network and find new job opportunities. Volunteering expands your life in ways that may surprise you. You may discover new abilities or find new interests.

Some places you can volunteer are:

- Senior living centers and nursing homes
- Humane societies
- Homeless shelters
- Food banks
- Local churches
- Reentry Programs

Call or visit these places to ask how you can help. You can also do a Google search for volunteer opportunities in your community. See the Resources Directory for more ideas.

———— 🙶 ————

"Don't give up. Do what you can to promote change. Take the time out to try to mentor some of these young people that are out here in the hopes that, one day, we can bring about changes. Instead of wondering when somebody else is gonna do something about it, I need to remember that I'm somebody and try to do what I can." – Anonymous

———— 🙷 ————

Part 5: County Specific Resource Directory

(This edition of the reentry guide is tailored specifically for individuals reintegrating into King County, and as such, the resource directory provided herein is primarily focused on King County.)

King County Resource Directory

Housing Resources - Transitional Reentry Housing

Name	Website	Contact	Description
2nd Chance Recovery House	N/A	(206) 229-0473	Men's transitional housing. Clean & Sober. DOC Approved. Non-S/O. Located in Auburn, WA.
AAHAA Sober Living	https://aahaasupportivehousing.com/	(253) 735-0665 | mark@aahaasupportivehousing.com	Coed transitional housing. Clean & Sober. Doc Approved. Non-S/O.
Ark House Ministries	https://arkhouseministries.com/	(206) 556-3165 | arkhouseministries1@gmail.com | 9456 13th Ave SW, Seattle, WA 98106	Faith-based transitional housing for men in reentry. DOC Approved. Non-S/O.
Arms Around You	https://www.armsaroundyou.org/	(206) 629-6405 | armsaroundyou.org@gmail.com | 506 2nd Avenue, Ste 1400, Seattle, WA 98104	Women's transitional housing for those in reentry. DOC Approved. Non-S/O.
Cheryl Bolton Housing	N/A	(206) 335-1685	Men's transitional housing. DOC Approved. S/O 1 & 2 Housing available.
Chief Seattle Club	https://www.chiefseattleclub.org/reentry	Front Desk: 206-715-7536 (7 AM - 2 PM Daily) | reentry@chiefseattleclub.org | 410 - Second Ave Extension S. Seattle, WA 98104	Welcome Home House - Men's transitional housing for those of Native American descent in reentry.
Communities of Belonging	https://communitiesofbelonging.org/	(206) 605-5351 | housing@communitiesofbelonging.org | 4701 SW Admiral Way, #172, Seattle, WA 98116	Men's transitional housing. DOC Approved. S/O Housing available. LGBTQ+ friendly.
Emanuel	N/A	(206) 498-1228 |	Faith-based men's transitional

Discipleship Ministries		setfreefee@gmail.com	housing, Clean & Sober. DOC Approved. Non-S/O. Located in Federal Way.
Fresh Start Housing	http://www.freshstarthousing.org/	(425) 780-3976 | freshstart_housing@yahoo.com | 4005 Rainier Ave. S., Seattle, WA 98118 (Seattle House)	Men's transitional housing. DOC Approved. S/O 1 & 2 housing available.
House of Mercy Ministries	http://houseofmercyministries.net	(206) 651-7840 | office@hom.church | 930 S. 336th St, Ste F, Federal Way, WA 98003 |	Faith-based men's transitional housing. Clean & Sober. 17 locations available in King County. S/O and non-S/O housing available. DOC Approved.
Jesus is God Ministries	https://www.jesusisgodministry.com/	(253) 362-3682 | 1814 S 266th Place Des Moines, WA. 98198	Faith-based transitional housing. ADA Accessibility. S/O housing available. DOC Approved.
Kate's House	https://kateshousefoundation.org/	(206) 743-5649	Two transitional houses located in Seattle, one male house and one female house. Clean & Sober. DOC Approved. Non-S/O.
One Nation Essential Needs Foundation:	https://www.onenfoundation.org/	(206) 852-4749 | clintonsaun@gmail.com | 6727 Rainier Ave S. #112, Seattle, WA, 98118 |	Coed transitional housing. Two locations available in King County. Clean & Sober. DOC Approved. Non-S/O.
Open Arms Services	N/A	(206) 841-4499	Men's transitional housing. Two locations in Seattle. Clean & Sober. DOC Approved. Non-S/O.
Oxford House Reentry	http://wa.oxfordhouse.us/docs/reentry.pdf	PO Box 27394 Seattle, WA 98165	There are 13 Oxford Houses in King County that are DOC approved. Write to them for a list of houses and an application.
Passage Point, YWCA	https://www.ywcaworks.org/locations/passage-point	(425) 270-6649 | 15900 227th Ave SE Maple Valley, WA 98038	Coed transitional housing for those with children. Clean & Sober. DOC Approved. Non-S/O.
Redwood Ministries	https://redwoodministry.org/	(206) 823-6362	Men's transitional housing. Two locations in King County. Clean & Sober. One location is wheelchair accessible. DOC Approved. S/O 1 & 2 housing available.
The Journey Project	https://www.thejourneyproject.info/	(206) 856-3125 | transition@thejourneyproject.info | 13504 Tukwila International Blvd, Tukwila, WA	Men's transitional housing. DOC Approved. S/O Housing available. LGBTQ+ friendly.

Trinity Housing	https://www.worldchangersnonprofit.org/services-4	(206) 413-0307 | anthonybaxter@worldchangersnonprofit.org | P.O. Box 98841 Des Moines, WA 98195	Men's transitional housing. Clean & Sober. DOC Approved. S/O 1-3 housing available.
WELD Seattle	https://www.weldseattle.org/	(206) 717-4687 | info@weldseattle.org | 1426 South Jackson Street, Seattle, WA 98144	Coed transitional reentry housing. Multiple houses in Seattle. Clean & Sober. Non-S/O.
Housing Resources - Emergency Housing			
Aloha Inn	https://ccsww.org/get-help/shelter-homeless-services/the-inn/	(206) 283-6070 | 1911 Aurora Avenue North Seattle, WA 98109	The Inn is a 24/7 enhanced shelter and related services for adults experiencing homelessness. This is a low barrier, harm reduction program. Services available include: Housing Counseling: Assistance in locating and applying for low-income, permanent housing. Counseling: Personal Counseling with a therapist offsite. Drug and Alcohol recovery support: Education and counseling groups and individual sessions onsite. Computer Lab: Drop in lab for resident use. Applications are received through referring partners.
Auburn Food Bank's Sundown Shelter	https://www.theauburnfoodbank.org/homeless	253-833-8925 | 2810 Auburn Way North, Auburn, WA 98002	Coordinates intake for a 45-bed shelter program for adults of all genders in the Auburn area.
Bread of Life Mission Men's Shelter	https://www.breadoflifemission.org/	206-682-3579 | 97 South Main Street, Seattle, WA 98104	Provides shelter for homeless men ages 18 and older; $5 per night, with two free nights per year; in-person pre-registration required. Registration is usually full by lunchtime.
Catholic Community Services Shelter and Homeless Services	https://ccsww.org/get-help/shelter-homeless-services/	(206) 328-5696 | 100 23rd Avenue S Seattle, WA 98144	Through day centers, emergency shelters and emergency services, we provide warm, safe refuge from the streets.
Compass Housing Alliance	https://www.compasshousingalliance.org/emergency-programs/	(206) 474-1000 | 210 Alaskan Way Seattle, WA	Enhanced non-congregate shelter model removes several barriers for people transitioning off the street by partnering overnight shelter with 24/7 on-site support services and intensive case management including housing navigation services. Blaine Center Men's Enhanced

			Shelter (downtown Seattle) Otto's Place Men's Shelter (downtown Seattle) Jan & Peter's Place Women's Shelter (Rainier)
Congregations for the Homeless	https://cfhomeless.org/shelter/	425-698-1295 | 13668 Southeast Eastgate Way, Bellevue, WA 98005	Provides year-round shelter for men ages 18 and older; no children. Men sleep in bunk beds. Services for clients also include showers, washer, dryer, case management, and a small storage locker. Register at Day Center. Those with severe medical vulnerabilities may be housed in a nearby hotel.
DESC Downtown Emergency Service Center	https://www.desc.org/what-we-do/survival-services/	(206) 464-1570 | 515 3rd Ave. Mary Pilgrim Inn — 14115 Aurora Ave. N The Gateway — 13300 Stone Ave. N (Seattle)	Call for latest updates on shelters and referral contact: (206) 464-1570
King County Regional Homelessness Authority	https://kcrha.org/regional-access-points/	Catholic Community Services – Seattle 100 23rd Ave. S., Seattle, WA 98144 206-328-5900 Multi-Service Center-Federal Way - 1200 S. 336th St., Federal Way, WA 98003 253-874-6718, then select Option 4 for the MSC Regional Access Point. YWCA Renton - 1010 S. 2nd St., Renton, WA 98057 425-523-1377 Solid Ground – North Seattle - 1501 N. 45th Street Seattle, WA 98103 (206) 694-6833 Catholic Community Services – Bellevue - The Salt House at Kirkland 11920 NE 80th St #100 Kirkland, WA 98033 Next to the New Bethlehem Shelter in Kirkland (206) 328-5900	The purpose of Coordinated Entry (CE) is to ensure that people experiencing homelessness have equitable access to housing resource connections to resolve their housing crisis.

Mary's Place Family Shelters	https://www.marysplaceseattle.org/get-help/shelters	206-245-1026 | info@marysplaceseattle.org | 3190 Martin Luther King Jr Way S, Seattle	Family shelters are 24/7 facilities that provide shelter for moms, dads, and children at night, and resources for housing, employment, and wellness each day. Local service providers are on site to make it easy for families to get the services they need.
REACH Center of Hope	https://reachrenton.org/center-of-hope	425-277-7594 | 7465 South 112th Street, Lakeridge Lutheran Church, Seattle, WA 98178	Provides intake for overnight shelter for families.Emergency Family Intake Line at 206-245-1026 to register and get started for shelter.
Salvation Army's NW William Booth Center - Enhanced Shelter Program	https://northwest.salvationarmy.org/	206-621-0145 | 811 Maynard Ave S, Seattle, WA 98134	Operates contracted shelter for homeless men, ages 18 and older; REFERRAL REQUIRED from FareStart, VA Hospital or King County Veterans' Program.
Salvation Army's Social Services Department in Seattle - Women's Shelter	https://northwest.salvationarmy.org/	206-338-5707 | 1101 Pike Street, Seattle, WA 98101	Provides shelter for single women. Length of stay is up to 90 days with possibility of extension; provides case management and support.
Seattle Indian Center's Inn at Roy Street Men's Shelter	https://seattleindiancenter.org/programs	206-329-8700 | 157 Roy Street, Seattle, WA 98109	Provides a nightly shelter for men ages 18 and older; includes breakfast and shower facilities. Register first at Drop-In Center on Dearborn Street. Expands capacity during severe weather. A few extra emergency beds are available during adverse weather.
Sophia's Way	https://sophiaway.org/sophia-place/	425-896-7385 | 3032 Bellevue Way Northeast, Bellevue, WA 98004	Provides a six-month shelter program for 21 women focused on case management and helping women move to transitional, supportive or permanent housing. Service animals permitted.Shelter intake line: (425) 598-2608
Union Gospel Mission Seattle	https://www.ugm.org/what-we-do/stabilization/	(206) 501-4357 | getHELP@ugm.org | 3800 South Othello Street Seattle, WA 98118	Men's Shelter, Hope Place for Women & Children, and KentHOPE Day Center for Women.
YWCA Seattle King Snohomish's Angeline's Center for Homeless Women	https://www.ywcaworks.org/programs	206-436-8650 | 2030 3rd Ave, YWCA Opportunity Place, Seattle, WA 98121	Operates nightly shelter for homeless women, ages 18 and older; includes intensive case management; no maximum length of stay; specifically designed for clients working toward stability and permanent housing.

Housing Resources - Supportive Housing & Housing Services			
Attain Housing	https://www.attainhousing.org/our-services/transitional-housing/	(425) 576-9531 | 125 State St. S Kirkland, WA 98033	Transitional housing and other supportive services for East King County for families with minor children. Must be referred by Regional Access Point, Catholic Community Services in Bellevue, by appointment only. Call (206) 328-5900 for an appointment, no drop-ins.
Bellwether Housing	https://www.bellwetherhousing.org/	(206) 623-0506 | 433 Minor Ave N, Seattle, WA	Permanent affordable rental housing. Find available apartments online, follow step-by-step guide to apply. Applicants must pay $35 and complete in-person appointment with Site Manager. More information about qualifications and income limits available online.
Catholic Housing Services	https://ccsww.org/get-help/housing/	(206) 328-5696 | 100 23rd Avenue S Seattle, WA 98144	Together, CCS and CHS provide a full spectrum of housing with 22 shelters, 17 transitional housing facilities and 52 permanent housing properties in Western Washington.
Chief Seattle Club	https://www.chiefseattleclub.org/permanent-housing	Front Desk: 206-715-7536 (7 AM - 2 PM Daily) | 410 - Second Ave Extension S. Seattle, WA 98104	Native-led agency providing basic needs and a day center, physically and spiritually supporting American Indian and Alaska Native people. Day Center in the Pioneer Square provides food, primary heath care, housing assistance, an urban Indian legal clinic, a Native art job training program, as well as frequent outings for members to cultural and community-building events.
Compass Housing Alliance	https://www.compasshousingalliance.org/affordable-housing/	(206) 474-1000 | applications@compasshousingalliance.org | 210 Alaskan Way Seattle, WA	Among their properties, they offer independent living for seniors, supportive housing for formerly homeless individuals, and affordable apartments for low-income and working-class households.
Community Roots Housing	https://communityrootshousing.org/find-apartment/	206-774-1600 | 1620 12th Avenue, suite 205, Seattle, WA 98122	Develops and maintains 45 properties of below-market and HUD-subsidized rental housing in Seattle; for moderate- to low-income families, couples and individuals.
DESC	https://www.desc.org/what-we-do/housing/	206-464-1570 | info@desc.org | 515 Third Avenue, Seattle, WA 98104	Today, DESC owns and manages 1,347 units of supportive housing throughout Seattle, and provides permanent supportive housing services to another 150 apartments in Keys to Home.

Housing and Essential Needs (HEN) – King County	https://ccsww.org/get-help/shelter-homeless-services/housing-and-essential-needs-hen/	(206) 328-5755 | Call or email for appointment henkc@ccsww.org | 100 23rd Ave S, Seattle, WA	Referral program through DSHS. Provides rent assistance, utility and transportation assistance, as well as hygiene and cleaning products. Serves adults (without minor children) who are unable to work due to a physical or mental incapacity. Program services are subject to funding availability and may be discontinued or reduced at any time. Call for more eligibility information and to determine if specific documents are required. No fees.
Housing Justice Project	https://www.kcba.org/?pg=Housing-Justice-Project	(206) 580-0762 | hjpstaff@kcba.org | King County Courthouse, 516 Third Ave., Room-W314	Providing free legal advice (legal consultations) for low-income renters with eviction related issues, answering questions about eviction paperwork, negotiating with landlords if you're a renter facing eviction, representing renters at courthouse eviction hearings (show cause hearings), sharing referral and resource information. Apply in person, online, call (206) 580-0762 to leave a message with staff or email at hjpstaff@kcba.org. Operated through King County Bar Association. For urgent issues please call 2-1-1.
Jubilee Women's Center	https://jwcenter.org/services/	206.324.1244 | apply@jwcenter.org | 620 18th Avenue East Seattle, WA, WA 98112	Offers a 2-year residential program for women; required technology and life skills classes. Case managers offer guidance and support as residents work toward a living-wage career and self-sufficiency. May have rooms available for pregnant women. Usually has a waitlist.
King County Housing Authority	https://www.kcha.org/	(206) 574-1100 | 600 Andover Park W Tukwila, WA	Rental housing and rental assistance. Provides subsidized housing and affordable housing; applications for Section 8 Housing Choice Vouchers in King County only
Low Income Housing Institute (LIHI)	https://www.lihihousing.org/housing	(206) 443-9935 | 1253 S Jackson St., Seattle, WA	All housing applications for LIHI properties are handled by the staff at the individual properties. Waiting list units are all rentals where rent is 30 percent of your household's monthly income. For wait-listed properties, fill out pre-application form. View website to see properties.
Mercy Housing Northwest	https://mercyhousing.org/northwest/	(206) 838-5700; See website or call for specific properties	Affordable housing for families, seniors and people with special needs. Each Mercy Housing

		and housing inquiries.	Multiple properties, see website.	property has its own leasing office and its own application process. Call the property directly for availability, requirements and how to apply.
Muslim Housing Services	http://www.muslim-housing.org/	(206) 723-1712	6727 Rainier Ave. S, Seattle, WA	Case management, homelessness prevention, transitional housing and rental assistance. Also offers food distribution, ESL for Arabic-speaking clients, furniture and household donations, school supplies, diaper distribution and youth soccer program. Serves refugees and second migration immigrants from East Africa, the Middle East, and other parts of Africa. Staff speaks multiple languages. Call for eligibility, application, and fee information. Services except food require ID and Social Security number to qualify.
Pioneer Human Services - Housing	https://pioneerhumanservices.org/housing/list?tid=5#0	(206) 768-1990	1733 Belmont Ave., Seattle, WA	Provides substance use disorder treatments, affordable housing, mental health counseling, job readiness training, and employment services. To apply call (206) 717-0240; email: housing@p-h-s.com; or visit in person.
Plymouth Housing	https://plymouthhousing.org/	(206) 374-9409 x139	rent@plymouthhousing.org	2113 3rd Ave., Seattle, WA	Provides permanent supportive housing for services tailored to each resident's individual needs, and may include: On-site nursing, medical care, behavioral health treatment, substance use treatment, hospice care, veterans counseling, family reunification, money management, community activities and outings. The first step for somebody seeking housing is to fill out a housing assessment at a Regional Access Point. In Seattle call (206) 328-5900 for appointment.
Seattle Housing Authority	https://www.seattlehousing.org/housing/sha-housing	(206) 615-3300	190 Queen Anne Ave. N, Seattle, WA	SHA provides long-term, low-income rental housing, such as conventional public housing and senior housing. Long waiting lists exist for all programs; no emergency housing. Preference given to applicants who are homeless and/or who have income at or below 30% of Area Median Income, but will consider those at or below 80%. Visit in person or visit the website to obtain an application. Once on a waiting list, check in

			monthly to confirm the need for housing. No fees for application.
Solid Ground - Housing Resources	https://www.solid-ground.org/get-help/housing/	(206) 694-6700 | 1501 N. 45th St., Seattle, WA	Solid Ground provides various housing program resources. Call (206) 299-2500 for Solid Ground's confidential Domestic Violence shelter services. Leave a voicemail at (206) 694-6833 for move-in cost assistance for people exiting homelessness. Other services available by referral through Coordinated Entry with 211. Whether you have lost your home and need shelter – or need support to stay in your current home – Solid Ground can connect you with information, resources and referrals to support your housing stability.
Tenants Union of Washington State	https://tenantsunion.org/	(206) 723-0500 | 5425 Rainier Ave. S, No. B, Seattle, WA	Phone hotline and walk-in service for tenants/renters. Informs and empowers tenants with the knowledge and skills needed to keep themselves and their families safely housed.

Housing Resources - Residential Recovery & Discipleship Programs

Acres of Diamonds - Compassion Transitional Houses	https://www.acresofdiamonds.org/	425-788-9999 | 26326 Northeast Kennedy Drive, Duvall, WA 98019	Provides Christian-based transitional housing for up to four households (single women and women with up to four children). Serves women transitioning away from addiction, domestic violence and other circumstances. Allows pets. NO REFERRAL NECESSARY.
Adult & Teen Challenge PNW - Seattle	https://teenchallengepnw.com/locations/seattle-metro-campus/	(877) 302-7149 | info.seattle@teenchallengepnw.com | 18611 148th Ave SE, Renton, WA 98058	Offers a low-cost Christian-based 12-month residential program assisting men with recovering from life-controlling addictions.
Conquest Unlimited	N/A	(206) 246-5263 | 4617 S 144th St, Tukwila, WA 98168	Operates a drug and alcohol sobriety house in South King County. Average stay is three to six months. DOC Approved.
Key Recovery and Life Skills Center	http://www.keyrecovery.org/our-services/	(206) 767-0244 | 10344 14th Ave S Seattle, WA 98168	Residential inpatient drug and alcohol treatment, focuses on individuals suffering from trauma and addiction. Programs include Long-Term Residential, Recovery House, After Care, and a program for residential treatment for families.
Multi-Service Center in Kent - Housing for	https://mschelps.org/gethelp/housing/recovery/	253-854-4406 | 24437 Russell Road, Suite 200, Kent, WA	Provides dormitory and apartment style housing, as well as case management, for women recovering

Women in Recovery		98032	from substance abuse and transitioning from a treatment facility. Must be below 30% of the area median income.
Pioneer Human Services' King County Housing Office - Clean and Sober Transitional Recovery Homes	https://pioneerhumanservices.org/housing	(206) 717-0240 | 1717 Belmont Avenue, Seattle, WA 98122	Provides drug- and alcohol-free transitional housing for those who have recently been incarcerated or in a treatment program for substance use disorder. Some locations accept families.
Praisealujah	https://praisealujah.org/	(253) 251-8971 | 20842 International Boulevard, Sea Tac, WA 98198	Provides a 6- to-12 month, faith-based treatment program. Open to adults of all genders.
Salvation Army, Adult Rehabilitation Program	https://seattlearp.salvationarmy.org/	(206) 587-0503 ext. 1 | 10750 Greenwood Ave. N	Offers a three-bridge approach that allows participants an intensive six-month in-patient recovery program, an additional two months of in-house work development, assistance finding a job, and an additional six months of independent living in the Adult Rehabilitation Program facility that provides a supportive sober community. All at no cost. Call program intake. Serves everyone, but Christian studies are offered as part of the program.
Sea Mar Community Health Center, Turning Point Adult Treatment Center	https://seamar.org/king-bh-turningpoint.html	(206) 219-5980 | 113 23rd Ave. S, Seattle, WA	Chemical Dependency Inpatient program specializes in service to Latino community, more than just a rehab facility; it is a leading provider of integrated and multidisciplinary health treatment. Provides clinically tailored, comprehensive and individualized treatment plans for each community member for a whole person approach, mind, body, and spirit.
Union Gospel Mission Seattle	https://www.ugm.org/what-we-do/recovery/	206-436-8650 | 2030 3rd Ave, YWCA Opportunity Place, Seattle, WA 98121	Our year-long, faith based recovery program helps men and women with counseling and relapse prevention curriculum.
Victory Outreach Church's Men's Home - Recovery Home for Men	N/A	206-781-1655	Provides Christian-oriented home for men leaving street life; requires 9-12 month commitment. NO REFERRAL NECESSARY.

ID Resources			
Washington State Dept. of Licensing - King County			
Name	Website	Contact	Description
Federal Way Driver Licensing Office	https://fortress.wa.gov/dol/dolprod/dsdoffices/OfficeInfo.aspx?cid=217&oid=32	253.661.5001 | 1617 S 324th St Federal Way, WA 98003-6004	<ul><li>Apply for a new driver license or instruction permit.</li><li>Get an ID card</li><li>Renew a driver license, ID card, or enhanced driver license/ID card (EDL/EID).</li><li>Change the name or address on your driver license.</li><li>Request a copy of your driving record.</li><li>Replace a lost or stolen driver license, ID card, or EDL/EID.</li><li>Apply for an enhanced driver license/ID card (EDL/EID).</li><li>No driver license testing or motorcycle testing.</li></ul>
Kent Driver Licensing Office	https://fortress.wa.gov/dol/dolprod/dsdoffices/OfficeInfo.aspx?cid=316&oid=26	253.872.2782 | 25410 74th Ave S Kent, WA 98032-6011	<ul><li>Apply for a new driver license or instruction permit.</li><li>Get an ID card</li><li>Renew a driver license, ID card, or enhanced driver license/ID card (EDL/EID).</li><li>Change the name or address on your driver license.</li><li>Request a copy of your driving record.</li><li>Replace a lost or stolen driver license, ID card, or EDL/EID.</li><li>Apply for an enhanced driver license/ID card (EDL/EID).</li><li>No driver license testing or motorcycle testing.</li></ul>
North Bend Driver Licensing Office	https://fortress.wa.gov/dol/dolprod/dsdoffices/OfficeInfo.aspx?cid=452&oid=28	425.888.4036 | 402 Main Ave S, Ste 11 North Bend, WA 98045	<ul><li>Apply for a new driver license or instruction permit.</li><li>Get an ID card</li><li>Renew a driver license, ID card, or enhanced driver license/ID card (EDL/EID).</li><li>Change the name or address on your driver license.</li><li>Request a copy of your driving record.</li></ul>

			• Replace a lost or stolen driver license, ID card, or EDL/EID. • Apply for an enhanced driver license/ID card (EDL/EID). • Driver license testing.
Redmond Driver Licensing Office	https://fortress.wa.gov/dol/dolprod/dsdoffices/OfficeInfo.aspx?cid=45&oid=23	425.649.4281 | 7225 170th Ave NE Redmond, WA 98052	• Apply for a new driver license or instruction permit. • Get an ID card • Renew a driver license, ID card, or enhanced driver license/ID card (EDL/EID). • Change the name or address on your driver license. • Replace a lost or stolen driver license, ID card, or EDL/EID. • Apply for an enhanced driver license/ID card (EDL/EID). • No driver license testing or motorcycle testing.
Seattle-Queen Anne Driver Licensing Office	https://fortress.wa.gov/dol/dolprod/dsdoffices/OfficeInfo.aspx?cid=583&oid=24	206.464.6845 | 450 3rd Ave W Suite 100 Seattle, WA 98119	• Apply for a new driver license or instruction permit. • Get an ID card • Renew a driver license, ID card, or enhanced driver license/ID card (EDL/EID). • Change the name or address on your driver license. • Request a copy of your driving record. • Replace a lost or stolen driver license, ID card, or EDL/EID. • Apply for an enhanced driver license/ID card (EDL/EID).
Seattle-West Driver Licensing Office	https://fortress.wa.gov/dol/dolprod/dsdoffices/OfficeInfo.aspx?cid=583&oid=30	206.764.4144 | 8830 25th Ave SW Seattle, WA 98106-3237	• Apply for a new driver license or instruction permit. • Get an ID card • Renew a driver license, ID card, or enhanced driver license/ID card (EDL/EID). • Change the name or address on your driver license. • Request a copy of your driving record. • Replace a lost or stolen driver license, ID card, or EDL/EID.

			• Apply for an enhanced driver license/ID card (EDL/EID). • No driver license testing or motorcycle testing.
Shoreline Driver Licensing Office	https://fortress.wa.gov/dol/dolprod/dsdoffices/OfficeInfo.aspx?cid=594&oid=22	425-670-8375 | 15809 Westminster Way N Shoreline, WA 98133	• Apply for a new driver license or instruction permit. • Get an ID card • Renew a driver license, ID card, or enhanced driver license/ID card (EDL/EID). • Change the name or address on your driver license. • Request a copy of your driving record. • Replace a lost or stolen driver license, ID card, or EDL/EID. • Apply for an enhanced driver license/ID card (EDL/EID).
Social Security Administration - King County			
Bellevue Office	www.ssa.gov	(800) 325-0778 | 636 120th Ave NE Ste 100, Bellevue, WA 98005	Get your Social Security Card
Burien Office	www.ssa.gov	(800) 772-1213 | 151 SW 156th St, Burien, WA 98166	Get your Social Security Card
Kent Office	www.ssa.gov	(800) 772-1213 | 321 Ramsay Way Ste 401, Kent, WA 98032	Get your Social Security Card
Seattle Office	www.ssa.gov	(866) 494-3135 | 915 2nd Ave Ste 901, Seattle, WA 98174	Get your Social Security Card
King County			
King County Vital Records Office	https://kingcounty.gov/en/dept/dph/certificates-permits-licenses/order-birth-certificate	(206) 837-0719 | 201 S Jackson St. Suite 220, Seattle, WA 98104	Order a birth certificate for someone born in King County or Washington state. 2nd floor in the East Lobby, open from 8:30 am to 4:30 pm.
WADOC, Reentry, and Advocacy Resources - King County			
WADOC			
Community Justice Center	https://doc.wa.gov/corrections/community/justice-centers/locations.htm#seattle	(206) 516-7600 | 1550 - 4th Ave. S. Seattle, WA 98134	A community justice center is a nonresidential facility staffed primarily by the department in which recently released individuals may

			access services necessary to improve their successful reentry into the community.
Auburn & Federal Way Office	https://doc.wa.gov/corrections/community/field-offices.htm#King	Auburn: (253) 333-5959 Federal Way: (253) 372-6470 | 2707 I St. NE, Suite A, Auburn, WA 98002	Community Field Office. Used for staff, programming and as places for individuals under community supervision to report.
Bellevue Office	https://doc.wa.gov/corrections/community/field-offices.htm#King	(425) 649-4331 | 23 148th Ave. SE Bellevue, WA 98007	Community Field Office. Used for staff, programming and as places for individuals under community supervision to report.
Burien Office	https://doc.wa.gov/corrections/community/field-offices.htm#King	(206) 835-7460 | 15111 8th Ave. SW, Suite 202 Seattle, WA 98166	Community Field Office. Used for staff, programming and as places for individuals under community supervision to report.
Kent & Renton Office	https://doc.wa.gov/corrections/community/field-offices.htm#King	Kent (253) 372-6440 Renton (253) 372-6470 | 1404 Central Ave S., Suite 101 Kent, WA 98032	Community Field Office. Used for staff, programming and as places for individuals under community supervision to report.
King County Administrative Unit, Special Assault Unit, Special Needs Unit, Seattle Metro Unit, S.E. Seattle Unit	https://doc.wa.gov/corrections/community/field-offices.htm#King	(206) 516-7600 | 1550 4th Ave. S Seattle, WA 98134-1510	Community Field Office. Used for staff, programming and as places for individuals under community supervision to report.
Northgate Office	https://doc.wa.gov/corrections/community/field-offices.htm#King	(206) 729-3326 | 9620 Stone Ave. N #102 Seattle, WA 98103	Community Field Office. Used for staff, programming and as places for individuals under community supervision to report.
West Seattle Office	https://doc.wa.gov/corrections/community/field-offices.htm#King	(206) 933-3402 | 6335 35th Ave. SW Seattle, WA 98126	Community Field Office. Used for staff, programming and as places for individuals under community supervision to report.
Reentry Housing Assistance Program - Section 5 King County	https://doc.wa.gov/docs/publications/400-BR012.pdf	(206) 423-2351 (206) 678-2673	Referrals for housing vouchers are made by the individual's case manager by submitting DOC Form 02-336. For ERD and Reentry Housing Vouchers referrals can be submitted 60 days prior to the individuals earned release date or once found releasable by the Indeterminate Sentence Review Board. For GRE and FOSA/CPA Housing Assistance, referrals can be submitted once approved for placement.

Reentry Programs & Resources			
Arms Around You Reentry Resources	https://www.armsaroundyou.org/	(206) 629-6405 | 506 2nd Avenue, Ste. 1400, Seattle, WA 98104	Provides re-entry support and navigation to a host of resources for those that are formerly incarcerated.
Bellevue College - Justice Involved Program	https://www.bellevuecollege.edu/mcs/justice-involve-returning-citizens-post-prison-education-program/	(425) 564-2423 | 3000 Landerholm Circle Southeast, Bellevue, WA 98007	Helps formerly incarcerated people transition successfully into college. Connects students to essential services. Provides supportive guidance as students make progress through their academic journey, and successfully exit into the labor force.
Chief Seattle Club - Drop-In Services	https://www.chiefseattleclub.org/reentry	206-715-7536 | 410 2nd Avenue Extension South, Seattle, WA 98104	Provides drop-in support services for adult American Indians and Alaska Natives, including clothing, nursing, health care, mental health, cultural programming, art programming, housing case management, DSHS support, and referrals to drug and alcohol counseling.
Divine Alternatives for Dads Services (DADS)	https://www.aboutdads.org/services	(206) 722-3137 | 411 12th Ave, Suite 300 Seattle, WA 98122	Help with Child Support. Help with a Parenting Plan. Navigating legal & relational barriers. Connecting with other Fathers. Becoming Dads Course. Support Groups.
Freedom Project - Reentry Support	https://freedomprojectwa.org/reentry-support/	(206) 460-2786 | reentry@freedomprojectwa.org | 227 ½ Wells Ave S Renton, WA 98057	Personal one-on-one support from someone who understands reentry in ways only we understand. Get help finding resources – like clothing, transportation, housing – from someone with lived experience who understands the barriers and needs.Inside Out Toastmasters.
Fresh Start Professional Services	https://freshstartps.org/	(206) 945-0686 | freshstartps.info@gmail.com | 1404 E Yesler Way #204, Seattle, WA 98112	Reentry/Transitional Strategy. Planning. Mentoring. Critical Thinking. Family/Children. Banking/Budgeting. Housing Choices (Transitional vs Permanent). Resources (Community). Educational/Occupational. Peer Engagement & Influence
House of Mercy Ministries - H.O.M.E. Reentry Program	http://houseofmercyministries.net	(206) 651-7840 | office@hom.church | 930 S. 336th St, Ste F, Federal Way, WA 98003 |	Comprehensive, faith-based reentry program that offers housing, case management, referral services, DSHS support, transportation services, basic needs, life skills classes, CBD program, digital equity program, peer-to-peer support, employment facilitation, workforce development, and discipleship program.

Interaction Transition		(206) 228-4639 | it@interactiontransiti on.org | 5300 4th Ave S, Seattle, WA 98108	Assists formerly incarcerated individuals in the reentry process and finding employment in areas such as warehouse, manufacturing, recycling, and auto-work. Must be 18 years of age and able to legally work in the U.S. No fees. Organization does not require ID, but employers likely will. Call or email for more information or to schedule an appointment.
Pioneer Human Services - (Reentry Resources)	www.pioneerhumanservices.org	(206) 768-1990 | Pioneertraining@p-h-s.com | 7440 West Marginal Way S. Seattle, WA 98108	Counseling. Treatment. Housing. Job Skills. Roadmap to Success Program.
Renton Technical College - Reentry Services	https://rtc.edu/re-entry-services	Contact: Gerald Bradford: 425-235-2352 x 5733 | reentry@rtc.edu | 3000 NE 4th St. Renton, WA 98056	Contact the Re-Entry Adviser for assistance with: Wraparound services. Pursuing higher education. Apprenticeship programs. Child support. Release planning and transition services. Resume and cover letter development.
Seattle Central College, Re-Entry Support Programs	https://seattlecentral.edu/campus-life/student-support-and-services/re-entry-support	206.934.4018 | Maria.Kang@seattlec olleges.edu | 1701 Broadway, BE3215 Seattle WA 98122	Provides services to refer reentry students to campus and community-based resources and partners specific to the variety of needs including housing, employment, clothing, personal finances and scholarship information. Safe space for peer-to-peer support, helps students with enrollment, registration, financial-aid.
Seattle Clemency Project	https://www.seattleclemencyproj ect.org/reentrysupport	206-682-1114 | info@seattleclemenc yproject.org | 20415 72nd Ave South, Suite 1-415, Kent, WA 98032	The Reentry & Mentoring Program provides Seattle Clemency Project clients with holistic reentry and transition support to promote their long-term success.
Seattle Public Library, Central Branch, Resources for the Formerly Incarcerated	https://www.spl.org/programs-an d-services/civics-and-social-servi ces/resources-for-the-formerly-in carcerated	206-386-4636 | 1000 Fourth Ave. Seattle, WA 98104-1109	Along with local organizations, we offer court-involved individuals, and their families, information and resources to help during and after incarceration. Free job search and career development programs are offered at the Central Library and Rainier Beach branch. Learn basic technology skills, how to use the Web, Microsoft Office programs and more. One-on-one, walk-in tutoring to help learners with test preparation, job readiness and life skills.

Sound Kent Clinic - Adult Services	https://www.sound.health/blog/programs/forensics-also-known-as-re-entry/	206-901-2000 | 841 Central Avenue North, #C-114, Kent, WA 98032	Provides assessment and short and long-term mental health services for King County residents experiencing current mental health symptoms. Offers re-entry services for those involved with the criminal justice system.
South Seattle College Justice Involved Solutions	https://southseattle.edu/programs/justice-involved-solutions	206.934.5206 | reentry.south@seattlecolleges.edu | 6000 16th Avenue SW Seattle, WA 98106	Provides services to refer reentry students to campus and community-based resources and partners specific to the variety of needs including housing, employment, clothing, personal finances and scholarship information. Safe space for peer-to-peer support, helps students with enrollment, registration, financial-aid.
The Journey Project	https://www.thejourneyproject.info/	(206) 856-3125 | transition@thejourneyproject.info | 13504 Tukwila International Blvd, Tukwila, WA	Housing. Case management. Life Skills Classes. Vocational Skills Training. Work Skills Training. Host of the Reentry Symposium. LGBTQ+ friendly.
Urban League of Metropolitan Seattle (ULMS)	https://urbanleague.org/	206-461-3792 | 105 14th Ave, Suite 200, Seattle, WA 98122	Housing. Workforce Development. Health. Entrepreneurship. Education. Advocacy. ULMS offers many services to those in reentry.
Weld Seattle	https://www.weldseattle.org/	(206) 567-9030 | 1426 South Jackson Seattle, WA	Services include housing, employment, peer support, community, and resources. Weld offers safe, dignified, clean and sober housing for people returning home from prison and those in recovery from addiction. Housing members are expected to be actively engaged in their reentry. They work, they volunteer, and they attend community meetings. Weld is a 501(C)3 nonprofit organization whose mission is to equip system-impacted individuals with housing, employment, and resources conducive to recovery and successful reintegration back into society.
WSDVA Reentry Program for Vets	https://dva.wa.gov/veterans-service-members-and-their-families/veterans-benefits/reentry-program-vet-court	Program Specialist (360) 725-2229 | timothy.koerschgen@dva.wa.gov | PO Box 41155, Olympia, WA 98504-1150 (206) 454-2799 | WDVA King County Veterans Programs Belltown Center	Re-entry and in-reach services for veterans who are currently incarcerated or exiting incarceration. Veteran benefits (applying for Service Connected Compensation, Non-Service Connected Pension, Social Security, and discharge upgrades) Military Family Outreach (working with veterans or current service members and their families and

184

		2106 2nd Ave Suite 100, Seattle, WA 98121	outreach services for veterans who are battling homelessness).
Advocacy Programs & Resources			
ACLU Washington	https://www.aclu-wa.org/	(206) 624-2180 | 705 2nd Ave Ste 300, Seattle, WA 98104	The ACLU of Washington is a non-partisan civil liberties organization dedicated to protecting and advancing freedom, equity, and justice for everyone in Washington.
Black Prisoners' Caucus	https://www.blackprisonerscaucus.org/	206-937-2701 | Black Prisoners' Caucus c/o Village of Hope PO Box 46485 Seattle, WA 98146	Mission: To promote cultural growth and provide incarcerated men and women the tools and platform to confront social issues that perpetuate discrimination, inequality, and oppression among prisoners and poor communities of color.
Columbia Legal Services	https://columbialegal.org/	(206) 464-5911 | 1301 5th Ave, Ste 1200, Seattle, WA 98101	Provides legal representation and advocacy for low-income individuals, including those involved in the criminal justice system.
Disability Rights Washington	https://www.disabilityrightswa.org/publications/reentry-resources-currently-and-formerly-incarcerated-individuals-disabilities-king-county/	(800) 562-2702 or (206) 324-1521; Language interpreters are available upon request. Please use 711 for Washington Relay Service (TTY). Collect calls from correctional facilities are accepted | info@dr-wa.org | 315 5th Ave S, Ste 850 Seattle, WA 98104	Disability Rights Washington provides free services to people with disabilities. They are a private non-profit organization that protects the rights of people with disabilities statewide. Their mission is to advance the dignity, equality, and self-determination of people with disabilities. We pursue justice on matters related to human and legal rights.
El Centro de la Raza	https://www.elcentrodelaraza.org/	(206) 957-4634 | 1607 S 341st Pl, Federal Way, Wa 98003	Builds community through unifying all racial and economic sectors; to organize, empower, and defend the basic human rights of our most vulnerable and marginalized populations; and to bring critical consciousness, justice, dignity, and equity to all the peoples of the world.
Financial Empowerment Network	https://www.fenwa.org/	360-830-6190 | 12819 SE 38th St, Bellevue, WA 98006	Financial Empowerment Network advances financial empowerment through partnerships that support access to affordable, effective, and relevant services, products, and other resources.
Freedom Education Justice Project	https://www.fepps.org/	(206) 729-2480 | learn@fepps.org | 918 S Horton St	FEPPS provides a rigorous college program for incarcerated women, trans-identified and gender

		#912, Seattle WA 98134	nonconforming people in Washington and creates pathways to higher education after students are released from prison.
The If Project	https://www.theifproject.org/	(425) 281-1142 | 6523 California Ave SW, Seattle, WA 98136	The IF Project is a collaboration of currently- and formerly-incarcerated adults, community partners, and law enforcement focused on holistic intervention and the reduction and prevention of incarceration and recidivism. Their work is inspired by and built upon people sharing their personal life experiences around incarceration.
King County Bar Association, The Records Project	https://www.kcba.org/?pg=The-Records-Project	(206) 267-7028 | 1200 5th Ave., No. 700, Seattle, WA	The Records Project provides free legal services to vacate eligible King County criminal convictions. A vacated conviction is removed from public background searches available to employers and potential landlords. Eligible persons include low-income people, homeless people, and immigrants (regardless of immigration status).
Northwest Immigrant Rights Project	https://nwirp.org/	206.587.4009 | 615 2nd Avenue, Suite 400 Seattle, WA 98104	Northwest Immigrant Rights Project promotes justice by defending and advancing the rights of immigrants through direct legal services, systemic advocacy, and community education.
Northwest Justice Project	https://nwjustice.org/home	206-464-1519 | 401 Second Avenue S, Suite 407 Seattle, WA 98104	Offers free legal services to low-income individuals, including assistance with criminal law matters
Peer Seattle	https://www.peerseattle.org/	(206) 322-2437 | 1520 Bellevue Ave, Seattle, WA 98122	Peer Seattle cultivates powerful, healthy lives by providing peer emotional support and development services to the LGBTQ community impacted by addiction, mental health and/or HIV.
POCAAN - Curb	https://www.pocaan.org/curb	(206) 322-7061 | autry@pocaan.org | 4437 Rainier Ave. S, Seattle, WA	Communities Uniting Rainier Valley and Beyond (CURB) provides systems navigation and trauma intervention activities for individuals harmed by the criminal legal system in Seattle who are between the ages of 18 to 24. Particularly for BIPOC (Black, Indigenous, People of Color) and LGBTQ.
Seattle Clemency Project	https://www.seattleclemencyproject.org/	206-682-1114 | info@seattleclemencyproject.org | 20415 72nd Ave South, Suite 1-415, Kent,	Seattle Clemency Project's mission is to increase access to justice for reformed individuals serving sentences that no longer serve a purpose and to prevent deportations

		WA 98032	that fracture our communities. They do this by matching their clients with free, high-quality, legal representation, afterward providing holistic reentry and transition support to promote their long-term success.
Seattle Office for Civil Rights	https://seattle.gov/civilrights/what-we-do	(206) 684-4500 | civilrights@seattle.gov | 810 3rd Ave., No. 750, Seattle, WA	Investigates civil rights discrimination and enforces laws against illegal discrimination in employment, housing, public accommodation, and contracting within Seattle City Limits. No fees.
Somali Community Services of Seattle	Somali Community Services of Seattle | SOMCSS	(206) 760-1181 | somcss@yahoo.com | 8810 Renton Ave. S, Seattle, WA 98118	Support refugees to undergo a smooth transitional process. Family and youth programs, housing referrals, senior programs including ethnic lunches, peer counseling, job search assistance, ESL classes, computer classes, Somali language classes and parenting education classes. Case managers can assist with the immigration process. Primarily serves refugees and immigrants. Call or visit in person. No fees. Need to have state ID, passport, green card or other identification.
YWCA Seattle | King | Snohomish	https://www.ywcaworks.org/	206-461-4888 | 1118 Fifth Ave, Seattle, WA 98101	YWCA works where we're needed most with people who face the greatest barriers to safety, stability, and opportunity. Racial and gender equity is at the center of our work to eliminate disparities in the most critical areas of people's lives.
Health, Mental Health, and Substance Use Resources - King County			
Asian Counseling and Referral Service, Health and Wellness	https://acrs.org/services/behavioral-health-and-wellness/	(206) 695-7511 | mhintake@acrs.org | 919 S King St, Seattle, WA	Primary care, acupuncture and Eastern practices, psychiatric services, medication management, substance abuse support, youth mental health, gambling treatment, and other health services offered. Also offers housing assistance and supported employment for people already enrolled in the mental health program.
Atlantic Street Center, Main Office	https://atlanticstreetcenter.org/	(206) 329-2050 | ascinfo@atlanticstreet.org | 2103 S. Atlantic St Seattle, WA 98144	The main office site focuses on resources for behavioral health and gender-based violence. Mental health services for those ages six through twenty-four. Primarily serving communities of color including African Americans, immigrants, and refugees, with the vast majority classified as low- and

			very low-income. Direct services include homelessness prevention, case management, therapy, education support, and domestic violence services.
Catholic Community Services, Pregnancy & Parenting Support (PREPARES)	https://ccsww.org/get-help/child-youth-family-services/	(206) 737-9264 | 100 23rd Ave. S, Seattle, WA	Counseling, case management, education, emergency assistance and material support for women and families with children 5 years and younger. Does not provide medical referrals. Call for phone intake. Interpreter services available by appointment only. No fees.
Cedar River Clinics	https://cedarriverclinics.org/seattle/	(800) 572-4223 | 509 Olive Way, #1454 Seattle, WA 98101 | Renton 601 S Carr Road Suite 200, Renton, WA 98055	Offers health care such as cancer screenings, STD testing and treatment, & HIV Testing. Offers transgender services such as hormone therapy, surgical referrals for gender reassignment, breast and cosmetic surgeries, post-surgical follow up and ID documentation. Serves clients identifying as LGBTQ. Call for more information or to make an appointment. Sliding scale fees. Accepts Apple Health (Medicaid) and most insurance plans. Documents required: Photo ID. Seattle location is telehealth only.
Chief Seattle Club	https://www.chiefseattleclub.org/	(206) 715–7536 | 410 - 2nd Ave Extension S Seattle, WA	Native-led agency providing basic needs and a day center, physically and spiritually supporting American Indian and Alaska Native people. Day Center in the Pioneer Square provides food, primary heath care, housing assistance, an urban Indian legal clinic, a Native art job training program, as well as frequent outings for members to cultural and community-building events.
Community Health Access Program (CHAP) - King County		1-800-756-5437 | (206) 284-0331 | chap@kingcounty.gov | Public Health — Seattle & King County; 401 5th Avenue, Suite 1000 Seattle, WA	CHAP is a telephone assistance program serving King County residents. Service enrolls people into health insurance, ORCA LIFT transportation, basic food, and other public benefit programs. Services are free and confidential. Equal access to health care regardless of income, ethnicity, language, or immigration status. Interpreters are available.
Community Living Connections		(206) 962-8467 | (844) 348-5464 | (toll-free) | info@communitylivingconnections.org	Phone line connecting social services for older adults, adults with disabilities, and their caregivers. Individual consultation, help planning for long-term care needs.

			Assistance accessing community resources such as: Medicaid, State and federal benefits, nutrition programs, family caregiver programs, kinship care, care coordination, minor home repair, transportation, more. Caregivers may qualify for caregiver support services. Other languages also available. Servicios ofrecidos en español.
Consejo Counseling and Referral Services	https://consejocounseling.org/our-locations/	(206) 461-4880 | 8615 14th Ave. South, Seattle, WA 98108 Additional locations in King County: Renton, Kent, Lake City, and Bellevue	Provides transitional housing program, domestic violence program, sexual assault program, children, youth and family services, mental health, substance use disorder treatment, and complementary medicine program and primary care. Primarily serves Spanish-speaking population. Call for intake.
Country Doctor Community Health Center/Dental	https://cdchc.org/ http://countrydoctor.org/dental	(206) 299-1600 | 500 19th Ave. E, Seattle, WA | (206) 299-1611 | 510 19th Ave. E, Seattle, WA	Provides health services for everyone. Interpretation services are immediately available. Offers full range of primary care services and the convenience of an on-site pharmacy. Offers prenatal and pregnancy care. Sliding scale fees. Accepts Medicare, Apple Health (Medicaid) insurance and uninsured patients. No one will be turned away due to inability to pay. Daytime appointments.
Country Doctor, After Hours Clinic	http://cdchc.org/clinic/after-hours-clinic/	(206) 709-7199 | 2101 E Yesler Way No.150, Seattle, WA 98122	After hours no appointment necessary, walk-ins welcome. Comprehensive health services and an after-hours clinic. Serves everyone. Interpretation services are immediately available. Offers full range of primary care services and the convenience of an on-site pharmacy. Offers prenatal and pregnancy care. Sliding scale fees. Accepts Medicare, Apple Health (Medicaid) insurance and uninsured patients. No one will be turned away due to inability to pay.
CReW (Counseling, Recovery, and Wellness) Program	https://ccsww.org/get-help/mental-health-services/crew-program/	Seattle/Eastside: Tasha Pharr, Access Specialist 206-956-9570 | South King County: Sharlene Insong, Psychiatric Care Coordinator (253) 246-2435 | 1902 2nd Ave,	CReW provides licensed outpatient mental health and substance use treatment services in a variety of settings where people are living, in order to reduce some barriers to ongoing care. They seek to assist adults with mental health, substance use, or co-occurring challenges to improve their quality of life and achieve increasing levels

		Seattle WA 98101 11920 NE 80th St, Kirkland, 98033 | 1229 W Smith St, Kent WA 98032 33505 13th Place S, Federal Way WA 98003	of stability in recovery.
Crisis Connections	https://www.crisisconnections.org/king-county-2-1-1/	2-1-1 For assistance within King County: 1 (800) 621-4636	Connects people with information on all health and human services in King County, such as housing assistance, help with financial needs, legal assistance, or help finding the nearest food bank, or hot meals. Provides pre-screening for food stamps. Call or submit a message on the 2-1-1 website. No fees.
DESC Downtown Emergency Service Center, James St./The Clinic at Hobson Place	https://www.desc.org/what-we-do/health-services/	(206) 464-6454 | 216 James St., Seattle, WA (206) 441-3043 | 2120 S. Plum St., Seattle, WA	Drop-In Center is open to all DESC clients that are enrolled in a Mental Health or Clinical program. Provides warm meal, access to hygiene services, rest, basic first aid, peer counselors, support groups, engagement activities, volunteer opportunities, monthly outings, connect with clinical team. SAGE case managers help secure and maintain housing, and improve clinical and social stability. Services include substance use disorder (SUD) issues, mental health case management, psychiatric treatment, medication monitoring, limited therapy and protective payee services. Call intake number and request the SAGE intake specialist. HOST provides intensive outreach and engagement for clients experiencing chronic homelessness.
Evergreen Treatment Services	https://www.evergreentreatment.org/seattle-clinic/	(206) 223-3644 | 1700 Airport Way S, Seattle, WA	The Seattle Clinic offers medication assisted treatment (MAT) for opioid use disorders to patients in King County and surrounding areas. Services combine the daily dispensing of methadone or buprenorphine with services like counseling and engagement with a medical provider.
Harborview Medical Center		(206) 744-9600 | 325 9th Ave., Seattle, WA	DUI evaluations, outpatient, intensive outpatient, treatment for co-occurring substance use disorder and mental health disorders and opiate replacement therapy serving everyone including patients with co-morbid medical

			issues. Can write prescriptions for Suboxone therapy. Agency provides Department of Behavioral Health and Recovery/DBHR-certified service(s). Call for more information or an appointment. Initial assessment is free. Sliding scale fees. Accepts Apple Health (Medicaid), Medicare and other eligible commercial or managed care plans. Accepts private pay.
HealthPointl, Midway (Des Moines)	https://www.healthpointchc.org/find-clinics/midway Clinics similar to this one are located all over King County, please use the following link to view all the clinic locations: https://www.healthpointchc.org/find-clinics	For Medical Call (206) 870-3590 | For Dental Call (206) 870-3600 | 26401 Pacific Hwy. S, No. 201 Des Moines, WA	Adult Dental Adult Medical Behavioral Health Children's Dental Children's Medical Diabetes Education Family Planning Immunizations Naturopathic Medicine Nutrition Obstetrics Pediatrics Pharmacy Physical & Annual Exams Whole Family Dental Whole Family Medical WIC and MSS (Women's, Infants & Children and Maternity Support Services)
International Community Health Services	https://www.ichs.com/ Clinics similar to this one are located all over King County, please use the following link to view all the clinic locations: https://www.ichs.com/locations	206.788.3700 | 720 8th Ave S Seattle, WA 98104	Culturally and linguistically appropriate health services. Staff is multilingual. Offers dental, vision, primary healthcare, behavioral health and recovery, STD testing and treatment, and family and maternity services. Suboxone treatment available to adults who call to schedule an assessment. No one is turned away due to inability to pay. Accepts Apple Health (Medicaid), Medicare, sliding scale fees are available. Photo ID and proof of insurance required, if insurance is to be billed. Call for appointment, same-day appointments available.
Key Recovery and Life Skills Center	http://www.keyrecovery.org/our-services/	(206) 767-0244 | 10344 14th Ave. S Seattle, WA	Residential inpatient drug and alcohol treatment, focuses on individuals suffering from trauma and addiction. Programs include Long-Term Residential, Recovery House, After Care, and a program for residential treatment for families. Programs are evidence-based, trauma-informed, teaches essential life skills for healthy, productive lives, offers job training for

			long-term financial stability, strives to heal and reunite families. Welcomes every race, color, gender, religion, national origin, sexual orientation or gender identity. Department of Behavioral Health and Recovery/DBHR-certified service(s), Apple Health (Medicaid).
King County Columbia City Center for Health	https://kingcounty.gov/en/dept/dph/health-safety/health-centers-programs-services/public-health-centers/columbia-city Clinics similar to this one are located all over King County, please use the following link to view all the clinic locations: https://kingcounty.gov/en/dept/dph/health-safety/health-centers-programs-services/public-health-centers	(206) 296-4650 | 4400 37th Ave. S, Seattle, WA 98118	General dental care for low-income children and adults. WIC services for low-income pregnant women and adults. Accepts Apple Health (Medicaid). For service with no insurance, private insurance, or if you are not a U.S. citizen, you must qualify for services based on low or no income. Photo ID required for WIC services. Photo ID for dental services preferred, but not required. Call to schedule an appointment before visiting.
King County Veterans Program	https://kingcounty.gov/en/legacy/depts/community-human-services/adult-services/veterans-service-members-families/programs-services.aspx	KCVP Seattle: 206-263-8387 | KCVP Tukwila: 206-263-8387 | 9725 3rd Ave NE, Suite 300 (Third Floor) Seattle, WA 98115 | 645 Andover Park W, No.100 Tukwila, WA	Services offered include emergency financial assistance, case management, employment, mental health counseling and housing system coordination. Serves veterans, service members and their legal dependents living in King County. Documents required include: Proof of service (prioir of current), Documentation of King County Residency, and proof of income eligibility for financial assisitance.
La Esperanza Health Counseling Services	http://laesperanzahcs.org/programs___services	Burien: (206) 306-2690; Lynnwood: (425) 248-4534 | info@laesperanzahcs.org | Burien: 15405 1st Ave. S, Burien, WA Lynnwood: 20815 67th Ave. W, No.201, Lynnwood, WA	Programs are bilingual (English and Spanish) and focus on Latino and immigrant communities. Alcohol and drug information school, DUI alcohol and drug assessments, outpatient substance use disorder treatment services, intensive outpatient treatment, Level 1 and 2 Anger Management classes, Domestic violence assessment and treatment, MRT treatment and Parenting Classes. Agency provides Department of Behavioral Health and Recovery/DBHR-certified service(s). Call for more information or to schedule appointment. Accepts private insurance and private pay. Sliding scale fees.
Lahai Health	https://lahai.org/	(206) 363-4105 x 230 | 2152 N. 122nd St. Seattle, WA 98133	Providing quality and compassionate health care to the underserved, showing Christ's love to everyone. Clinic provides health care, full medical exams, resources

			to obtain low to no cost prescription drugs, laboratory tests, imaging services, intensive nursing case management and referrals to medical specialists. Also offers Professional Mental Health Counseling. Cannot provide urgent care. Call for an appointment. Does not bill patients or insurance. See website or call for multiple service locations.
Matt Talbot Center	https://www.mtcseattle.org/	(206) 256-9865 | 2313 Third Ave. Seattle, WA 98121	Offers services and support to individuals ready to commit to their recovery with an intensive clinical outpatient treatment program offered in a Christian context. Supervised by a Certified Substance Use Disorder Professional (SUDP), this recovery and relapse prevention program addresses the physiology, psychology, and sociology of addiction.
Narcotics Anonymous	https://seattlena.org/	(206) 790-8888 | Location varies.	Support groups and a 24-hour helpline for anyone who has a desire to stop using drugs. Call for support and for information on meeting times and sites, or text your zipcode to (206) 790-8888 for an auto-response with five meeting times and locations in your area. No fees.
Navos - Mental Health Wellness Center	https://www.navos.org/ To find a clinic: https://neighborcare.org/clinics/	(206) 248-8226 | 1210 SW 136th St., Burien, WA	Intensive outpatient treatment and mental health treatment for King County residents, DBHR-certified services. Treatment for chemical dependency. Will not serve patients who need detoxification or who require inpatient care. Family and child intensive therapy services, outpatient therapy, case management, infant mental health services, information and referral, and counseling. Apple Health (Medicaid) is required. Call for intake, early in the morning is best.
Neighborcare Health	https://neighborcare.org/	(206) 548-5710 | Multiple locations. Call for appointments.	Medical, dental, mental health, pharmacy, social work, and many other services for patients of all ages at various locations around Seattle.
New Traditions	http://new-traditions.org/	(206) 762-7207 | intake@new-traditions.org | 9045 16th Ave. SW, Seattle, WA 98106	Chemical dependency treatment for pregnant women. Usually serves women who are low income and many are transient or homeless. Offers comprehensive outpatient

			services. Agency provides DBHR-certified service(s). Call for an appointment. No fees if client meets criteria for Apple Health (Medicaid). Sliding fee and private pay for non-Medicaid clients.
Odessa Brown Children's Clinic, Othello	https://www.seattlechildrens.org/clinics/odessa-brown/	(206) 987-7210 | 3939 S Othello St., No. 101, Seattle, WA 98118	Services for for infants, children and adolescents (under the age of 18). Offers medical care, immunizations, dental care, and mental health services, and WIC (a nutrition program that helps pregnant women, new mothers, and young children eat well). Also offers social worker referrals for connection to community programs such as cooking classes, swimming lessons, and local school services with many programs like student support groups.
One Health Clinic	https://www.onehealthclinic.org/	(206) 428-3020 | 2709 3rd Ave., Seattle, WA	The One Health Clinic provides free veterinary care and (in collaboration with Neighborcare Health) free human healthcare to youth and young adults experiencing homelessness.
Pioneer Square Medical Clinic	https://www.uwmedicine.org/locations/pioneer-square	(206) 744-1500 | 206 3rd Ave. S, Seattle, WA 98104	Serves adults 18 and older who are low income, homeless, or without health insurance. Free for people experiencing homelessness. Services include podiatry/foot care, social services, dietician consultations and health education. An on-site pharmacy fills prescriptions by clinic providers. Mental healthcare, specialty services, and hospitalization are available to patients if needed.
POCAAN - Breaking the Chains of Addiction	https://www.pocaan.org/breaking-addiction	(206) 322-7061 | olivette@pocaan.org | 4437 Rainier Ave. S, Seattle, WA	Who It's For: BIPOC (Black, Indigenous, People of Color) individuals living with HIV and struggling with addiction. What it Provides: A comprehensive counseling program that offers a safe way to recover from addiction with support services from a certified Substance Use Disorder Professional who has first-hand experience with addiction and recovery.
Praisealujah	https://praisealujah.org/about-us	Office (206) 504-8845 Women's program (206) 226-5994; Men's program (206) 307-9166 | 20832	Faith Based Treatment facility to assist men and women who are struggling with opioid, fentanyl, and other substance abuse, situations/circumstances caused by alcohol addiction, drug addiction,

		International Boulevard SeaTac, WA	abuse, homelessness, emotional trauma, loss, and hopelessness. Intensive 6 month to one-year program, with faith-based perspective. Also food assistance.
Recovery Cafe	https://recoverycafe.org/	South Lake Union: 206-374-8731	2022 Boren Ave, Seattle, WA 98121	SODO: 206-333-2314	4202 6th Ave S, Seattle, WA 98108	A community of individuals who have been traumatized by homelessness, addiction and other mental health challenges. The Café is about community, and a place to gather together for a refuge for healing and hope. Members receive meals, recovery classes, peer support and referrals. Visit to sign up for a New Member Introduction, serves everyone.
Salvation Army, Adult Rehabilitation Program	https://seattlearp.salvationarmy.org/	(206) 587-0503 ext. 1	10750 Greenwood Ave. N, Seattle, WA	Offers a three-bridge approach that allows participants an intensive six-month in-patient recovery program, an additional two months of in-house work development, assistance finding a job, and an additional six months of independent living in the Adult Rehabilitation Program facility that provides a supportive sober community. All at no cost. Call program intake. Serves everyone, but Christian studies are offered as part of the program.
Sea Mar Community Health Centers	https://seamar.org/services-king.html	Administrative Offices: (206) 762-3730	1.855.289.4503	1040 S. Henderson St. Seattle, WA 98108	Medical, dental, mental health, pharmacy, social work, and many other services for patients of all ages at various locations around King County..
Seattle Indian Health Board	https://www.sihb.org/	(206) 324-9360	info@sihb.org	611 12th Ave. S, Seattle, WA 98144	124 Second Ave S. Seattle, WA 98104	12736 33rd Ave NE, Suite 200, Seattle, WA 98125	Provides health and human services to its patients, while specializing in the care of Native people. Medical, dental, mental health, chemical dependency, outpatient services, community education services, and housing assistance services. Offers maternal and infant health services as well as the WIC program. Provides emergency assistance and safety planning for victims of domestic violence. Offers programs and care for elders, and veterans. Sliding scale fees for qualifying native American or Alaskan with correct documentation.
Seattle Intergroup	https://www.seattleaa.org/	Call any time (206) 587-2838		Helps people become acquainted with Alcoholics Anonymous, locate

		5507 6th Ave. S, Seattle, WA	meetings, and make sober connections.
Seattle's Union Gospel Mission, Dental Clinic	https://www.ugm.org/what-we-do/stabilization/dental-services/	(206) 621-7695	dentalclinic@ugm.org	318 2nd Ave Extension South Seattle, WA 98104	Dental services serving adults 18 and older with income at or below 200 percent of the Federal Poverty Level. Call for an appointment. Documents required: Photo ID, food stamp award letter, or documentation of income for the last two months. Fees are $20 per visit, debit or credit only. Call for more information.
Seattle's Union Gospel Mission, Recovery Programs	https://www.ugm.org/what-we-do/recovery/	Administrative Offices: (206) 723-0767	mission@ugm.org	3800 South Othello Street Seattle, WA 98118	Drugs and alcohol can destroy people. They keep people on the streets, unable to escape the cycle of homelessness. UGM's faith-based recovery programs help people leave their addictions behind and give them the foundation for starting a new life. Different recovery programs in different locations, visit website or call to find the right program for you.
Sound Health	https://www.sound.health/locations/	(206)-901-2000	marketing@sound.health	Multiple locations. Call for appointments.	Sound's services include individual and group therapy, addiction treatment and substance use services, domestic violence and a range of children and family programs, vocational services, school-based programs, criminal justice, and re-entry services, services for the deaf, services for individuals with cognitive and developmental disabilities, crisis support services, services for those with private insurance, military and veteran's programs, supported housing services (for eligible clients), and residential services for clients with acute needs.
Third Avenue Primary Care Clinic	https://www.uwmedicine.org/locations/third-avenue-center	(206) 521-1231	2028 3rd Ave., Seattle, WA 98121	Primary care clinic and mental health services for homeless, low-income, and at-risk people without health insurance or a primary care provider. Services include psychiatric consultations, medication management, and recommendations for continued psychiatric care. Visit in person; established clients may call. Accepts Medicare, Apple Health (Medicaid) and private insurance. Financial counseling is available. For psychiatry must have primary care physician referral (within Harborview). Do not take Tri-Care. Dental but no vision services.

Uplift Northwest, Vision Clinic	https://www.upliftnw.org/	(206) 728-5627 | 2515 Western Ave., Seattle, WA	Weekly eye clinic September through June. Can receive a pair of glasses once per year. Serves those without vision insurance who are at or below 200 percent of the Federal Poverty Level. Call for appointment. Documents required: ID. No fees. Showers and laundry for clients. Computer lab for WorkSource support. Three meals served. Places clients into temporary day labor and full time hired jobs. Offers bus tickets for work assignments. Documents required: valid state or government issued photo ID and a Social Security card. Background check is done. First-time clients apply in person. Visit in person. No fees.
Valley Cities - Behavioral Health Services	https://www.valleycities.org/	(253) 833-7444 | Multiple locations. Call for appointments.	Valley Cities provides inpatient and outpatient mental health and substance use disorder treatment, along with support services for adults, children, and families living in King County.
YMCA - Counseling Services	https://www.seattleymca.org/social-impact-center/counseling-services	(206) 382-5340 | counseling@seattleymca.org	Licensed therapists for people of all ages. Remote and in-person counseling for stress, anxiety, depression, family and relationship issues, grief, loss, substance use and addiction, self-harm, gender identity, body image, conflict resolution, court requirements related to mental health or substance use, foster support, adoption support. Sliding scale which allows everyone to have affordable access to services, and accepts Medicaid.
Resources to Meet Basic Needs - King County			
Anchor – South King County Shelter System - Catholic Community Services	https://ccsww.org/get-help/shelter-homeless-services/anchor-south-king-county-shelter-system/	Kent: (253) 854-0077 x5104; Federal Way: (253) 893-7895 | Kent Community Engagement Center 1229 W Smith St, Kent WA 98032 | Federal Way Day Center 33505 14th Place S No. D Federal Way, WA 98003	Offers 24/7 shelter and essential needs support such as meals, toiletries and access to other basic needs items. Supportive case management services for education, employment, family reunification, mental health and addiction recovery.
Asian Counseling and Referral Service, Food	https://acrs.org/services/aging-services-for-older-adults/acrs-food-bank/	(206) 695-7510 | miguels@acrs.org | 800 S Weller St., Seattle, WA 98104	Distributes foods that cater to Asian American and Pacific Islander diets, including healthy and nutritious staples like rice, tofu, soy milk,

Bank			noodles, canned proteins and produce.
Ballard Food Bank	https://www.ballardfoodbank.org/	(206) 789-7800 | 1400 NW Leary Way Seattle, WA 98107	Food bank styled like grocery store. Clients must register to use food bank service, but ID is not required. Can shop in the grocery store once a week, receive a free meal at the cafe once a day, and access non-food resources in the Hub like mail services, ID vouchers, and more. Non-perishable food bags offered. Also offers grocery home delivery and financial assistance for those living in 98109, 98119, 98199, 98103, 98133, 98107, 98117, and 98177.
Ballard Sunday Dinners	http://www.bflcs.org/	(206) 784-1306 | Ballard First Lutheran Church, 2006 NW 65th St., Seattle, WA	Sunday night dinners, free.
Bethany Community Church	https://churchbcc.org/missions/localmissions	(206) 524-9000 | 8023 Green Lake Dr. N, Seattle, WA	Food bank and hot meals offered Mondays in the Community Life Center (CLC) building. Serves everyone. No fees.
Bike Works - BikeMobile	https://bikeworks.org/event/bikemobile/	(206) 673-0840 | adultprograms@bikeworks.org | 3709 S Ferdinand St Seattle, WA	Repair comes to you. From spring to fall, the BikeMobile travels around the Seattle area, primarily visiting areas designated as "bike deserts", where bike shops are few and far between. All repair services are performed for free, or on a sliding scale. Most bike parts are offered at cost and offers used parts to fit almost any budget. The BikeMobile was created to increase access for: Youth, People from low-income households, Black, Indigenous, People of Color, Women, Trans, non-binary individuals, Immigrants and Refugees, People experiencing homelessness, People with disabilities, and People dependent on their bike for daily transportation.
Blessed Sacrament Food Program	https://www.blessed-sacrament.org/st-vincent-de-paul	(206) 930-6005; (206) 767-6449 | 5050 8th Ave. NE, Seattle, WA 98105	Sunday meal has limited indoor seating or pick-up and take to go. All are welcome to the Friday Food Pantry (modified in-person shopping). No proof of ID required and no fees. Grocery delivery is available for residents that are physically unable to visit the Food Pantry and must reside within our Parish boundaries. Visit in-person or call for delivery requirements.

Bread of Life Mission Shelter	https://www.breadoflifemission.org/emergency-services-overview	(206) 682-3579 | info@breadoflifemission.org | 97 S Main St., Seattle, WA 98104	Services include clothing distribution, showers for women only as needed, mail service, bus passes, storage lockers with monthly fee, hot lunch, computers, dinner. Overnight shelter available only for men age 18 and older. Valid state ID and shower required to stay, $5 fee. Hot dinner offered Mon. – Sat., 7:15 p.m. Chapel hours Tues. – Sat., 6:30 – 7:10 p.m. Doors close at 8:15 p.m.
Byrd Barr Place	https://byrdbarrplace.org/	(206) 812-4940 | 722 18th Ave, Seattle, WA 98122	Energy assistance (PSE HELP and LIHEAP), food pantry, financial empowerment courses, and resource referral to the Seattle area. May visit the Market for food once per week. Home delivery available only to residents of ZIP codes 98102, 98112, and 98122; call for information on how to arrange. Proof of current address required. Offers energy assistance once per program year and temporary shelter assistance (eviction prevention) when available. Serves Seattle residents with income at or below 125 percent of the Federal Poverty Line. Available October through August as funding allows. Call or go online for application instructions. No fees.
Compass Housing Alliance Day Center Services	https://www.compasshousingalliance.org/emergency-programs/compasscenternavigation/	(206) 474-1630 | 210 Alaskan Way S Seattle, WA	Homeless adults 18 and older can seek refuge, meals, and basic services as well as connect with housing navigation support, case management, entitlements, and other benefits, mental health counseling, and nursing services. Additional day services such as laundry, showers, mail, and banking are also available on-site.
Congregations for the Homeless	https://porchlightcares.org/	office (425) 289-4044; shelter (425) 502-9958 | 515B 116th Ave NE (at Lincoln Center) Bellevue, WA	Men's programs offer permanent housing, rotating shelter, emergency shelter, day center, and case management. Shelter space first-come, first-served basis, priority going to men who spent the previous night at the shelter. Enhanced shelter includes three meals a day, showers, laundry, storage, mail, haircuts, computers, etc. Offers limited case management services, housing navigation, employment navigation, medical and dental care, and professional mental health and addiction supportive services.

Des Moines Area Food Bank	http://www.myfoodbank.org/	(206) 878-2660 | 22225 Ninth Ave. S, United Methodist Church (lower level) Des Moines, WA	Food pantry and commodities. May visit food pantry once per month for full pantry. No limit on bread and produce room – Mon. – Fri. 9 a.m. – 2:30 p.m. Verify addresses served on website. Visit in person. No fees. Meals programs for kids, check website for information.
Digital Equity Program - Seattle Information Technology (Seattle IT)	https://seattle.gov/tech	(206) 684-8498 | digitalequity@seattle.gov | 700 5th Ave., No. 2700, Seattle, WA	Provides help with low-cost internet options, the Affordable Connectivity Program (ACP), cable customer assistance, and referral to community computer and training services. The priority strategic areas of the digital equity work are: skills training; connectivity; devices & technical support.
Disabled American Veterans Network	https://www.dav.org/get-help-now/medical-transportation/	(206) 341-8267 | 915 2nd Ave., No. 1040, Seattle, WA	Transportation to medical services at the Veterans Administration Hospital. Appointments are required one week in advance. Veterans can bring an escort or service dog with a doctor's note. Serves veterans with disabilities. Not wheelchair accessible. No fees. Located at the VA Medical Center.
Discount Smart Phones - Seattle Information Technology Office	https://seattle.gov/tech/internet-and-devices/discounted-computers-and-phones	(206) 684-8498 | digitalequity@seattle.gov | 700 5th Ave., No. 2700, Seattle, WA	Lifeline Discount Smart Phone Programs. Lifeline is a government benefit program that provides monthly telephone service discounts for eligible consumers in all of Washington State living on low incomes, helping create access to the opportunities and security that phone service affords - including being able to connect to jobs, housing, family and 9-1-1. Website lists information on phone companies that participate in this program, and income eligibility.
Dress for Success Seattle	https://seattle.dressforsuccess.org/	(206) 461-4472 | office@dfsseattle.org | 600 Pine St., No. 310, Seattle, WA	Services include Employment Retention Programs, Career Center, one-on-one Career Coaching, and Career Wardrobe. Must have referral and schedule an appointment. See website, or phone (206) 461-4472 for information on getting a referral. Email office@dfsseattle.org.
DSHS King County Locations	https://www.dshs.wa.gov/office-locations?field_geofield_distance%5Bdistance%5D=100&field_geofield_distance%5Bunit%5D=3959&field_geofield_distance%5Borigin%5D=King+County	(877) 501-2233 | There are many locations in King County, please follow the website link or call the number above to find the	Apply for assistance Do a review, report a change, or have questions about cash, food, Housing and Essential Needs referral, Medicaid (for people who are 6 and older, blind or disabled, receiving SSI or eligible for

		right location for you.	Medicare). Washington Connection How to apply for services	DSHS (wa.gov)
Edible Hope Kitchen	https://stlukesseattle.org/edible-hope/	(206) 784-3119	5710 22nd Ave. NW, Seattle, WA lower level	Weekday morning free hot breakfast.
El Centro de la Raza - Food Pantry	https://www.elcentrodelaraza.org/el-centro-food-bank/	(206) 973-4401	2524 16th Ave S, Seattle, WA 98144	The food bank provides nutritious, emergency and supplemental food to low-income individuals and families in the Seattle area three days a week. We also have dedicated navigators on-site to assists people in securing food stamps and other non-emergency food resources. Our food bank is open to all. Many of our seniors consider coming to the food bank as a time to socialize and connect to their cultures through food.
Elizabeth Gregory Home	https://eghseattle.org/	(206) 729-0262	University Lutheran Church 1604 NE 50th St., Seattle, WA	Day center with light case management services for anyone 18 and older who identifies as female. Showers, laundry, sleeping room, computer access and mail program. Breakfast, lunch, food to take with you. UDSM (University District Street Medicine.) Weekly clothing giveaway. Call to request interpreter services. No fees. Transitional housing and case management for sober single women 18 and older who are experiencing homelessness. Anyone who identifies as female is welcome. Openings are limited. Please visit day center to apply.
FamilyWorks, Greenwood & Wallingford Food Banks	https://familyworksseattle.org/food-banks/#hours	(206) 647-1780	9501 Greenwood Ave. N, Seattle, WA	1501 N 45th St., Seattle, WA	Offers a food bank. Serves residents of zip codes 98103, 98115, 98107, 98133, 98117 and 98177. Will serve additional zip codes outside of these areas. Visit in person. Documents requested: photo ID and current proof of address. No fees.
Filipino Community of Seattle	https://www.filcommsea.org/programs	(206) 722-9372	info@filcommsea.org	5740 Martin Luther King Jr Way S, Seattle, WA 98118	Cultural home for the Filipino Community as well as immigrants, refugees. Lunch program and affordable low-income housing for seniors.
First Covenant Church	https://www.firstcovenantseattle.org/	(206) 322-7411	400 E Pike St., Seattle, WA 98122	Free full breakfast for all.

First United Methodist Church of Seattle	https://firstchurchseattle.org/events/shared-breakfast/	(206) 622-7278 | Fellowship Hall 180 Denny Way, Seattle, WA	Community breakfast served seated at tables. All welcome. Visit in person. No fees.
Highline Area Food Bank	http://highlineareafoodbank.org/need-help/	(206) 433-9900 | 18300 Fourth Ave. S, Manhattan Community Ctr. Burien, WA	Food pantry that clients may visit once per week. Serves residents of the Highline area. Visit in person or call for information about service area. Documents required: photo ID, proof of residence and verification of family size. No fees.
Hopelink	https://www.hopelink.org/programs/	(425) 869-6000 | 8990 154th Ave. NE Redmond, WA 98052	Hopelink operates services, at multiple locations, that serve homeless and low-income families, children, seniors and people with disabilities in north and east King County. Hopelink also provides transportation services throughout King and Snohomish Counties. All of their services are provided within the state of Washington. Their Administrative team members are currently housed in Redmond. If you have general questions about Hopelink, or if you are not sure where to call, try their administrative office at 425.869.6000.
Housing and Essential Needs (HEN)	https://ccsww.org/get-help/shelter-homeless-services/housing-and-essential-needs-hen/	(206) 328-5755 | henkc@ccsww.org Call or email for appointment	Referral program through DSHS. Provides rent assistance, utility and transportation assistance, as well as hygiene and cleaning products. Serves adults (without minor children) who are unable to work due to a physical or mental incapacity. Program services are subject to funding availability and may be discontinued or reduced at any time. Call for more eligibility information and to determine if specific documents are required. No fees.
Hyde Shuttle - Sound Generations	https://soundgenerations.org/our-programs/transportation/hyde-shuttle/	(206) 727-6262 | info@soundgenerations.org | 2208 Second Ave., #100 Seattle, WA 98121	Free lift-equipped, door-to-door transportation for people 55+; and also younger persons with disabilities. Must live within one of the neighborhood service areas: Auburn, Burien and Highpoint, Bryn Mawr-Skyway, Kent, Federal Way, Des Moines and Normandy Park, Seattle, Renton, Seatac, Shoreline, Sno Valley, and Tukwila.
Immanuel Community Services	https://www.icsseattle.org/	(206) 622-1930 | 1215 Thomas St., Seattle, WA	Provides a food bank, community lunch, and a hygiene center with laundry and shower services. Services available to all adults. No

			children. No fees and no ID requirements of any kind. Sign-up in person on-site. Recovery program shelter available for up to one year for up to 15 men going through recovery, offered in partnership with the Matt Talbot Center.
Jewish Family Service - Polack Food Bank	https://www.jfsseattle.org/get-help/polack-food-bank/	(206) 461-3240 | fb@jfsseattle.org | 1601 16th Ave., Seattle, WA	Kosher friendly food bank.
Jubilee Women's Center	https://jwcenter.org/	(206) 324-1244 | 620 18th Ave. E Seattle, WA	Offers low-income and homeless, female-identifying adults up to two bags of clothing every 3 months with no ID required. Call to make an appointment. No fees. Offers a two year transitional housing program, female–identifying adults without children in care. For application, call, visit in-person, or visit website. Residents pay $680/month with subsidies available for the first 6 months. Vaccination and proof of income required for housing. Limited wheelchair access.
King County Metro Transit Regional Reduced Fare Permit (RRFP)	https://kingcounty.gov/en/dept/metro/travel-options/accessible-services	(206) 553-3000; TTY: (206) 684-2029 | 201 S Jackson St., Seattle, WA	The Regional Reduced Fare Permit (RRFP) entitles senior riders (age 65 or older), riders with a disability and Medicare card holders to reduced fares on public transportation systems in the Puget Sound region. Note: ID required for age-specific service like a Youth Card or a Senior Permit.
LIHI Urban Rest Stop, Ballard & Downtown	https://urbanreststop.org/	Ballard: (206) 258-3626 | 2014-B NW 57th St., Seattle, WA | Downtown: (206) 332-0110 |1924 9th Ave., Seattle, WA	Restrooms, showers, laundry facilities for adults and youth of all genders. Showers are ADA compliant. No intoxication allowed. The downtown URS has private shower rooms, washer and dryer units, and large men's and women's restrooms. Patrons receive free toiletries. No fees. Laundry sign-up is over the phone or in person and shower sign up is only in-person only.
Mary's Place Day Center for Women	https://www.marysplaceseattle.org/get-help/day-center	(206) 812-8559 | 1830 Ninth Ave., Seattle, WA	A drop in center for women. Showers, laundry, housing and health resources, breakfast and lunch, groups and community.
Multi-Service Center in Federal Way		253-838-6810 | 1200 South 336th Street, Federal Way, WA, 98003	Provides supplemental and emergency food to individuals living in the Federal Way School District; special no-cook options are available for those experiencing

			homelessness. Also provides formula, cereal, baby food and diapers for infants as available.
New Bethlehem Day Center	https://sacredheart.org/Parish/pastoral-care-social-concerns/new-bethlehem-day-center/	(425) 679-0350 | 11920 NE 80th St., No. 100 Kirkland, WA	Provides families (adults with children under 18, present) essential services including: showers, laundry, computers, social services, snack and dinner. Provides grab-and-go meals navigation to shelters and other emergency resources and social services. Serving families only, adults must have at least one child under 18 or younger in attendance.
North Helpline - Lake City & Bitter Lake	https://northhelpline.org/	Lake City Location: (206) 367-3477 | 12736 33rd Ave NE Seattle WA 98125 | Bitter Lake Location: (206) 413-8192 | 13000 Linden Ave N Seattle WA 98133 ,	Services include food banks, hygiene supplies, baby cupboard, referral services, mail services, winter time services, tenant education, financial assistance for eviction and utility shut off prevention (206) 365-8043, and free health clinic. Food bank and emergency service center for homeless or residents who reside in 98125, 98133, 98177, 98155, 98115, 98011 and 98028. Homeless clients can receive one no cook bag per day. Visit in person. No fees.
Northwest Harvest, SODO Community Market	https://www.northwestharvest.org/our-work/community-programs/sodo-community-market/	(206) 625-0755 | 1915 4th Ave. S, Seattle, WA	Food bank services. No ID, no proof of income, and no residency information is required to shop with us. Clients may visit once per day. Visit in person. Baby cupboard serves families with children 5 and younger. No fees.
ORCA Cards - King County Metro Transit Bus	https://kingcounty.gov/en/dept/metro/fares-and-payment/ways-to-pay/orca-cards	(888)-988-6722 | 201 S Jackson St., Seattle, WA	Provides an ORCA card to pay your transit fare on buses, trains and ferries throughout the Puget Sound. Available for youth, seniors, low-income, people with disabilities, or people receiving certain state benefits.
Phinney Ridge Lutheran Church - Direct Assistance and Food Bank	https://prlc.org/phinney-ridge-lutheran-church-food-bank	(206) 783-2350 | 7500 Greenwood Ave. N, Seattle, WA	Direct financial assistance for individuals or families in need of help including help with rent, a utility bill, or gasoline for a car. Email outreach@prlc.org to be screened for assistance. Food Bank is open to all without any zip code restrictions. ID required. Food for a variety of different needs.
Pike Market Food Bank	https://www.pmsc-fb.org/food-bank	(206) 626-6462 | 1531 Western Ave. (Level P5 of Pike Place Market parking	Serves residents of all ages in the 98101, 98104, or 98121 zip codes, and people who are homeless living in downtown Seattle. Groceries

		garage)	available once per week. Bring ID (if you have it, ID is not a requirement), and a grocery bag if you have it (we have paper ones if you don't). Notify staff/volunteers if you have mobility issues and cannot stand in line. Visit in person. No fees.
Praisealujah	https://praisealujah.org/community-based-services	(206) 504-8845 | 20832 International Boulevard SeaTac, WA	Food Bank
Providence Regina House	https://www.providence.org/locations/wa/regina-house	(206) 763-9204 | 8201 10th Ave S, Suite 6, Seattle, WA 98108	Weekly food and clothing bank at South Park Neighborhood Center Food pantry. May visit every week. Serves those who are homeless or in ZIP codes 98108, 98148, 98168 and 98188. Documents required: ID and proof of current address. No fees.
Queen Anne Food Bank	https://sacredheartseattle.org/qafb	206 216-4104 | info@qafb.org | 205 Second Ave North, Seattle, WA	Meals, sack lunches and a food pantry. Visit in person. Meals serves everyone. Offers hats, socks, toiletries when available. No fees.
Queen Anne Helpline	https://www.queenannehelpline.org/	(206) 282-1540 | 311 W McGraw St., Seattle, WA	Adult clothing, non-perishable food, bus tickets, and other no-fee resources available for pickup once every 30 days. Financial assistance (rent, utilities, and/or move-in costs) for low-income residents housed within zip codes 98109, 98119, and 98199. Call anytime.
Rainier Valley Food Bank	https://www.rvfb.org/	(206) 723-4105 | 9021 Rainier Ave S, Seattle, WA	Documents Required: None, No fees. Mission is to nourish with good food, empower with knowledge, and serve with compassion. Outreach Coordinator on site to assist with help finding and applying for benefits such as SNAP, housing, clothing, transportation, and healthcare. ID or specific documents are required to access non-food services. No fees.
Salvation Army, White Center	https://seattlewhitecenter.salvationarmy.org/	(206) 767-3150 extension 1 | 9050 16th Ave. SW, Seattle, WA	Provides groceries, as well as diapers and pet food when available, to homeless and low-income individuals and families in White Center. To qualify, must have low-income and live within the following zip codes: 98106, 98108 (west of the Duwamish, in the South Park neighborhood), 98116, 98126, 98136, 98146, 98148, 98158, 98166, 98168, 98188 and 98198 (north of 216th). Requests the

			following verification documents: Proof of income, verification of family size, proof of address and Photo ID. Serves everyone.
Salvation Army, Central Seattle Food Pantry	https://seattle.salvationarmy.org/	(206) 447-9944 extension 2 | 1101 Pike St., Seattle, WA	Pick out your own food, and food bags for non-cook, requests ID for adults, but okay if no ID. No fees.
Seattle Indian Center	https://seattleindiancenter.org/	(206) 329-8700 | admin@seattleindian .org | 624 S Dearborn St., Seattle, WA	Primary focus is serving the American Indian/Alaska Native community, and also serves people of color as well as anyone in need. Provides a multi-service center with advocacy and support services. Programs include outreach and engagement, drop-in center, food bank, and community hot meals. For community shelter services, call for intake and location.
Seattle Public Library, Central Branch, Social Services & Help for Those in Need	https://www.spl.org/programs-and-services/civics-and-social-services/social-services-referrals	(206) 386-4636 | 1000 4th Ave., Seattle, WA	Specializing in services for the insecurely housed. The Community Resource Specialist can help you find shelter, mental health counseling, job training, food assistance, legal help, domestic violence support, medical help, and a social work team. Also offers to loan Wi-Fi hotspots and books to those living in encampments. Hotspots can be reserved online by any borrower, but the Library sets aside hotspots specifically for homeless communities to use and share.
Seattle's Open Meal Service provided by OSL	https://www.oslserves.org/	(206) 919-7468 | info@oslserves.org | 2515 Western Ave., Seattle, WA	No-cost hot meal service, three times per day, seven days a week. All are welcome.
Shoreline Community Care	https://shorelinecommunitycare.org/get-help/	(206) 496-3116 | Berean Bible Church, 2345 N 185th St., Shoreline, WA	Financial assistance for rent, utilities and other essential needs. May receive assistance once every 6 months. Serves residents of the city of Shoreline. No walk-ins, by appointment only. Leave a voicemail stating: first and last name, address, contact phone number, and best time to call. Documents required: photo ID, monthly budget, and, depending on help needed, a utility bill and/or landlord contact info. No fees. Agency holds a Christian worldview but serves non-Christians and does not require church attendance.
Shower	https://atyourservice.seattle.gov/	(206) 386-1030 |	Free hot showers provided by

Hotline, City of Seattle	2022/02/25/2022-hygiene-shower-trailer-locations/	Call for weekly updated locations	Seattle Public Utilities in shower trailers for 30-45 minutes. Single occupancy, sanitized between each use, secure storage while using, pets secured while using. Call for instructions and weekly updated locations.
Solanus Casey Center	https://ccsww.org/get-help/shelter-homeless-services/solanus-casey-center/	(206) 223-0907 | 804 9th Ave., Seattle, WA	Walk-in hospitality and referral center that provides services to help people get an identification card (ID), administrative and financial help for people who have had their Washington state IDs stolen or lost, confiscated or not returned by law enforcement. Use the 9th & Columbia entrance of St. James Cathedral.
Solid Ground	https://www.solid-ground.org/get-help/	DSHS Benefits Help: (206) 694-6742; Tenant Info Hotline: (206) 694-6767 | 1501 N 45th St., Seattle, WA	Legal services to help clients obtain and retain public benefits like SNAP food stamp/EBT, Medicaid/health insurance, government cash assistance, and more. Provides information and referral for tenants facing eviction or struggling with other rental issues. Provides references to food and nutrition assistance programs, as well as rental assistance and shelter diversion through 211. Serves low-income residents of King County. No restrictions for advice and referrals. No fees.
St. Francis House	https://www.stfrancishouseseattle.org/	206-268-0784 | info@stfrancishouseseattle.org | 169 12th Ave, Seattle, WA 98122	Free clothing, socks, underwear, masks, toiletries, and sanitizer for men, women and children. May receive assistance once every 30 days. Visit in person, no appointment necessary. ID required.
St. James Cathedral	https://www.stjames-cathedral.org/outreach/kitchen.aspx	General Line: (206) 264-2091 | Immigrant Assistance: (206) 382-4511 | 907 Columbia St., Seattle, WA 98104	Meal serving everyone. St James Immigrant Assistance provides ESL/English language instruction, comprehensive naturalization assistance, immigrant legal services, citizenship preparation classes. Call for an appointment for services. No fees.
St. Luke's Episcopal Church	https://stlukesseattle.org/edible-hope/	(206) 784-3119 | 5710 22nd Ave. NW, Seattle, WA	Light breakfast and food bags serving everyone. Serving Meals Monday-Friday, 8:00-10:00am. Visit in person. No fees. A warm place to enjoy the meal.
St. Vincent de Paul of Seattle, Georgetown	https://svdpseattle.org/get-help/food-bank/	(206) 767-6449 | 5972 4th Ave. S, Seattle, WA 98108	Food bank distributing boxes and bags of food. Offers "Community Connectors" that provide

Food Bank			information about and help you apply for housing assistance, aid for utilities, health care, job readiness, education, and other benefits. For those experiencing homelessness, a special program, FACES (Food, Assistance, Compassion & Emergency Services), is available every Friday. See food bank staff for details on availability and intake. Visit in person. No fees.
The Bikery	https://www.thebikery.org/	info@thebikery.org | 845 Hiawatha Pl. S, Seattle, WA	Free bikes program for those experiencing homelessness. Helps you fix your bike yourself. You will have access to a wide range of tools and volunteer knowledge to help you as much (or as little) as you need. Refurbished discount bikes available to purchase. Bikes are donated by community members and refurbished by volunteers. They get donations every week and inventory changes quickly, so check back often.
The Bridge Care Center	https://www.bridgecarecenter.org/	(206) 789-0220 | info@bridgecarecenter.org | 1401 NW Leary Way, Seattle, WA 98107	Offers adult clothing for all genders, hygiene items. Outdoor gear offered when available. Outreach case managers are available to provide guidance on useful resources for unhoused individuals in the Ballard and Greater Seattle area. Phone use is available. No ID or referral requirements.
The Giving Room Food Bank	https://thegivingroomseattle.org/	(206) 552-9586 | givingroom@epiclifechurch.org | 10510 Stone Ave N, Seattle, WA 98133	The Giving Room food bank offers food, friendship, prayer, and a door into community. Epic Life Church in north Seattle hosts this grocery-store-style shopping experience where guests can shop for free groceries (e.g., produce, dairy, frozen meat, dry goods) and personal items. We all have something valuable to offer the world—come give and receive!
Transform Burien	https://transformoutreach.org/	(206) 839-6620 | admin@transformburien.org | 15623 Des Moines Memorial Dr., Burien, WA | Laundry: 15006 SW Ambaum Blvd., Burien, WA	Transform Burien provides free food, clothing, laundry, and more. Shower truck and towels, clean underwear, shampoo and soap are provided. Showers have a 15 minute limit. Laundry located at listed address, volunteers will put quarters into the machines for those in need to do their laundry. Detergent, bleach, and dryer sheets are provided. Also provides a medical and dental van twice a month.

Tukwila Pantry		(206) 431-8293 | operations@tukwilap antry.org | Riverton Park United Methodist, 3118 S 140th St., Tukwila, WA	Operates a food pantry program for residents of Tukwila, SeaTac, Burien and Boulevard Park. No fees. First-time registrants and clients returning for their first visit of the new year must bring confirmation of address. Doesn't require proof of income. Proof of address can be a utility bill, lease, hotel/motel rental receipt. ID required.
United Way - Food Delivery	https://www.uwkc.org/need-help/f ood-delivery/	(253) 237-2019 | fooddelivery@uwkc.o rg	United Way of King County is offering free, weekly home delivery of groceries. This a free service available to anyone in King County who is unable to afford groceries and cannot access their local food bank. You can participate in this program regardless of your citizenship or immigration status. No information about citizenship status is collected during enrollment. Apply online, or phone, or email. To participate in this program, you must: Live in King County, Washington; Be unable to access your local food bank in person; Be unable to afford groceries. May be a wait list; If you need immediate assistance with getting food, please call 2-1-1.
University District Food Bank	https://www.udistrictfoodbank.org /services/	(206) 523-7060 | 5017 Roosevelt Way NE, Seattle, WA 98105	Food pantry, baby cupboard and home delivery. Offers fresh fruits and vegetables, dairy, frozen meat, canned and dried goods, toiletries, baby formula, diapers, and pet food plus connections to important community resources. Visit once a week. Serves the unhoused and any residents in ZIP codes 98102, 98103, 98105, 98112, 98115 and 98125. Visit in person. Call for home delivery. Documents required: photo ID and proof of address. No fees.
Washington state's Basic Food program- King County	https://kingcounty.gov/en/dept/dp h/health-safety/health-centers-pr ograms-services/access-outreac h-program/basic-food-program	1-800-756-5437 | chap@kingcounty.go v | Public Health — Seattle & King County 401 5th Ave., Suite 1000 Seattle, WA	Basic Food is a food and nutrition program for individuals and families who meet the low income guideline, to afford healthier foods by providing monthly benefits to buy food. Basic Food will also qualify you for Free or Reduced School Meals for your child.
West Seattle Food Bank/Clothesli ne	https://westseattlefoodbank.org/	(206) 932-9023 | Foodbank:3419 Southwest Morgan Street Seattle, WA	Operates a food pantry, baby cupboard and home delivery. May visit food pantry once per week. Serves those that are homeless or

		98126 | 4425 41st Avenue Southwest Seattle, WA 98116	ZIP codes 98106, 98116, 98126 and 98136. Visit in person. Arrive early to get a number. Documents required: photo ID and proof of address (unless homeless). No fees.
White Center Food Bank	https://www.whitecenterfoodbank.org/	(206) 762-2848 | 10829 Eighth Ave. SW Seattle, WA 98146	Food pantry, food bags, baby supplies and food delivery. Food bags for everyone, pantry serves ZIP code 98146, as well as parts of 98106, 98126, 98136 and 98168. Call to confirm geographic eligibility. Visit in person. Home-bound clients can call. Documents Required: photo ID and proof of address. No fees. 3 visits per month.
Women's Wellness Center	https://ccsww.org/get-help/	(206) 256-0665 | 100 23rd Ave. S Seattle, WA	Showers, laundry facilities and toiletries. Nurse visits once a week. Serves adult women. Visit in person. No fees.
YWCA - Angeline's Day Center	https://www.ywcaworks.org/programs/angelines-day-center	(206) 436-8650 | 2030 Third Ave. Seattle, WA	Provides drop-in services like meals, laundry, showers, lockers, and connections to community resources. Offers advocates to help with tasks like getting an Identification card/ID or completing SSI or DSHS paperwork.
YWCA - Central Area Food Bank		mboyce@ywcaworks.org | foodbank@ywcaworks.org | 2820 E Cherry St. Seattle, WA 98122	Distributes free food and groceries weekly to residents in YWCA emergency shelter and transitional housing, as well as low-income families from the community 2 - 3 p.m.
Employment & Education Resources - King County			
ANEW - Pre-Apprenticeship Program	https://anewcareer.org/	(206) 381-1384 | 18338 Andover Park West, Tukwila, WA 98188	They offer high-quality, pre-apprenticeship training programs that help individuals obtain careers in construction trades. They partner with many registered apprenticeship programs in the Seattle area and expose students directly to their training facilities. ANEW also provides placement assistance and retention services for two years after graduation.
Asian Counseling and Referral Service	https://acrs.org/services/employment-and-training-services/	(206) 695-7600 | 3639 MLK Jr. Way S, Seattle, WA	ACRS promotes economic self-sufficiency by providing job-seekers with skills training, placement and retention services. Their goal is to help people find long-term employment that pay living wages and offer advancement opportunities.

Bellevue College	https://www.bellevuecollege.edu/	425-564-1000 | 3000 Landerholm Circle Southeast, Bellevue, WA, 98007	Provides post-secondary education within a community college setting. Online classes are available. Some childcare is available on a fee basis for enrolled students.
Bellevue College - Center for Career Connections at	https://www.bellevuecollege.edu/careers/	425-564-2212 | 3000 Landerholm Circle Southeast, Bellevue, WA, 98007	Offers help with: - Exploring college majors - Planning a career path - Finding an internship or job - Finding resources to fund education Educational Planning and Advising offers: - Transfer advising - Schedule planning - Educational goal setting Human Development Studies provides courses in: - College survival - Assertiveness training - Self-esteem training - Personal growth groups - Interpersonal relations - Stress management
CARES of Washington	https://www.caresofwa.org/	(206) 938-1253 | wehr@caresofwa.org | 1833 N 105th St., #202 Seattle, WA 98133	Career coaching, financial planning, benefits counseling and asset development services serving people 18 and older who are legally eligible to work in the U.S. Serves people with disabilities and people with barriers to employment. Call, apply online or apply in person. No fees.
Cascadia College	https://www.cascadia.edu/	425-352-8000 | 18345 Campus Way Northeast, Bothell, WA, 98011	Offers two-year degrees, certificate programs, adult basic education courses and two Bachelors of Applied Science degrees in sustainable practices and mobile applications. Also offers Running Start and GED programs. Running Start allows high school students to enroll at the college and get both high school and college credit for courses taken.
Casa Latina - Job Skills Training	https://casa-latina.org/work/job-skill-trainings/	(206) 956-0779; Employment Services/Servicios de Empleo: (206) 686-2554; ESL/Clases de Inglés: (206) 686-2618 | 317 17th Ave. S, Seattle, WA	Offers free English classes, day labor dispatching, housecleaning dispatch, community support and help reclaiming stolen wages. Serves the Latino immigrant community. Visit in person. Documents required: Photo ID. Membership for job dispatch: $25/year.
Dress for Success	https://seattle.dressforsuccess.org/	(206) 461-4472 | office@dfsseattle.org	Services include Employment Retention Programs, Career Center,

Seattle		| 600 Pine St., No. 310, Seattle, WA	one-on-one Career Coaching, and Career Wardrobe. Must have referral and schedule an appointment. See website, or phone (206) 461-4472 for information on getting a referral. Email office@dfsseattle.org.
DVR Division of Vocational Rehabilitation - King County	https://www.dshs.wa.gov/office-locations?field_geofield_distance%5Bdistance%5D=100&field_geofield_distance%5Bunit%5D=3959&field_geofield_distance%5Borigin%5D=King+County&field_office_type_tid%5B%5D=9654	View website to find the right location for you. Additional resources can be found at: https://www.dshs.wa.gov/dvr/resources-job-seekers	DSHS Department of Vocational Rehabilitation strives to provide the best services and resources possible to our customers helping them keep, find, and maintain employment. Services include vocational rehabilitation counseling, guidance and assessment Services, assistive technology and independent living services, job-related services, and more for people with disabilities who seek employment services.
FareStart Adult Culinary Program	https://www.farestart.org/job-training	(206) 787-1502 | 700 Virginia St., Seattle, WA	Sixteen weeks of culinary arts job training, followed by six months of support services for adults 18 and older. The program provides assistance with housing, transportation, wrap around case management services, job placement and more. No fees.
Goodwill - Job Training and Education Center	https://evergreengoodwill.org/job-training-and-education	(206) 329-1000 | 700 Dearborn Pl. S, Seattle, WA	Support services, work readiness classes and vocational training in retail, customer service and warehouse logistics. Call for more information. No fees.
Green River College	https://www.greenriver.edu/students/academics/getting-started/	253-833-9111 | 12401 Southeast 320th Street, Auburn, WA, 98092	Offers a variety of courses and programs that can lead to an associate's degree, certificate or diploma for academic transfer or a professional or technical field.
Highline College	https://admissions.highline.edu/	206-592-3181 | 2400 South 240th Street, Des Moines, WA, 98198	Coordinates academic transfer programs involving two years and four years of study in business, arts, science, etc. Provides opportunities for vocational degrees, certificates and short-term job training. Students may use child care service while working or in class (not for drop-in appointments).
Hopelink - Employment Services	https://www.hopelink.org/programs/employment-services/	425-250-3030 | HEP@hopelink.org	Hopelink's Employment Program provides several options to meet all your employment goals. The Career Coaching program aims to create a partnership between clients and employment specialists to reflect on and identify the skills, knowledge, and resources needed to find

			employment. Hopelink uses a collaborative approach where clients meet with their dedicated employment specialist once a week to review progress.
Lake Washington Institute of Technology	https://www.lwtech.edu/	425-739-8381 | 11605 132nd Avenue Northeast, Kirkland, WA, 98034	Offers professional, career and technical training to students who wish to improve basic skills, build on existing professional abilities, or change careers. Focus is on students learning quickly while mastering the skills of their chosen discipline. Child care is available to students. Evening classes may be available. Offers programs in the areas of bachelor and transfer degrees, applied design, business and service, computer/information technology, energy and technology, culinary arts, health science, manufacturing and transpiration technology. Job Skills Improvement Classes: Classes are offered to improve the job skills of persons employed in an occupation who wish to broaden their knowledge or upgrade their skills. Transfer Programs: Students may complete certain programs to transfer to several universities in the area.
Neighborhood House - Employment and Adult Education	https://nhwa.org/employment-and-adult-education/	206-923-6480 | info@nhwa.org | 1225 South Weller Street, Suite 510 Seattle, WA 98144	Neighborhood House connects community members with meaningful employment at livable wages and training opportunities to support their career advancement. Career Specialists help set goals and viable steps to achieve them. They also team up with local community colleges and other partners to connect individuals to vocational training, internship programs, and help with job placement. Their citizenship and English language classes provide pathways to future opportunities for immigrants and refugees.
North Seattle College	https://www.northseattle.edu/	206-934-3663 | 9600 College Way North, Seattle, WA, 98103	College offers academic, vocational and remedial education services including the following: - College transfer programs - Career training programs - Continuing education programs - Pre-college programs - High school programs - 5 bachelor of applied science degrees - Over 60 professional-technical degrees and certifications

			Student support services include - Career counseling - Accommodations for students with disabilities - Tutoring - Limited child care
Northwest Education Access (NWEC)	https://www.nweducationaccess.org/	(206) 523-6200 | info@nweducationaccess.org | 6920 Roosevelt Way NE No. 355, Seattle, WA 98115	Northwest Education Access provides the individualized guidance, connections to resources, and financial support that low-income young people need to earn higher education degrees. Services include Applying to College, Finding GED/High School Completion Sites, Placement Test Preparation, College Readiness Skill Building, Career + Program Exploration, Finding Funding, Scholarships + Financial Aid, Connect to Campus + Community Resources, Completely free! Much more!
Orion Industries - Job Placement and Follow-up	https://orionworks.org/	253-661-7805 | 1590 A Street Northeast, Auburn, WA, 98002	Placement specialist assists clients in job placement. Follow-up continues for at least three months.
Pioneer Human Services - Job Readiness Training	https://pioneerhumanservices.org/job-skills/Job-readiness	(206) 768-7333 | 7000 Highland Park Way SW, Seattle, WA	Helps develop skills to find and maintain employment. Five days per week for three weeks. Referrals accepted by a probation/corrections officer, case manager, therapist or self. Offers connections to apprenticeships programs. Seattle and Spokane Roadmap to Success job readiness training programs accepting applications for virtual and in-person programs.
Port of Seattle's Office of Port Jobs - Airport Jobs	https://portjobs.org/our-programs/airport-jobs	206-787-7501 | 17801 International Boulevard, Seatac Airport Mezzanine Level, SeaTac, WA, 98188	Operates as a central recruiting source for Seattle Tacoma International Airport employers and for job seekers.
Pre-Apprenticeship Construction Training (P.A.C.T.)	https://woodtech.seattlecentral.edu/programs/pre-apprenticeship-construction-training	(206) 934-5460 | jerry.jordan@seattlecolleges.edu | Wood Technology Center Seattle Central College 2310 S. Lane Seattle, WA 98144	Designed to help adults gain the skills needed to make them successful competitors for entry-level jobs in construction trade apprenticeship programs. The program is focused on providing basic carpentry skills and terminology, shop math, and effective and safe operation of power tools. Participants also learn and receive certification in forklift operation, road flagging, OSHA 10 safety, and first aid/CPR. The

			program is 22 credits long and takes approximately one quarter to complete.
Prison Scholar Fund	https://www.prisonscholars.org/	(206) 734-5425 | 1752 NW Market Street, #953 Seattle, WA 98107	The Prison Scholar Fund is a non-profit organization that provides education and employment assistance to incarcerated individuals to help them succeed and thrive in society while avoiding homelessness and the revolving door of reincarceration. They also advocate for reform in correctional education to increase access to all. Their core program provides access to postsecondary distance education, mentoring, and advising. They also offer a coding program for justice-involved humans, digital equity training, and affordable connectivity programs
Renton Technical College	https://rtc.edu/	425-235-2352 | 3000 NE 4th St, Renton, WA, 98056	Offers specialized professional and technical training programs to people 18 years of age and older. Certificate of Completion, Associate of Applied Science degree and Associate of Applied Science-Transfer degrees are offered. Other services include financial assistance, counseling and testing.
Shoreline Community College	https://www.shoreline.edu/	206-546-4101 | 16101 Greenwood Avenue North, Shoreline, WA, 98133	Provides comprehensive post-secondary and continuing education programs, including adult basic education, English as a Second Language classes, parenting classes, vocational education and many other programs.
SKCAC Industries and Employment Services	https://www.skcac.org/employment-services/	253-395-1240 | info@skcac.com | 19731 Russell Road, Kent, WA 98032	Provides training and job placement for people with disabilities, primarily serves those with developmental disabilities. Maintains ongoing support and follow-up services during and after job placement. Conducts job interviews in the community to assess the clients' interests and abilities.
Real Change	https://www.realchangenews.org/	(206) 441-3247 | 96 S Main St., Seattle, WA	Immediate low-barrier work opportunity for all, earning income by selling the weekly newspaper. No ID required. Provides access to services for participants of work program including case management, food assistance, referrals, medical and veterinary care, mailboxes, computer lab, and

			more. Creates and distributes this guidebook. Also available online at www.emeraldcityresourceguide.org
Seattle Central College	https://seattlecentral.edu/	206-934-3800 | 1701 Broadway, Seattle, WA, 98122	College credit academic courses offer a full spectrum of college transfer courses that apply toward a four-year program of study. Students are encouraged to attain their Associate of Arts (AA) or Associate of Science (AS) degree at SCCC for greater ease of transfer to a four-year institution. Individual classes may also be transferable. It is recommended that students confer with an academic advisor to ensure course transferability. Professional and Technical Studies provides training and certificate courses in a wide range of trades and technical fields.
Seattle Jobs Initiative	https://www.seattlejobsinitiative.com/job-seekers/	(206) 628-6975 | social@seattlejobsinit.com | 1200 12th Ave. S, No. 160, Seattle, WA	Seattle Jobs Initiative (SJI) supports job seekers in acquiring the skills, training, and support needed to enter a career that offers a living wage, and benefits in the fields of manufacturing, healthcare, diesel, ironworkers, and maritime welding. Provides a career navigator, help with goal setting, communication, interview preparation, and support services – such as housing, childcare and transportation.
Seattle Public Library, Central Branch, Job Resources	https://www.spl.org/programs-and-services/civics-and-social-services/job-resources	(206) 386-4636 | 1000 4th Ave., Seattle, WA	Resources for discovering a new career path, gaining new job skills, creating a cover letter and resume, and finding job opportunities. Free job search and career development programs will be available at Ballard Branch, Rainier Beach Branch, and on level 7 at the Central Library (special job search computers only at Central).
South Seattle College	https://southseattle.edu/	206-934-5300 | 6000 16th Avenue Southwest, Seattle, WA, 98106	Offers two-year degrees, short-term certificates and courses for college preparation and college transfer. Also offers two bachelor's degrees, in Hospitality Management and Sustainable Building Science Technology. Limited child care may be available.
TRAC Associates	http://tracassoc.com/our-programs.html	(206) 443-9999 | 215 6th Ave N., No. 100, Seattle, WA	TRAC Associates assist all disadvantaged job seekers: disabled, veteran, homeless, public benefit recipients, Limited English Proficient (LEP) , low-basic skills, illiterate, mature workers (55+),

			minority (including race, ethnicity, and religion), and long-term unemployed.
Union Jobs at MLK Labor	https://www.mlklabor.org/union-jobs/	(206) 441-8510	Online list of open union jobs for living wages and benefits. Full time or part time, many entry level union jobs such as customer service, hospitality field, food service, cashiering, working in a grocery store, barista, cooks, retail sales, painter, human services, airport agents, hotel attendants, warehouse processing, and many others. Shows description of employer company, each union, job duties, pay compensation and details. Apply online by registering to log in. After applying for a job online, MLK Labor offers, when possible, to advocate for qualified applicants to be hired, just let them know at unionjobs@mlklabor.org
United Way - Student Benefits Hub	https://www.uwkc.org/benefitshub/	(206) 649-8124 | 720 2nd Ave., Seattle, WA	Program for King County community or technical college students to help with everyday financial tools to keep you in school. Services include help paying for groceries, Utility bill assistance, Access to food, Paying for the bus, Financial coaching, Financial aid application assistance, Emergency financial grants, help with taxes, help with legal services, Housing supports, and more. Schedule an appointment online, or for more information phone or email.
Uplift Northwest	https://www.upliftnw.org/job-seekers/	(206) 728-5627 | 2515 Western Ave. Seattle, WA	Uplift Northwest is on a mission to provide dignified jobs and job-readiness services to men and women experiencing poverty and homelessness in the Puget Sound Region. We connect men and women with life-changing job opportunities. Common job opportunities include: landscaping, hospitality, food service and prep, warehouse, sanitation, housekeeping, moving assistance, and more. Helps earn and pays for food industry certifications. For Uplift workers, Uplift offers lockers services, housing assistance, and career training opportunities, as well as access to community partner-provided: meals, medical, dental, and cell phone services.
Urban League	http://urbanleague.org/priorityhire	(206) 461-3792 |	Assists individuals to enter

Metropolitan Seattle - Construction Trades Program	/	105 14th Ave. Suite 200 Seattle, WA	pre-apprenticeship programs and access to work in the construction industry. Provides wraparound support services. Must be 18 or older, WA state resident, have a serious interest in construction, and attend an information session after applying. Apply online, or phone for more information. For program participants, provides: financial assistance for learning supplies, work clothes, transportation, union dues, initiation fees, soft skills training, skills re-licensing and certification; additionally provides referrals to: credit counseling, digital literacy, and housing assistance.
Urban League of Metropolitan Seattle (ULMS) - Career Bridge	http://urbanleague.org/careerbridge/	(206) 461-3792 | 105 14th Ave. Suite 200 Seattle, WA	Career Bridge program is to help individuals with multiple barriers access education, employment, economic career opportunities in order to improve their quality of life. Provides job portfolio assistance (resume, cover letter, career planning, interview prep), wrap-around services, job placement assistance, transportation assistance. ULMS empowers African Americans and other diverse underserved communities to thrive by securing educational, economic opportunities. Open to any individual with a diverse background, including those with criminal histories, those experiencing homelessness, Veterans. Apply online, or phone for more information.
Vadis in Seattle	https://www.vadis.org/	253-863-5173 | 16000 Christensen Road, Suite 240 Tukwila, WA 98188	Offers community-based employment services including job placement and competitive employment.
Weld Seattle Employment Connection	https://weldworks.org/	206-571-4938 | Jay@weldseattle.org | 1426 South Jackson Street, Seattle, WA, 98144	Provides transitional and permanent labor program for individuals that have been impacted by the criminal legal system. Acts as a liaison between clients and the business community. Program includes: - Safety training - Safety equipment/ clothing - Transportation assistance Employment opportunities include: - Construction - General labor services - Manufacturing

			- Warehouse - Retail - Recycling
WorkSource Seattle-King County	https://www.worksourceskc.org/	Locations: Auburn, Downtown Seattle, North Seattle College, South Seattle College, Redmond, Rainier. https://www.worksourceskc.org/locations	Provides Computer Lab, Job Bank, Job Search Assistance, Resumé assistance, Interview preparation, Career Planning, Training, GED preparation, apprenticeship opportunities, internet access, Copiers, printers, phones, and faxes, Unemployment Insurance Application, Basic Support. Job fairs, Employer hiring events, Mock interviews, In-person ADA accessible technology, Translation or interpretation services, Website offers online job search. No fees.
YMCA - Employment Assistance and Training	https://www.seattleymca.org/social-impact-center/youth-young-adults/employment-education	Apply online; or call (206) 749-7550.	Serves ages up to 25 years old. Services include Better interview skills/mock interview, employment training program, filling out job applications, guidance on how to get a state ID or social security card, guidance on where to apply for unemployment, information on businesses that are currently hiring, and referrals to resources. Apply online or call (206) 749-7550.
YWCA - BankWorks	https://www.ywcaworks.org/programs/bankworks	(253) 736-2301 | bankworks@ywcaworks.org | 11215 Fifth Ave. SW Seattle 98146 | Auburn Learning Center 313 37th St SE Auburn, WA 98002	Prepares low-income job seekers for banking positions as a first step on the career ladder in the financial services industry, consists of 8 weeks of free industry-specific job training with a strong customer service and sales focus followed by direct job placement into positions at partner banks and credit unions. Provides instruction, career navigation, coaching, and mentoring for up to one year after placement. Operates in Seattle, Auburn, Bellevue, White Center, online.
YWCA - Eastside Employment	https://www.ywcaworks.org/programs/eastside-employment	(425) 556-1353 | mlreter@ywcaworks.org | 16601 NE 80th St. Redmond, WA	Employment advocates work with participants to make a plan for college classes or vocational training, and access additional support services. For homelessness employment program contact struong@ywcaworks.org. Through case management, participants get the tools and resources to support them to secure a living wage job and gain stability.
YWCA - Economic Resilience	https://www.ywcaworks.org/programs/economic-resilience-initiative	(206) 336-7000 | eri@ywcaworks.org | 9720 Eighth Ave.	Financial classes, workshops, coaching, and resources to help women and families build economic

		SW Seattle, WA	stability and empowerment, with many offered in both English and Spanish. Build skills and confidence with their personal finances. Vocational Training in various sectors, basic skills and ESL training, short-term vocational training, computer literacy skills, job and career search assistance, and various services for youth. All services are provided in multiple languages and are focused on helping White Center and South King County residents obtain the education, career skills, financial capability, and support they need in order to thrive.
Initiative/Green bridge Learning Center	https://www.ywcaworks.org/programs/greenbridge-learning-center		

Legal, Immigration, & Refugee Resources - King County			
ACLU Washington	https://www.aclu-wa.org/	(206) 624-2180 | 705 2nd Ave Ste 300, Seattle, WA 98104	The ACLU of Washington is a non-partisan civil liberties organization dedicated to protecting and advancing freedom, equity, and justice for everyone in Washington.
Asian Counseling and Referral Service, Legal Clinic	https://acrs.org/legal-services/	(206) 695-7639 or general legal clinic (206) 267-7070 | info@acrs.org | 3639 MLK Jr. Way S, Seattle, WA 98144	Legal services for Asian American Pacific Islanders. Specializes in detention and deportation defense, asylum and refugees, human trafficking, domestic violence. Call for an appointment.
Benefits Law Center	https://benefitslawcenter.org/	(206) 686 – 7252 | info@benefitslawcenter.org | 1404 E. Yesler Way # 203 Seattle, WA 98122	Benefits Law Center provides Social Security legal advocacy to people living with physical and mental disabilities who are homeless or low-income. Services include Applying for SSI and SSDI, and Appealing denials. The Disabled Homeless Advocacy Project (DHAP) delivers legal aid at local shelters, libraries, and sites accessible to the homeless population. DHAP helps provide resources necessary to help keep clients engaged in medical treatment and in their disability claim. Proof of income eligibility required.
Catholic Immigration Legal Services	https://ccsww.org/get-help/specialized-services/refugee-immigration-services/	(206) 328-6314 | 100 23rd Ave. S, Seattle, WA	Immigration legal services, including citizenship assistance, green cards, DACA and family-based petitions serving low-income refugees, asylees and immigrants in Washington. Call for initial screening. Will not deny services due to inability to pay.
City of Seattle,	https://seattle.gov/iandraffairs	(206) 727-8515 |	City of Seattle Office of Immigrant

Office of Immigrant and Refugee Affairs		700 5th Ave # 1616 Seattle, WA	and Refugee Affairs programs include Citizenship access, ESL and Job Training, Legal Defense Fund and Network, Immigrant Family Institute, Language Access Program, Ethnic Media Program, and COVID 19 Disaster Relief Fund for Immigrants. City employees do not ask about citizenship status and serve all residents regardless of immigration status.
Columbia Legal Services	https://columbialegal.org/	(206) 464-5911 | 1301 5th Ave, Ste 1200, Seattle, WA 98101	Provides legal representation and advocacy for low-income individuals, including those involved in the criminal justice system.
Housing Justice Project	https://www.kcba.org/?pg=Housing-Justice-Project	(206) 580-0762 | hjpstaff@kcba.org | King County Courthouse, 516 Third Ave., Room-W314, Seattle, WA	Providing free legal advice (legal consultations) for low-income renters with eviction related issues, answering questions about eviction paperwork, negotiating with landlords if you're a renter facing eviction, representing renters at courthouse eviction hearings (show cause hearings), sharing referral and resource information. Apply in person, online, call (206) 580-0762 to leave a message with staff or email at hjpstaff@kcba.org. Operated through King County Bar Association. For urgent issues please call 2-1-1.
Ingersoll Gender Center	https://ingersollgendercenter.org/	(206) 849-7859 | 911 E Pike St. #221, Seattle, WA	Ingersoll Gender Center is an organization by and for transgender and gender nonconforming people providing mutual support through peer led support groups, resource navigation, community organizing, and education. Offering gender affirming Healthcare Provider Database, Job Board, Rural Resource Guides, Transgender Tenant Rights, Shelter and Housing Guide, and a Guide to Amending your Identity Documents in King County. Peer support groups for people to come together for information and mutual support.
International Rescue Committee	https://www.rescue.org/united-states/seattle-wa	(206) 623-2105 | seattle@rescue.org | 1200 S 192nd St., No. 101 SeaTac, WA	Serves everyone with routine immigration matters such as applying for green cards, employment authorization, and citizenship. Offers resettlement services, family reunification assistance, social service access, and employment services to immigrants, refugees, and asylees. Direct services to victims of human

			trafficking and other crimes with no ID required. Eligibility and document requirements for all other services vary.
King County Bar Association, Free Legal Assistance	https://www.kcba.org/?pg=Free-Legal-Assistance	(206) 267-7100 | 1200 5th Ave., No. 700, Seattle, WA	The King County Bar Association Pro Bono/free Services department works with over 1400 volunteer attorneys, paralegals, law students and community members to provide free legal assistance for low income King County residents. Provides assistance for General Legal Advice, Debt and Bankruptcy, Family Law, Vacating Criminal Records, and The Housing Justice Project provides free legal assistance to renters facing eviction in King County.
King County Bar Association, The Records Project	https://www.kcba.org/?pg=The-Records-Project	(206) 267-7100 | 1200 5th Ave., No. 700, Seattle, WA	The Records Project provides free legal services to vacate eligible King County criminal convictions. A vacated conviction is removed from public background searches available to employers and potential landlords. Eligible persons include low-income people, and homeless people, and immigrants (regardless of immigration status).
King County Department of Public Defense	https://kingcounty.gov/en/legacy/depts/public-defense.aspx	Office: (206) 296-7662; 24/7 On-Call Attorney: (206) 477-8899; financial eligibility screening: (206) 477-9727 | 710 2nd Ave., No. 200, Seattle, WA	Legal representation for people who are found to be income-eligible and are charged with a crime in King County. Financial interview required, with no appointment necessary. Representation is also provided to youth, those involved in a dependency proceeding, people facing civil commitment, and others. Does not accept cases from Seattle Municipal Court. The 24/7 on-call attorney service is available to anyone in custody in King County or under investigation who is seeking the advice of an attorney.
King County Law Library		(206) 477-1305 | 516 3rd Ave., Room W621, Seattle, WA	King County Law Library aids all persons with their need for legal information by providing legal materials, training, education, and services in a welcoming and positive environment.
Lavender Rights Project	https://www.lavenderrightsproject.org/	(206) 639-7955 | 911 E Pike St. #314, Seattle, WA	Lavender Rights Project elevates the power, autonomy, and leadership of the Black intersex & gender diverse community through intersectional legal and social services. We utilize the law as an organizing principle to affirm our

			civil rights and self-determination. Our organization disrupts oppressive systems that target Black gender diverse and intersex communities of color and lead to disproportionate levels of poverty, housing disparities, and gender-based violence, especially among Black and Indigenous people.
Living with Conviction	https://livingwithconviction.org/lfo-help	(206) 307-3028 | info@livingwithconviction.org | P.O. Box 17392, Seattle, Wa 98107	Legal Financial Obligation reduction/waiver guidance.
MAPS - Muslim Community Resource Center (MCRC)	https://mapsredmond.org/	Office: (425) 947-7146; services: (888) 404-6272 | 16307 NE 83rd St., No. 10 Redmond, WA	Emergency assistance referral, legal clinic, counseling, refugee assimilation, elder services and Islamic funeral services. Provides rental and utility assistance and help with eviction notices or final notices, and transitional housing options that are socially and culturally appropriate for single women. Serves the Muslims of Puget Sound. Call or visit website for more information. Services require a photo ID.
Neighborhood Legal Clinics	https://www.kcba.org/?pg=Neighborhood-Legal-Clinics	(206) 267-7070 | Location varies	Coordinates legal clinics across King County. No income restrictions. Serves King County residents or those who have a case filed in King County. Clients must call for an appointment. Bring any pertinent documents to the appointment. No Fees.
Neighborhood Legal Clinics, Asian Pacific American Legal Clinic	https://kcll.org/legal-clinics/guide-to-free-low-cost-legal-help-in-king-county/asian-pacific-american-legal-clinics-resources/	(206) 695-7639 | 3639 MLK Jr. Way S, Seattle, WA View website for additional locations.	Serves Asian and Pacific Islander clients who have a case filed in King County. Call the appointment line and leave a message. No fees. Appointments are only scheduled seven days in advance. Legal consultation, advice and referrals for a wide range of civil legal issues including, but not limited to, living wills/ advance directives, powers-of-attorney, wills, estate planning, rights to public benefits /Apple Health (Medicaid), etc. Accommodations for disability and interpreters are provided free.
New Holly Learning Center	https://southseattle.edu/programs/newholly-learning-center	(206) 934-6642 | 7058 32nd Ave. S, No. 201, Seattle, WA	Offers assistance to individuals seeking U.S. citizenship including citizenship and ESL classes. Provides bilingual case management, free HIV education,

			as well as counseling, testing and referrals, early childhood education programs and general employment and adult education services. Serves low-income community members, public housing residents, immigrants and refugees. Call for information. No fees.
Northwest Immigrant Rights Project	https://nwirp.org/get-help/	(206) 587-4009 | 615 2nd Ave., No. 400, Seattle, WA	Direct legal representation in court, visa application support, and defends the rights of people to gain safety through asylum. Services for children and youth rights, and the right to become a U.S. citizen. Direct representation for immigrant survivors of violence, and DACA (Deferred Action for Childhood Arrivals). Detention and Deportation Defense offers representation in immigration court. Also works for systemic change, and offers Community Education such as Know Your Rights Presentations, and Immigration 101 Training for Service Providers.
Northwest Justice Project	https://nwjustice.org/get-legal-help	Eviction help: 1-855-657-8387 Office: (206) 464-1519 | 401 2nd Ave. S No. 407, Seattle, WA	Legal services for low-income people particularly vulnerable populations, including farm workers, Native Americans, Western State Hospital patients, veterans, victims of crime, survivors of domestic violence, and persons over 60 years old. Apply online or call 211 for a referral, or call CLEAR (Coordinated Legal Education, Advice and Referral) 1-888-201-1014. Services include public housing discrimination, workplace conditions, home foreclosure, access to government benefits, education and employment issues, lost wages, medical debt, access to courts, general civil rights. Website information is available in multiple languages.
OneAmerica	https://weareoneamerica.org/about/about-oneamerica/	Office: (206) 723-2203, Hotline: (844)-RAID-REP | 1225 S. Weller Street No. 430, Seattle, WA	One America advocates Immigrant Defense Funds for immigrants who may not be able to afford an attorney, facilitates Know-your-rights trainings, direct action, grassroots organizing, and legislative action. By calling 1-844-RAID-REP and texting JOIN to (253)-201-2833, the community can protect itself. Sign up to stay tuned for action alerts and other opportunities to get involved.

Q-Law LGBTQ Legal Clinic	https://www.qlawfoundation.org/	Appointment line: (206) 235-7235	clinic@qlawfoundation.org	1216 Pine St., No. 300, Seattle, WA	Offers FREE consultation with a volunteer attorney on LGBTQ+ issues. Legal clinic designed to address the needs of lesbian, gay, bisexual and transgender individuals and couples. No fees.
Refugee Federation Service Center	https://www.rfsc.org/	(206) 501-4121	1209 Central Ave S suite 134, Kent, WA	Employment and training services, citizenship application and advocacy, assistance with immigration paperwork, ESL classes, information and referral, family counseling and translation services, serving low-income refugees and immigrants. No fees.
Refugee Women's Alliance (REWA)	https://www.rewa.org/	(206) 721-0243	4008 MLK Jr. Way S, Seattle, WA	Provides refugee and immigrant women and their families with culturally and linguistically appropriate services. Provides services to become independent. Programs for family empowerment, English as a Second Language (ESL), employment and vocational training, housing and homelessness prevention, domestic violence intervention, and support for sexual assault survivors, licensed behavioral health, naturalization and legal services, senior nutrition and wellness, early Learning Centers, and youth programs. No fees.
Seattle Clemency Project - Immigrant Post-Conviction Relief	https://www.seattleclemencyproject.org/immigrant-post-conviction-relief	206-682-1114	info@seattleclemencyproject.org	20415 72nd Ave South, Suite 1-415, Kent, WA 98032	Seattle Clemency Project partners with the Northwest Immigrant Rights Project and Khmer Anti-Deportation Advocacy Group to obtain the legal assistance they need to stay in their community and keep their families intact.
Seattle Office for Civil Rights	https://seattle.gov/civilrights/what-we-do	(206) 684-4500	810 3rd Ave., No. 750, Seattle, WA	Investigates civil rights discrimination and enforces laws against illegal discrimination in employment, housing, public accommodation, and contracting within Seattle City Limits. No fees.
Seattle Public Library, Central Branch, Immigrant & Refugee Services	https://www.spl.org/programs-and-services/civics-and-social-services/immigrant-and-refugee-services	(206) 386-4636	1000 4th Ave., Seattle, WA	Free classes and online tools for citizenship and English language learning. Books, CDs and DVDs in many languages. Free public computers. As an immigrant or new citizen, you have the right to fair treatment when you vote, worship, travel or express your views. The pocket-sized "Know Your Rights" cards explain your freedoms. You can pick one up at any Library location.

Solid Ground	https://www.solid-ground.org/get-help/	DSHS Benefits Help: (206) 694-6742; Tenant Info Hotline: (206) 694-6767 | info@solid-ground.org | 1501 N 45th Street, Seattle, WA 98103	Legal services to help clients obtain and retain public benefits like SNAP food stamp/EBT, Medicaid/health insurance, government cash assistance, and more. Provides information and referral for tenants facing eviction or struggling with other rental issues. Provides references to food and nutrition assistance programs, as well as rental assistance and shelter diversion through 211. Serves low-income residents of King County. No restrictions for advice and referrals. No fees.
St. James Cathedral	https://www.stjames-cathedral.org/immigrant/default.aspx	General Line: (206) 264-2091 St. James Immigrant Assistance: (206) 382-4511 | 907 Columbia St., Seattle, WA	Meal serving everyone. St James Immigrant Assistance provides ESL/English language instruction, comprehensive naturalization assistance, immigrant legal services, citizenship preparation classes. Call for an appointment for services. No fees.
Tenant Law Center	https://ccsww.org/get-help/specialized-services/tenant-law-center/	(206) 324-6890 | 100 23rd Ave. S, Seattle, WA (Randolph Carter Family Center)	Tenant Law Center provides free legal representation to tenants facing evictions or subsidy termination. If you are a low-income renter in Seattle and you have received an eviction notice, subsidy termination letter or a payment plan from your landlord, call for appointment. Also provides legal advocacy for homeless families, and free legal representation services to all Rapid Re-Housing providers in King County. If you need help with any other housing issue, please call intake line at 206-324-6890 for a referral. Does not accept walk-ins. Operated by Catholic Community Services.
The Redemption Project of Washington	https://www.redemptionwa.org/about		The mission of RPW is to increase access to counsel, ensure defenders have resources to deliver effective advocacy, and provide reentry support in trial-level post-conviction cases.
Unemployment Law Project	https://unemploymentlawproject.org/	(206) 441-9178 | 1904 Third Avenue, Suite 604 Seattle, WA 98101	Legal counseling and representation at administrative hearings for persons denied unemployment benefits. Provides information on your employment and unemployment rights, guidance when navigating quitting your job or being terminated, and legal advice on employment and employee/employer relations. Office

			is closed for in-person appointments. Aides in legal representation for anyone who has opened a claim or is eligible to open a Washington state unemployment claim. Call for intake interview. No fees for information or advice with an attorney. Charges $200 if representation is successful.
Washington Innocence Project	https://wainnocenceproject.org/	(206) 636-9479 | PO Box 85869, Seattle, WA 98145	Washington Innocence Project, a 501(c)(3) nonprofit organization, uses direct legal representation to get innocent people out of prison, advocates for policy change to keep people from being wrongfully convicted in the first place, and offers support services to the wrongfully convicted and their families.
Family & Children Resources - King County			
Catholic Community Services, Kinship Program	https://ccsww.org/get-help/services-for-seniors-people-with-disabilities/kinship-services/	(206) 328-6858 | 100-23rd Ave. S, Seattle, WA	For families who are raising grandchildren, nieces, nephews, siblings etc. who are in need of assistance navigating resources to help the families become stable . Assists with applying for TANF, Child Tax Credit, finding medical or mental health services and assistance with applying for medical insurance. Some financial support services for rent, utilities, etc once a year; quarterly legal clinics to explore adoption/guardianship.
Catholic Community Services, Pregnancy & Parenting Support (PREPARES)	https://ccsww.org/get-help/child-youth-family-services/	(206) 737-9264 | 100 23rd Ave. S, Seattle, WA	Counseling, case management, education, emergency assistance and material support for women and families with children 5 years and younger. Does not provide medical referrals. Call for phone intake. Interpreter services available by appointment only. No fees.
Changes Parent Support Network	https://cpsn.org/	888-468-2620 | office@cpsn.org | PO Box 31862, Seattle, WA 98103	Changes Parent Support Network is a structured, peer-led program that provides support to parents struggling with children who are engaging in oppositional and self-destructive behaviors. Changes offers hope, help, support and relief from feeling overwhelmed and alone. We give back freely to the community in recognition and thanks to those that walked this path before us and helped us. We are a registered 501 (c) 3 non-profit organization.

Child Care, City of Seattle	https://seattle.gov/education/for-parents	(206) 386-1050 | 700 Fifth Ave., #1700 Seattle, WA	Child care through Seattle Preschool Program (SPP) or Child Care Assistance Program (CCAP). Financial assistance for families in need of child care for low income families with children 13 and under. Call for further information about requirements (206) 386-1050, or email education@seattle.gov. You can apply online at listed website.
Child Welfare Services at Washington State Department of Children, Youth, and Families in King West	https://www.dcyf.wa.gov/services/child-welfare-system/cps	800-609-8764 | 100 W Harrison St, South Tower, Suite 200, Seattle, WA, 98119 See website for additional locations.	Provides both permanency planning and intensive treatment services to children and families who may need help with chronic problems such as on-going abuse and neglect or intensive medical needs.
Childhaven	https://childhaven.org/programs/	(206) 957-4841 | 1025 S 3rd Street Renton, WA 98057 | 1345 22nd St NE Auburn, WA 98002	Childhaven is addressing the epidemic of childhood trauma and adversity through relationship, partnership, and innovation. Offers a variety of programs for children from birth to age 24 and their families where they live, learn, and play, including their homes, early learning centers, pediatric and family health settings, community centers, and schools. Childhaven's skilled and caring staff work collaboratively with families to develop care plans that are individualized, family-centered, and culturally relevant. Multiple program services including art, trauma care, counseling, early learning, and support for infants and toddlers. Income statements required for Early Learning (ECEAP, Early ECEAP); Insurance is required for some programs.
Children's Home Society of Washington	https://www.childrenshomesociety.org/northking	(206) 364-7930 | nsfc@chs-wa.org | 2611 NE 125th St., #145 Seattlem, WA	National organization with centers in this state offers resources for families. Services include support groups, nutrition program for Women, Infants, Childre (WIC), prevention by partnering with families earlier to get ahead of problems before they occur at home, health and maternity support for pregnant women, occasional parenting classes, child and family counseling, and early learning for children ages 0-5, at home. Also, some advocacy for foster care placement and reuniting children with parents if they are child

			protective services involved families. Interpreters available with advance notice. Serves low-income families. Call for appointment.
Divine Alternatives for Dads Services (DADS)	https://www.aboutdads.org/services	(206) 722-3137 | 411 12th Ave, Suite 300 Seattle, WA 98122	Help with Child Support. Help with a Parenting Plan. Navigating legal & relational barriers. Connecting with other Fathers. Becoming Dads Course. Support Groups.
Early Childhood Education and Assistance Program - City of Seattle	https://seattle.gov/education/for-parents/child-care-and-preschool/early-childhood-education-and-assistance-program	(206) 684-0296 | 700 5th Ave, No. 1700, Seattle, WA	The Early Childhood Education and Assistance Program (ECEAP), funded through the State of Washington's Department of Early Learning and the City of Seattle, offers part-day and full-day, high-quality, culturally and linguistically appropriate preschool services for eligible 3- and 4-year-olds and their families. The primary goal is to help participating children develop the skills they need to be ready for school and acquire a passion for lifelong learning. Families have access to information, resources, and training that support them in moving towards their individual and family goals.
Families of Color Seattle (FOCS)	https://www.focseattle.org/parent-groups-register	(206) 317-4642	Offers Family Programs and Parent Groups. Gatherings are eight to ten weekly, two-hour sessions. Curriculum includes dialogue on racism, identity, and tools to best support raising strong, compassionate children of color. Facilitators are parents with lived experience. Sharing experiences, pain, trauma, and liberation to be equipped with tools to protect and inform children of color.
Family Resource Center	https://familyworksseattle.org/	(206) 647-1790 | theteam@familyworksseattle.org | 1501 N 45th St., Seattle, WA	Resource center programs and services are free. Kids basics: clothing, books, diapers, toys. Drop in play group for children 0-5, parents or caregivers. Navigation services, and hygiene supplies.
Gifts of Hope	https://www.givinggiftsofhope.org/	(206) 486-7171 | info@givinggiftsofhope.org	Gifts of Hope is a non-profit organization that was founded in 2017 in response to the homelessness in South Seattle and its effects on children. Through community networks it has expanded assistance, and desires not to enable but encourage those in need by providing them with basic needs, such as food and

			clothing, as well as haircuts, empowerment classes, cooking and craft classes, holiday support and resources for housing, medical care and referrals for counseling.
Guided Pathways – Support for Youth and Families	https://www.guidedpathways.org/	253.236.8264 | connect2gps@guidedpathways.org | 6625 S. 190th St., Suite B102, Kent, WA 98032	They empower and support families and youth struggling with behavioral, emotional or substance abuse challenges in navigating resources to achieve wellness and resilience.
Northwest Family Life	http://northwestfamilylife.org/suvivor-services/	(206) 363-9601 24/7 hotline: 1-800-244-5767 | 12360 Lake City Way NE, No. 420, Seattle, WA	Serves women and children who are experiencing or have experienced abuse. Offers advocacy based counseling, safety planning, education on domestic violence and referrals to legal, housing, employment and spiritual resources. Weekly support groups. Call for appointment. No fees.
Southeast Youth & Family Services	https://seyfs.org/	(206) 721-5542 | 3722 S Hudson St., Seattle, WA	Individual and family counseling, employment assistance, case management, advocacy, information and referral and crisis intervention. Serves African and Asian immigrant and refugee individuals and families. Dedicated to helping youth and families overcome traumas of economic and educational inequality, disparities in foster care and the criminal justice system, and other forms of institutional racism. Call for appointment. No fees for most services.
Incarcerated Parents Project	https://defensenet.org/case-support/incarcerated-parents-project/	206-623-4321 | 810 3rd Ave, Suite 258 Seattle, WA 98104	IPP envisions that keeping parents in the community, not in jail or prison, ensuring incarcerated parents are able to maintain meaningful connections with their minor children if they are imprisoned, and removing stigma associated with parental incarceration will keep their families and our community safer.
You Grow Girl !	https://www.yougrowgirl.org/	(206) 417-9904 | South Seattle/Mt. Baker: 2200 Rainier Ave S, Suite 201, Seattle, 98144 | Kent/Covington: 15215 SE 272nd Street, Kent, 98042	You Grow Girl! is a nonprofit organization serving female-identifying youth and families. Commitment to empower sisters and families by providing comprehensive, wraparound services. Through the 'Whole Sister, Whole Family Pathway' adolescents, youth and adults are able to reach their authentic selves through the development of life skills, advocacy and self-respect.

			Programs include youth leadHERship and career focused mentoring, behavioral health services include case management (ages up to-24), individual and family counseling (ages up to-30), psychoeducation and support groups (ages up to-30), WISe and wraparound services (ages up to-21).
YWCA - Parent Child +	https://www.ywcaworks.org/progr ams/parent-child-plus	(206) 209-5662 | awarsame@ywcawor ks.org | 3800 S Myrtle St. Seattle	Educational home visiting program for families with children between 16 months and 2 1/2 years old. Early learning specialists will visit with you and your child twice a week for 30 minutes. Each week your child will receive a free book or toy. Parent Child + specialists speak English, Somali, and Tigrinya.

Cultural & Veteran Resources - King County

Cultural Resources

Call BlackLine	https://www.callblackline.com/	1 (800) 604-5841	Call BlackLine® provides a space for peer support, counseling, reporting of mistreatment, witnessing and affirming the lived experiences for folxs who are most impacted by systematic oppression with an LGBTQ+ Black Femme Lens. Call BlackLine® prioritizes BIPOC (Black, Indigenous, and People of Color). By us for us.
Chief Seattle Club	https://www.chiefseattleclub.org/	Front desk: (206) 715–7536 Housing: (206) 677–0912 | 410 - 2nd Ave Extension S Seattle	Native-led agency providing basic needs and a day center, physically and spiritually supporting American Indian and Alaska Native people. Day Center in the Pioneer Square provides food, primary heath care, housing assistance, an urban Indian legal clinic, a Native art job training program, as well as frequent outings for members to cultural and community-building events.
Chinese Information and Service Center	https://cisc-seattle.org/	(206) 624-5633 | 611 S Lane St. Seattle, WA	Multi-service family support center includes naturalization assistance, healthcare navigation, housing assistance, ESL classes, case management to older adults and people with disabilities and family counseling, and more. Hosts free legal clinic. Primarily serves limited-English-speaking immigrant Chinese and other Asian households. Visit in person. Call for fee information.

Council on American-Islamic Relations: CAIR	https://cairwa.org/	(206) 367-4081 | 1511 3rdAve., No.701, Seattle, WA	Advocates on behalf of those who have experienced religious discrimination, defamation or hate crimes. Serves practicing Muslims and those perceived as Muslims. Call for more information. No fees. Services by appointment only, no walk-ins.
East African Community Services	https://www.eastafricancs.org/	(206) 721-1119 | 7050 32nd Ave. S, Youth Building, Seattle, WA	EACS offers wrap around services for East African refugee and immigrant families. Provides Pre—K to 12th Grade After school and summer programs. Also provides innovative STEM mentorship through the MathCode+Robotics and Strong Girls Powerful Leaders. Provides Parent Leadership Training (PILTI) and Advocacy and U.S. Citizenship Classes. Engagement and family resourcing provides rental assistance, diapers and culturally appropriate food. Diversion and reentry support for youth returning to community from incarceration. No fees.
El Centro de la Raza	https://www.elcentrodelaraza.org/	(206) 957-4634; Veterans Specialist: (360) 986-7046 | 2524 16th Ave. S, Seattle, WA	Multi-service center offers ESL classes, a bilingual legal clinic, life skills and job readiness education, child and youth programs, a bilingual child care/preschool program, maternity services, crisis advocacy and homeless prevention. Services for veterans, especially women veterans and veterans of color. Serves veterans of all discharge types. Operates a food pantry, serves everyone, provides a community a meal for adults over 60. Benefits navigator available on site limited hours each week.
Entre Hermanos	https://entrehermanos.org/	(206) 322-7700 | 1621 S Jackson, No. 202, Seattle, WA	Promotes the health and well-being of the Latino Gay, Lesbian, Bisexual, Transgender, and questioning community in a culturally appropriate environment. Services include support group, and social workers provide referrals. Immigration Department for direct legal services, asylum, immigration relief, for those detained. Provides a range of services related to HIV/AIDS prevention, care, and support, Free HIV Testing, Community Forums, Latino PrEP Navigator who can help you access PrEP (Pre-Exposure Prophylaxis), and Condom Distribution. Providing Advocacy and Civic Engagement,

			and registering new voters.
Filipino Community of Seattle	https://www.filcommsea.org/	(206) 722-9372 | 5740 MLK Jr. Way S, Seattle, WA	Serves Filipino and other communities in Greater Seattle and beyond. Provides culturally appropriate services for educational support and mentorship, social interaction, counseling and support. Cultural home for the Filipino Community as well as immigrants, refugees. Lunch program and affordable low-income housing for seniors. Youth programs with families, schools, and BIPOC members of the community.
Helping Link	http://www.helpinglink.org/program-services/	(206) 568-5160 | 1032 S Jackson St., No. C, Seattle, WA	Empowers Vietnamese American social adjustment, family stability, and self-sufficiency, offers Citizenship Classes, ESL classes, computer and iPad training classes, information and referrals. Serves the Vietnamese community. Call to confirm hours. Register in person. No fees.
Horn of Africa Services	https://hoas.org/	(206) 760-0550 | 5303 Rainier Ave. S, No. D, Seattle, WA	Serves the East African immigrant and refugee community. Social services, educational assistance, youth programs, and economic empowerment to address the needs of the community. Offers citizenship classes, housing assistance, job search assistance, benefits assistance, more. After school programs available for kindergarten through 12th grade. Call main office or visit in person to complete an application. No fees.
IDIC Filipino Senior & Family Services	https://www.idicseniorcenter.org/	(206) 587-3735 | 7301 Beacon Ave. S, Seattle, WA	Filipino organization that provides advocacy in healthcare and social services to underserved elderly, immigrant and vulnerable families. Helps seniors 50 years of age and older apply for benefits, job training, affordable housing, and interpretation. Assistance with immigration, activities such as games and fitness opportunities, hot meals, and a food bank. Also serves adults with disabilities. No required fees. Suggested that you show photo ID or other proof of King County residence, but not required for services. Call for more information.
Jewish Family Service	https://www.jfsseattle.org/	(206) 461-3240 | 1601 16th Ave., Seattle, WA	Assistance for Jewish community and general community impacted by trauma, poverty and disability.

			Provides program to support survivors of domestic violence, including safety planning, legal, housing, financial assistance and support groups. Also offers counseling program focused on healing for people with mental health challenges, addiction, past or current trauma. Also offers services for older adults and family caregivers, refugees and immigrants. Some utility assistance as well. Operates a food bank offering Kosher options. Serves people of all backgrounds regardless of zip code. Documents required: ID. No fees.
MAPS - Muslim Community Resource Center (MCRC)	https://mapsredmond.org/	Office: (425) 947-7146; services: (888) 404-6272	16307 NE 83rd St., No. 10 Redmond, WA	Emergency assistance referral, legal clinic, counseling, refugee assimilation, elder services and Islamic funeral services. Provides rental and utility assistance and help with eviction notices or final notices, and transitional housing options that are socially and culturally appropriate for single women. Serves the Muslims of Puget Sound. Call or visit website for more information. Services require a photo ID.
Mother Nation	https://www.mothernation.org/	(206) 722-2321	4250 S Mead St., Seattle,	Native American organization offering culturally informed healing services, advocacy, mentorship and homeless prevention. Emergency transportation for victims of domestic violence, safety planning, public benefit application assistance, housing referrals, referrals to employment, advocacy with Indian child welfare, domestic violence court and Tribal courts, and weekly women's healing circles. Serves Native families. Call for an appointment. Documents required: tribal ID or other documentation of native descent. Free.
Peer Kent	http://peerkent.org	(253) 277-4942	216 W Gowe St., No. 300 Kent, WA	Peer Kent cultivates powerful, healthy lives by providing peer emotional support and development services to the lesbian, gay, bisexual, transgender, queer (LGBTQ) community impacted by addiction, mental health and/or HIV. Services include peer coaching. Also offers employment support and referrals to resources such as housing or medical care.

Peer Seattle	https://www.peerseattle.org/	(206) 322-2437 | 1520 Bellevue Ave., No. 100	Peer emotional support and development services to the LGBTQ+ community impacted by addiction, mental health and/or HIV. Peer coaching for recovery and goals, and peer facilitated support groups to become part of a community. Offers employment support and referrals to resources such as housing or medical care.
Seattle Indian Center	http://seattleindiancenter.org	(206) 329-8700 | admin@seattleindian.org | 624 S Dearborn St., Seattle, WA 98134	Primary focus is serving the American Indian/Alaska Native community, and also serves people of color as well as anyone in need. Provides a multi-service center with advocacy and support services. Programs include outreach and engagement, drop-in center, food bank, and community hot meals. For community shelter services, call for intake and location.
Somali Community Services of Seattle	http://somcss.org	(206) 760-1181 | 8810 Renton Ave. S, Seattle, WA	Support refugees to undergo a smooth transitional process. Family and youth programs, housing referral, senior program including ethnic lunches, peer counseling, job search assistance, ESL classes, computer classes, Somali language classes and parenting education classes. Case managers can assist with the immigration process. Primarily serves refugees and immigrants. Call or visit in person. No fees. Need to have state ID, passport, green card or other identification.
Ukrainian Community Center of Washington	https://uccwa.org/	(425) 430-8229 | 13470 MLK Jr. Way S., Seattle, WA	Immigration assistance with green cards, naturalization and citizenship classes. Provides individual and family counseling, case management and advocacy. Social services include domestic violence screenings, assessments and intervention, parenting education, assistance accessing state and federal benefits and assistance with Native Countries documents. Seniors have access to a daily lunch program, nutrition education, enhanced fitness and counseling services. Serves Eastern European refugee and immigrant communities. Some services are offered free of charge to low-income families.
United Indians of All Tribes	http://unitedindians.org	(206) 285-4425 | 5011 Bernie	Social service provider, community center, and cultural home for the

| | | Whitebear Way, Seattle, WA | urban Indigenous community. Offers family services, support for expectant families, school readiness, economic self-sufficiency, employment services program, housing stability, and health and well-being. Native Workforce Services Program; Emerging Native Artists Cohort to develop professional skills and businesses; Labateyah Youth Home, Foster Care, Homelessness Prevention, Preschool, Native Elders Program; Native Veterans Program. Offers free online Daybreak Star Radio accessible through the website to reconnect heritage, belonging, and significance as a people. |
| Foundation | | | |

Veteran Resources			
Catholic Community Services, Michael's Place	https://ccsww.org/get-help/housing/transitional-housing/michaels-place/	(206) 726-5688 | 1307 E Spring St., Seattle,WA	Transitional housing for homeless adult male veterans who have a mental health diagnosis or are in recovery and eligible for transitional housing through the Veterans Administration Puget Sound Health Care System (VA Hospital). Application is done via the VA system or King County Veterans organizations. Residents must pay 25 percent of their gross income.
Compass Housing Alliance, Shoreline/Rent on Veterans Center	https://www.compasshousingalliance.org/affordable-housing/veterans-center-shoreline/ https://www.compasshousingalliance.org/affordable-housing/veterans-center-renton/	(206) 474-1880 | 1301 N 200th St. Shoreline, WA | 419 S 2nd St. #4 Renton, WA	Shoreline Veterans Center (SVC) provides permanent supportive housing and case management for 21 men and 4 women who are Veterans. The center's technology lab offers computer classes and helps residents apply for benefits, look for a job, and access resources online. If you are currently a homeless Veteran or at risk of losing housing, please call the VA's Homeless Outreach Clinic at 425-203-7200.
Department of Veteran Affairs Community Resource and Referral Center	https://www.va.gov/puget-sound-health-care/	(206) 764-5149 | 305 S Lucille St., Seattle, WA	Provides referrals to resources for healthcare, housing, and more for U.S. military veterans. May provide short-term case management as needed and resource information outside of veteran-specific resources.
Disabled American Veterans Network	https://www.dav.org/get-help-now/medical-transportation/	(206) 341-8267 | 915 2nd Ave., No. 1040, Seattle, WA	Transportation to medical services at the Veterans Administration Hospital. Appointments are required one week in advance. Veterans can bring an escort or service dog with a

			doctor's note. Serves veterans with disabilities. Not wheelchair accessible. No fees. Located at the VA Medical Center.
King County Veterans Program, North & South	https://kingcounty.gov/en/legacy/depts/community-human-services/adult-services/veterans-servicemembers-families/programs-services.aspx	(206) 477-8282 | North: 9725 3rd Ave. NE, No. 300, Seattle, WA	Provides emergency financial assistance, housing system coordination, case management, and social work, as well as education and employment resources. Documents required include proof of service (prior or current) as an active duty or reservist member; documentation of King County residency, and proof of income eligibility for financial assistance.
Operation: Welcome One Home, For Veterans	https://kcrha.org/regional-access-points/	(877) 904-8387 206-454-2799 | WA State Department of Veterans Affairs (WDVA) office: 2106 2nd Ave., No. 100, Seattle, WA 98121; or VA Puget Sound Community Outreach and Housing Services (CHOS) Renton Walk-in Clinic: 419 S 2nd St., No. 2, Renton, WA 98057	The Washington State Department of Veteran Affairs Information and Assistance Call Center is the "Command Center" for Veterans and Neighbors to call to connect homeless Veterans to services.
Seattle Central College Veterans Services	http://seattlecentral.edu/campus-life/student-support-and-services/veterans	(206) 934-6352 | 1701 Broadway No. BE3215, Seattle, WA	Assists veteran students, their dependents and partners with the tools and resources to successfully navigate the transition from military to college life. Benefits include: 50 percent off tuition waiver for qualified military personnel and veterans, help with housing referrals, educational programs and scholarships, job search assistance, resume prep, advising, career center, childcare assistance, counseling, disability resources, tutoring, and TRiO student support services.
Seattle Public Library, Central Branch, Veterans Services	http://spl.org/programs-and-services/civics-and-social-services/veteran-services	(206) 386-4636 | 1000 4th Ave., Seattle, WA	Offers drop-in help for veterans who are currently homeless or living on low incomes. Veteran specialists from Supportive Services for Veteran Families connect veterans with social services to help them find housing and get the support they need to stay in their homes. The Help for Veterans events offer rapid access to housing,

			counseling, financial planning and legal assistance.
Seattle Vet Center	http://va.gov/seattle-vet-center	(206) 764-5130; after hours: (877) 927-8387 | 305 S Lucile St., Seattle, WA	Offers benefit counseling, job service referrals and bereavement counseling. Mental health intake assessments for veterans who experienced PTSD, and/or sexual trauma in the military. Offers short-term trainings on living/coping skills as well as long-term multiple-focus trainings. Will refer to other agencies. Serves veterans and sometimes veterans' families. Call or visit site. If available, bring medical discharge and separation (DD214) papers. No fees.
Veterans Affairs Crisis Line		(800) 273-8255 | 24/7	Connects Veterans and Service members in crisis and their families and friends with qualified, caring VA responders through a confidential toll-free hotline, online chat, or text.
Washington Department of Veteran Affairs	http://dva.wa.gov	(206) 454-2790 (206) 454-2799 | 2106 2nd Ave., 1st floor, Seattle, WA	Re-entry and in-reach services for veterans who are currently incarcerated or exiting incarceration. Veteran benefits (applying for Service Connected Compensation, Non-Service Connected Pension, Social Security, and discharge upgrades) Military Family Outreach (working with veterans or current service members and their families and outreach services for veterans who are battling homelessness).
William Booth Center	http://northwest.salvationarmy.org	(206) 621-0145 | 811 Maynard Ave. S Seattle, WA	Transitional housing with case management for homeless men 18 and older. Maximum stay varies by program. Performs background checks. Entry done through a process established by the VA. Fees are determined on a case-by-case basis. Referral from a partner organization required. Partners are King County Veterans' Program, FareStart and Salvation Army off-site shelter.
YWCA - Supportive Services for Veteran Families	http://ywcaworks.org/programs/supportive-services-veteran-families	(425) 264-1426 | ltiffin@ywcaworks.org | 1010 S Second St. Renton, WA	Assists Veterans towards housing stability, including currently homeless veterans with a desire to find and maintain permanent housing who served active duty.

Matthew 7:24

"Everyone then who hears these words of mine and does them will be like a wise man who built his house on the rock."

House of Mercy

Made in United States
Troutdale, OR
09/21/2024

22997269R20135